THE
COMPLETE
OUTDOOR
COOKBOOK

THE COMPLETE OUTDOOR COOKBOOK

Yvonne Young Tarr

QUADRANGLE/THE NEW YORK TIMES BOOK CO.

Library of Congress Catalog Card Number: 72–90453

International Standard Book Number: 0–8129–0334–X

PRODUCTION BY PLANNED PRODUCTION
DESIGN BY BEN FEDER

*I dedicate this book to all of those people,
agencies and societies devoted
to the preservation of the ecology
in our endangered world.*

*With a special thanks to Ruth Grossman,
my editorial assistant,
and Ruth Haughwout, my general assistant.*

Contents

CONTENTS

Camping 139

Cooking by the Sea 193

Picnics Hot and Cold 227

Hiking and Backpacking 263

Introduction

WHEN THE FIRST really warm day slips upon us, when the buds on the trees are suddenly full-fledged leaves, when the children begin to talk about summer vacation, when we look out in the full light of day and notice the car needs washing, we know, finally, that summer is really here. At that moment, all across the nation, thousands of minds and palates lightly turn to thoughts of food cooked over glowing coals. The season's first "cookout" is afoot.

What strange impulse causes us to burst from our paneled, tiled and superbly equipped kitchens and rush lemming-like to our backyard terrace and blackened grills? Why this ritual outdoor broiling of meats and vegetables?

One of the reasons undoubtedly is the zest that fresh air adds to our appetite. The heady odor of charcoal-broiled steaks and 'burgers is enough to make even the most jaded of winter palates wake up to the taste sensation in store. Then too, our outdoor cooking equipment is the finest in the world. Myriad grills, fireplaces and hibachis, not to mention electrically operated spits, skewers, fryers, skillets, etc., make cooking out under the open skies in our own backyard more pleasure than pain. Here the whole family is together and re-laxed, and age differences are forgotten in the enjoyment of eating succulent meats, fish, vegetables, fruits, delicious biscuits and desserts, served forth hot and flavorful . . . "right off the grill."

One important thing to realize is that the cook who serves the most delicious foods is usually the cook who is aware of the quality and freshness of the food she or he buys. In winter it is often difficult to find vegetables that are truly fresh. But once the growing season comes, there is a whole sequence of fresh foods available. Asparagus in May, peas in June, lettuce, scallions, squash in July. Once August and September have come there is a veritable cornucopia: corn, broccoli, tomatoes, peppers, eggplant, green beans, limas, potatoes. Remember that warm weather means vegetables and fruits are growing and ripening in the fields—and it is well worth your while to look for them at greengrocers, specialty vegetable markets or roadside stands. When you buy food of the highest quality and freshness, you need to do little to it. Its "just-picked" good-ness guarantees delicious flavor.

Many of these stores will carry fresh herbs, too—rosemary, thyme, fennel, sage, chives, parsley, and also horseradish and ginger roots. These fresh herbs are considered a must by most gourmet cooks.

If you have access to soil where you can grow vegetables and herbs you are fortunate indeed, and your reputation as a cook is assured. There can be no vegetables fresher than the ones you pluck from living plants—served a few hours later, their vitamin content and their flavor intact.

Even if you live in town you can have fresh herbs, most of which grow like weeds when planted in either a garden or a flowerpot. So try to buy or grow fresh herbs—you'll be amazed at the subtle difference they make, especially when used with fresh vegetables. Fresh herbs are specifically called for in many of these recipes. However, in most you may substitute dried if necessary, and this has been indicated.

This book has been written with the hope that it will intro-duce you to new and more interesting meals that can be

INTRODUCTION

cooked and served out-of-doors. Whether your favorite outdoor meal is one eaten in the backyard, around a campfire, at the beach or on a picnic or hike, these pages attempt to tell you how to feed your family, your friends, and yourself distinctive and more tantalizing food in the beauty and carefree surroundings of nature.

There are unlimited possibilities for cooking a tempting variety of dishes outdoors at home; because of the accessibility of your kitchen here you can use your stove and oven for preparing a part of the meal. And of course you have running water for washing up. The recipes for cooking outdoors away from home (where you will not have these amenities) are, on the whole, simpler in terms of ingredients, utensils and cooking steps required. However, many of the recipes in the at-home section *can* be made over a campfire or at the beach, and the reader is urged to use imagination in selecting ones that will be appropriate to the situation.

TERRACE
AND
BACKYARD
COOKING

Barbecue
Equipment
and
Techniques

BARBECUE UNITS for backyard, porch or patio cooking come in a variety of sizes and price ranges; in general, the more expensive they are, the more versatile they are too. Many are equipped with elaborate attachments for cooking in the grand manner. Grills of simpler construction, while not as impressive, will enable you to turn out steaks, chops and roasts that taste equally delicious. What you choose to buy depends on your familiarity with the techniques of outdoor cooking, the number of people you'll be serving and the kinds of cooking you will do—whether broiling, spit-roasting or baking.

If you've never prepared a complete dinner for eight over glowing charcoals, it might be wise to forget about that large, expensive and accessory-laden barbecue which looks so appealing. Begin rather with one of the smaller brazier-type barbecues. As you advance in your firebuilding and outdoor culinary skills, your initial investment will repay you with many years of usefulness as a supplementary grill for broiling appetizers or for beach or picnic use.

There are important special features to look for when buying a barbecue of any size or price. Consider the size of your

3

family and the cooking capacity of the barbecue. Your new unit should be of sturdy construction, substantial enough to give you years of service. Look for heavy gauge metal and a chrome-plated grill—these are designed to last. Your unit should have some provision for ventilation built in, such as dampers to lower or increase the heat, and an efficient and easy-to-operate mechanism for lowering the firepan or raising the grill. The grill rods themselves should be closely spaced, so that foods can be managed more easily. You may feel that a hood is essential—hood or partial hoods protect your fire from wind and assure even cooking by reflecting the heat. Descriptions of some of the available kinds of barbecue units follow.

Small Portable Barbecues

Folding grills are the simplest type of barbecue unit. Excellent for beach or picnic, they are lightweight with folding wire legs that make them easy to pack. Most are equipped with fireboxes underneath the grills for holding coals, and some even have a simple lowering and raising mechanism.

4

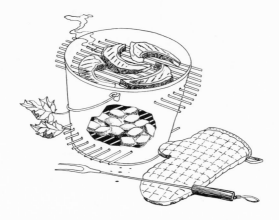

Bucket broilers are pail-shaped units. The coals are set on the bottom, just below the ventilation openings. The limited cooking capacity of these broilers can be increased by using a skillet over the grill. Bail handles and lightweight construction make them ideal for picnic or beach.

Hibachis are easily portable, although they are usually made of cast iron. They require few coals to produce a good fire. Their size somewhat limits their usefulness, but they make ideal supplementary units for broiling kebabs or hors d'oeuvres.

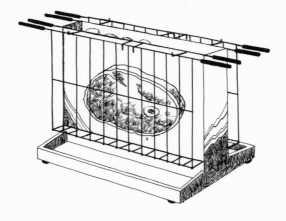

Vertical grills have one or two center fireboxes in which the coals are set. Steaks or chops are locked in racks on either side of the firebox, where they broil while hanging in front of the fire.

Braziers range in size from small, shallow, portable table-top units set on a tripod, all the way up to the deeper-bowled cast-iron 30-inch models, which often have wheels on 2 of their

3 or 4 legs. Such specialized features as handles or cranks for lowering or raising the grill, hoods or partial hoods, electrical attachments for spit-roasting, large cooking capacity and good working height make the versatile brazier a popular barbecue unit.

Covered barbecues assure easy heat control. Reflected heat from the dome cover cooks the food faster and more evenly. Adjustable dampers in both the top and bottom enable the covered barbecue to simulate your kitchen stove, and will snuff out good leftover charcoal after your food is cooked, for use some other time. Both size and the addition of accessories, such as electric spits, built-in temperature thermometers, extra grills and built-in electric coils for starting the coals, add to the cost of these units. However, their efficiency and ability to roast a larger cut in a shorter time with fewer coals make for some economy.

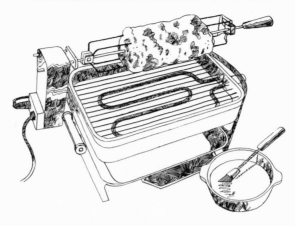

Electric barbecues appeal to many who want the pleasure of outdoor cooking without the bother of building a fire. Although purists may shudder at the lack of excitement these provide, they do produce even heat and superb results. Electric barbecues have all the standard features of charcoal grills: foods can be broiled, spit-roasted or baked; their capacity for accommodating the larger roasts is, however, limited. Efficient electric barbecues heat almost at once, are easy to clean and maintain, and are doubly useful since they may be used indoors.

The electric skillet, cooker, deep fat fryer, blender or mixer that you use in your kitchen will make the transition to porch or patio with no trouble. In addition, any of these may be used as a supplementary cooking unit as you grill the main course over charcoal. Electric hot trays or tables are handy for keeping food warm.

Barbecue Tools

Having the right tools on hand will make a considerable difference in the success of your outdoor cooking efforts and enable you to work with ease. Keep your equipment accessible and in good working order, ready for you to begin cooking. Basic items are:

—Two sets of tongs, one for lifting coals and one for turning food

—Hinged wire baskets of different depths

—Long-handled fork, spoon and pancake turner

—Long skewers

—Long-handled basting brush or glass tube baster

—Pair of asbestos mitts

—Set of sharp knives: paring knife, carving knife, steak knives, roast slicer

—Set of heat-proof pads

—Meat thermometer

—Large salt shaker and pepper mill

—Seasonings and spices

—Wire brush with scraper to clean the grill

—Liquid starter or electric starting rod

There are literally dozens of other fascinating devices available for outdoor cooking. Such refinements may appeal to the gadget-minded but are not necessary.

Cooking Over Charcoal

Experience is, naturally, the most valuable teacher in learning fire-building techniques, but novice outdoor cooks need to know a few basic rules for fire and heat control.

The kind of barbecue you use and the size of the particular food you will cook are both important factors in determining the size of the fire you will need. A lidless barbecue grill uses more coals than one with a hood. Longer-cooking roasts will require more coals than small chops or steaks. Fast-burning charcoal is best for steaks or chops. Briquettes burn hot and long: use them for roasts, whole birds or other foods that need time to cook.

Line the grill bed with a sheet of aluminum foil; this helps to regulate the heat since the foil reflects heat upward, and it also keeps the barbecue clean. Place a single sheet of newspaper over the foil, arrange the charcoal or briquettes in a shallow layer, making sure to cover an area only slightly larger than the surface of the food to be cooked. Douse both paper and charcoal with liquid starter. When you set a match to the paper the briquettes will ignite evenly.

For kebabs, line up your hot charcoal or briquettes in parallel rows—this is more efficient, and puts the heat right where the cooking's going on. In rotisserie roasting, set your coals for briquettes in a circle slightly larger than the size of the roast, surrounding a drip pan in the center directly underneath. The heat can then be regulated by moving the coals outward to slow the cooking, or closer to increase the temperature and keep flare-ups to a minimum.

Light your fire as described and wait for the coals to turn ash-gray (or glow red if it's after dark) before beginning to cook. If your fire is cooperative, this should take about 1/2 hour. When cooking a large roast, extra briquettes may be added to an established fire by setting them first on the outside of the burning coals and then raking them toward the center as they begin to catch fire.

Even heating temperatures are best for charcoal cooking. Broiling requires a higher temperature than roasting. A popular method for judging whether the temperature of your fire is slow, medium or high is to hold your hand just over the grill at the level at which the food will be cooking. Immediately count aloud by seconds: "one thousand one" equals one second, "one thousand two" equals two seconds, and so on. If your hand can withstand the heat for only 1 or 2 seconds, your fire is very hot; 3 or 4 seconds indicates a medium fire, and 5 or 6 seconds means the fire is slow.

When your coals are ready, begin your cooking by raising the broiling surface to its highest level, adjusting it closer to the coals as they cool. If your grill does not have a raising and lowering mechanism, regulate the heat by spacing out the coals, or by cooking in a long-handled hinged wire basket held over the grill. For campfires, the grill may be raised by shoring up the sides of the fireplace with additional rocks. Heat for longer-cooking foods may also be regulated by moving the food off to the side of the grill away from the center of the heat, where it will cook more slowly.

Keep in mind that when too much gray ash covers the briquettes, this covering acts as an insulator and reduces the amount of heat generated. Tap the briquettes lightly with your fire tongs from time to time while cooking, to maintain a constant heat. Knock the white ash from the tops of dying coals if your food needs just a bit more cooking. This will bring the coals back to life temporarily.

The hood on a covered barbecue helps to regulate cooking by trapping and reflecting the heat. An effective substitute cover for a lidless grill may be easily constructed from several layers of heavy-duty aluminum foil. Foil may also be used to make a windscreen for your grill or campfire, or to provide an improvised reflector oven for faster and more even cooking.

Remember—your fire is in ideal condition when the briquettes are red, glowing and covered with gray ash.

PREVENTING FLARE-UPS

Here are several hints to reduce the inevitability of those searing, smoky flare-ups and the possibility of burned meals.

Always make sure that your coals have reached the gray ash stage before beginning to cook. Coals or briquettes still flaming or spotted with black are sure to flare and smoke and produce uneven heat. Even ash-gray coals will flame or smoke from sizzling fat or the oil from your marinade or basting sauce. Trim your meat of excess fat before barbecuing and use a drip pan directly underneath your roasts. Surround the drip pan with a ring of hot coals. The indirect heat will produce even cooking and a minimum amount of smoke. In spit-roasting, arrange the spit so that the bottom of the roast turns towards you and the top turns away—all fat should then fall into the drip pan. Use a pair of fire tongs to space your coals 1/2-inch to an inch apart after they are heated; this way most of the fat from steaks or chops will fall on the empty spaces instead of on the coals. Another trick is to slightly tilt your grill down to one side so that the fat will run off. Keep a sprinkler-top bottle full of water at hand should flare-ups occur despite your best efforts. Sprinkle the water over the coals, but take care not to soak them or the fire may reduce in intensity or go out altogether. However, a really experienced, efficient fire keeper will not need to resort to this method.

USING FOIL

Versatile aluminum foil is a marvelous convenience for the outdoor cook. Properly wrapped foil packages of meat, fresh vegetables or fruits, or any combination of these, seals in the flavor and juices, and eliminates pan washing or grill cleaning.

A drip pan which can be easily constructed of aluminum foil is a must for spit-cooking over charcoal. It also provides the added advantage of conserving juices for gravy, and may, if proper care is taken, be used more than once.

The drip pan needs to be only slightly larger than your roast, but you may want to extend it the length of your grill. To make a drip pan, use a sheet of heavy-duty foil doubled and a bit larger than the meat. Crease each of the sides to a 1-1/2-inch width; flatten the sides after creasing them. Begin at one corner and raise the two adjoining creased edges, pulling them together, and bend the point down inside to anchor it and provide an unbroken surface. Reinforce the corners by pinching them firmly. Repeat this procedure until all corners are secure.

Recipes
for the
Open
Grill

Broiling Meat, Poultry and Fish*

THIS PORTION of the book is especially designed for would-be backyard chefs, for others whose outdoor culinary efforts have been for the most part confined to steaks, hamburgers and hotdogs, and even for those of you who may have ventured a little deeper into the more adventurous techniques of cooking over charcoal. Choose among the many different and equally delicious cuts of beef, pork or lamb; the fish and shellfish; the chicken, duck or turkey recipes; try the marinades or sauces recommended with your choice of a main course, or experiment with any combination that appeals to you. The marinades and

* Here I would like to note that the cooking times given in this book are based on the particular day they were tested by me. Your grill, your fire, your climate and/or wind velocity on any given day may vary from the conditions on my patio. It is advisable, therefore, to check the cooking progress of your recipe from time to time to determine the degree of doneness, etc., of your foods.

sauces may be made in your kitchen, or out-of-doors. You may be surprised to discover that almost all of the cooking methods you use in your own kitchen may be adapted to your charcoal grill—all you really need is a little experience.

Steaks, chops, roasts—beef, lamb, pork, fowl—in combination with the marinades and sauces provide an infinite variety of possibilities for your pleasure, all fit feasts for the out-of-doors! Use a meat thermometer or the "cut and peek" system to determine when your meat is ready to eat. *Accurate* charts for broiling cannot be given because of the difference in the intensity of heat from fire to fire and the amount of wind or draft on any given day.

BEEF STEAKS

Tender, top-quality steaks from the loin or rib will provide you with lavish eating, but don't neglect the less-expensive cuts. With a little help from a spicy marinade, a not-so-tender steak may turn into a succulent treat.

Sirloin Steak. Cut from the upper part of the loin, this largest of steaks is the traditional king of the barbecue.

Top Sirloin Steak is the trimmed and boneless sirloin.

Porterhouse Steak, cut from the thick end of the short loin, has a T-bone and a sizable piece of tenderloin as its distinguishing features. The tenderloin, sometimes termed *New York* or *strip steak,* is also sold separately.

T-Bone Steak is a trimmed and slightly smaller version of the porterhouse.

Club Steak. The rib end of the short loin supplies these smallest of loin steaks.

Rib Steak from the tender rib section is noted for the marbling of fat that contributes so much to its flavor and tenderness. When sold boneless the rib eye is variously called *Delmonico* or *Spencer* steak.

Top Round Steak is tender despite its lean appearance. The tender upper part of the round is popularly sold as London broil. Bottom round should be tenderized before cooking.

Blade or Chuck Steak, cut from just below the rib section, may be broiled just as it is if it comes from the first two ribs. Otherwise this inexpensive but flavorful steak should be marinated or tenderized.

Flank Steak. This very lean, flat steak cut from the intersection of the ribs and hip may be scored and marinated before cooking. Slice diagonally when carving.

Skirt Steak comes from the inside rib cage, resembles a smaller flank steak, and may be stuffed and rolled before broiling.

BEEF ROASTS

All roasts to be barbecued will profit from being cooked covered with a barbecue hood or a layer of foil. Have boned or rolled roasts tied securely at 1-inch intervals so that the meat holds together while cooking. Lean roasts will be tastier if covered with a layer of fat before being tied. Insert a meat thermometer into your roast to ensure that the degree of doneness will be to your liking.

Standing Rib Roast is both flavorful and tender; usually requires a little less cooking than a boneless roast.

Rolled Rib Roast is a rolled and tied standing rib roast minus the ribs.

Top Sirloin Roast is a tender cut from the top of the loin. Its boneless, flat shape makes it ideal for cooking directly on the grill with the lid closed or lightly wrapped with foil.

Rib Eye Roast comes from the center of the rib section. It is a choice, tender, boneless cut. Other terms for the rib eye are *Spencer Roll* or *Market Roast.*

Beef Tenderloin or *Fillet* is the tenderest, and usually most expensive roast. Fat-shy, it should be tied with a layer of fat before cooking.

Sirloin Tip Roast, with a flavor and texture similar to sirloin steak, is ideal for rotisserie broiling.

Top Round Roast may be barbecued on a spit, but requires tenderizing. Slice very thinly for serving.

Eye Round Roast needs tenderizing and an extra layer of fat before being trussed for rotisserie cooking.

Rump Roast, cut in different shapes from the fleshy hindquarters, is a less-expensive roast needing tenderizer or marinade and an extra layer of fat.

Cross Rib Roast, also known as *English Cut* or *Shoulder Clod,* is cut from the beef shoulder. This less-expensive roast, cross-grained with a thin thread of muscle, needs to be marinated before cooking.

LAMB

Tender, juicy lamb chops and lamb steaks of all shapes, sizes and prices are ideal for barbecuing, either as is or refrigerated first in your favorite marinade. Lamb is tastiest when slightly underdone—brown on the outside yet still pinkish in the center.

Rib Chops are best barbecued when they are cut to double thickness. This keeps them juicy.

Loin Chops have more meat and less bone than rib chops. They will reward you with good eating if cut extra thick. Two loin chops cut together as a large double chop without severing the backbone are known as *Saddle Chops.*

Saratoga Chops are boneless cuts from the lamb shoulder usually held secure by wooden skewers.

Shoulder Chops are meaty, less expensive, and come in 2 easily identifiable varieties: the round bone and the blade bone.

Lamb Leg Steaks or *Chops* are the largest and meatiest of the chops.

Leg of Lamb is usually cut between the upper butt or sirloin portion and the lower shank end. It may be cooked with the bone or boned, rolled and tied for spit-cooking; cut into shish kebab; or boned and cooked flat, butterfly-fashion, directly over the coals.

Lamb Breast may be grilled flat, without boning, or it may be boned and have a pocket made for stuffing.

PORK

Pork cuts of all descriptions have long been favorites for outdoor cooking, but pork *must* be well cooked before serving—no pink should show. Allow plenty of time—the wait will be worth it.

Pork Chops and *Steaks* cut to a 1-inch thickness do nicely barbecued either directly on the grill or secured in a wire basket.

Pork Spareribs and *Backribs* usually require long cooking but provide delicious eating when basted with any of a variety of barbecue sauces during the last 15 to 30 minutes of cooking. Be sure to bring your basting sauce to the boiling point before serving it as a dunking sauce for the ribs.

Pork Shoulder may be boned and tied for spit-cooking, cooked butterfly-fashion directly over the grill, or cut into cubes for kebabs.

Fresh Pork Leg needs long cooking. Use a meat thermometer and cover your grill. The roast may be barbecued whole, or boned and tied.

Ham or *Ham Slices* usually are sold fully or partly cooked, require less cooking time, and may be marinated and then barbecued over slow coals, basting with sauce toward the end of the cooking.

Bacon responds best to grilling when cut in thick slices.

Pork Sausages must be thoroughly cooked unless they're the brown-and-serve variety.

FISH

Kinds of fish are discussed on pp. 196–202. The main thing to remember in cooking fish over open coals is that the flesh cooks quickly and tends to fall apart. Use a hinged wire basket for small fish or wrap the fish in foil to hold it together.

MARINADES

Most pork, beef, lamb, poultry and fish may be cooked over coals or electric grills, rotisseries, etc., without the benefit of the flavoring or tenderness a marinade imparts. Some of the above-mentioned, however, benefit tremendously from an hour, a day or even several days of marinating. Game, particularly furry animals, should be marinated for at least two to three days, and often a week of marinating is not too much.

All of the following marinades may be used for basting, and many also serve as sauces for the cooked meat. When the marinade is to be used as a baste or a sauce, it should be simmered a few minutes first. Pork, chicken or fish marinades *must* be boiled before being used as a sauce.

Enamel or glass pans and dishes are the best receptacles for marinating; however, plastic bowls may also be used. Do not use earthenware as many of the glazes have lead as a primary ingredient.

If you are camping and/or living off the land, wine, vinegar, lemon juice and spices help to preserve meats that cannot be refrigerated.

Apple-Ginger Marinade

For beef, pork, lamb or poultry: marinate 2 to 3 hours.

1/4 cup apple juice or cider
1 tablespoon minced fresh ginger, or 1/4 teaspoon powdered
1/4 cup cider vinegar

1/3 cup salad oil
1/3 cup soy sauce
1/3 cup honey
2 cloves garlic, crushed

Mix all ingredients together.

Mustard-Citrus Marinade

For beef, lamb, poultry or shrimp: marinate 2 to 3 hours.

2 tablespoons French-style mustard
3 cloves garlic, crushed
3 tablespoons soy sauce

3 tablespoons lemon juice
3 tablespoons lime juice
3 teaspoons vegetable oil

Beat together all of the ingredients with the exception of the

18

oil. Add the oil a 1/2 teaspoon at a time, beating vigorously after each addition.

Tangy Brown-Sugar Marinade

For beef, pork or poultry: marinate 2 to 3 hours.

3 tablespoons vegetable oil
1/4 cup brown sugar
1/4 cup Worcestershire sauce

3/4 cup catsup
1/2 cup cider vinegar
1 teaspoon salt

Mix all ingredients together in a saucepan and bring to just under a boil over medium heat. Cover, reduce the heat, and allow the marinade to simmer for about 5 minutes. When cool, pour the marinade over the meat and refrigerate. The marinade may also be used to baste the meat if it is brought to a boil.

Spicy Sherry-Soy Marinade

For beef, pork, chicken or fish: marinate 2 to 3 hours.

3 tablespoons dry sherry
1/3 cup soy sauce
1/3 cup vegetable oil
4 cloves garlic, crushed

1/2 teaspoon chili powder
Freshly ground black pepper to taste

Mix together all ingredients.

Herb-Wine Marinade

For beef or lamb: marinate overnight.

3/4 cup red wine
1/3 cup vegetable oil
3 tablespoons wine vinegar
1/4 cup tomato juice
3 cloves garlic, minced

1 tablespoon sugar
3/4 teaspoon salt
3 bay leaves
1 teaspoon dried thyme
1/2 teaspoon dried sage

Place all ingredients in a saucepan. Mix well and bring to a boil. Stir thoroughly and let the mixture cool before pouring it over the meat. Before using for basting, bring to a boil and discard the bay leaves.

Citrus-Soy Marinade

*For pork. Cut lean pork into 3/4-inch slices or
1 1/4-inch cubes. Marinate for 1 hour.*

Juice of 1 lime
Juice of 1 lemon
1/4 cup soy sauce

2 tablespoons melted butter
3 tablespoons brown sugar

Mix together all ingredients.

Chinese Oyster Sauce Marinade

*For pork. Cut lean pork into 3/4-inch slices or
1 1/4-inch cubes. Marinate for 1 hour.*

1/3 cup Chinese oyster sauce

2 large cloves garlic, peeled and crushed
1 tablespoon brandy

Mix together all ingredients.

Tart Garlic Marinade for Shish Kebab

For lamb: Marinate overnight.

5 cloves garlic, minced
2 onions, chopped
1 1/2 cups vinegar
2 cups water

3 bay leaves
1 1/2 teaspoons salt
12 peppercorns

Place all ingredients in a saucepan, stir well, and bring to just under a boil. Cover and simmer over low heat for 1 hour. Allow the marinade to cool before adding it to the meat.

Lamb Marinade

*Marinate for three days, turning the meat occasionally.
For lamb chops or leg of lamb cut into 2-inch cubes.*

3/4 cup lemon juice
6 tablespoons honey
4 bay leaves, crumbled

3/4 cup mint leaves,
chopped

Mix together all ingredients and pour over the meat. Refrigerate. Broil the meat until pink and serve hot with Honey-Mint Yoghurt Sauce (page 24).

Hunter's Marinade

*For beef or game: marinate overnight or for
several days.*

1 cup white wine
1/3 cup tarragon vinegar
1/3 cup olive oil
2 small onions, sliced

8 bruised peppercorns
6 juniper berries
1/4 teaspoon thyme
1/4 teaspoon sage

Mix together all ingredients.

Venison Marinade

Marinate 24 hours, turning the meat frequently.

2 medium-sized onions,
thinly sliced
2 medium-sized carrots,
thinly sliced
2 small stalks celery
3 cloves garlic, sliced
3/4 cup red wine vinegar
3/4 cup vegetable oil

1 1/2 teaspoons freshly
ground black pepper
2 small bay leaves
2 teaspoons thyme
5 or 6 juniper berries
2 tablespoons finely
chopped parsley
2 cups red wine

Trim the tops from the celery and discard them. Chop the celery coarsely. Place the vegetables in a bowl and pour the vinegar and oil over them. Add the pepper, bay leaves, thyme, juniper berries and parsley. Stir in the wine. Mix all ingredients thoroughly.

Citrus Marinade

For fish: marinate for 4 hours while refrigerating.

1 cup lime juice
1/2 cup orange juice
1/4 cup lemon juice
1 onion, sliced

3 tablespoons olive oil
Salt and freshly ground pepper to taste

Mix together all ingredients.

Tart White Wine Marinade

For fish: marinate 3 to 4 hours.

2 tablespoons olive oil
1/2 cup white wine
2 small lemons, peeled and thinly sliced
1 teaspoon fresh thyme

3 small bay leaves
10 peppercorns, slightly minced
1/4 teaspoon salt

Mix together all ingredients.

SAUCES

South Seas Sauce

Dip charcoal-broiled ham, chicken, pork or shrimp in this unusually tasty sauce. It may also be used as a marinade.

2 cloves garlic, crushed
1 cup soy sauce
1 tablespoon crushed red pepper

3 tablespoons molasses
1/2 cup crushed pineapple, drained

Mix together all ingredients. Refrigerate for at least 1 hour.

Sweet-and-Sour Sauce

Try this unusual sauce on everything from grilled hamburgers to pork and shrimp.

1 cup light brown sugar
2 cups cold water
1 teaspoon white vinegar
2 fresh peaches, peeled, pitted and chopped
3/4 cup finely chopped sweet pickles

3/4 cup finely chopped pineapple chunks
6 tablespoons finely chopped pimiento
1 teaspoon soy sauce

Place the sugar, water, vinegar and chopped peaches in a saucepan. Bring to a boil over medium heat and continue to boil until the mixture thickens and is syrupy. Add the pickles, pineapple, pimiento and soy sauce; boil 1 minute more. Chill the sauce overnight.

Red Hot Mustard-Kumquat Sauce

Hot enough to make you cry, but tasty enough to make you smile—an unusual sauce for pork or duck.

1 10-ounce jar preserved
 kumquats
8 teaspoons dry mustard
2 1/3 tablespoons sherry

2 tablespoons kumquat
 syrup
4 1/2 tablespoons soy sauce

(Makes 2 4-ounce glasses)

Drain the kumquats and reserve 2 tablespoons of the syrup. Finely chop the kumquats, discarding the seeds. Mix together the mustard and sherry to make a paste. Add the chopped kumquats to the mustard-wine paste; add the reserved kumquat syrup and the soy sauce. Stir thoroughly to blend all of the ingredients.

Honey-Mint Yoghurt Sauce

A delicious dressing for fruit salads or any lamb dish. This yoghurt concoction is cool and exotic.

3 tablespoons honey
2 tablespoons chopped
 mint leaves

1/4 cup apple or orange
 juice
1 cup plain yoghurt

(Makes approximately 1 1/2 cups)

Simmer the honey, mint and fruit juice for 1 or 2 minutes. Allow to cool, then gently stir in the yoghurt. Chill.

Caper Sauce

Try this with lamb, fish or shellfish.

1/2 cup wine vinegar
1/2 teaspoon salt
1/8 teaspoon white pepper
1 cup olive oil

2 tablespoons capers,
 minced
2 tablespoons chopped
 pimiento

(Makes approximately 1 1/2 cups)

24

Measure the vinegar into a small bowl and stir in the salt and pepper. Add the olive oil, the minced capers and the pimiento. With a fork or a wire whisk, mix together all of the ingredients.

Mayonnaise

4 teaspoons white vinegar	2 1/2 teaspoons Worcestershire sauce
2 teaspoons French-style mustard	4 1/2 tablespoons lemon juice
4 large egg yolks	1/4 teaspoon salt
Dash of salt	Freshly ground black pepper to taste
1 cup vegetable oil	
1 cup olive oil	

(Makes about 2 cups)

Put the vinegar, mustard, egg yolks and a few grains of salt together in an electric blender. Whirl at medium speed for several minutes. Very gradually add the vegetable oil and olive oil to the eggs and blend at high speed until thick and creamy. Remove from the blender and briskly beat in the Worcestershire sauce, lemon juice, salt and pepper. Chill well and serve cold.

Garlic Mayonnaise

8 cloves garlic	1 1/2 cups olive oil
1/2 teaspoon salt	2 lemons
3 egg yolks	

(Makes 2 cups)

Peel the garlic cloves. Place them in a mortar with the salt and mash them thoroughly with a pestle until reduced to a smooth paste. Separate 3 eggs, and place the yolks in a large bowl. Add the garlic and salt mixture and stir gently to blend. Gradually add the olive oil, a few drops at a time, and with a wire whisk, beat the mixture energetically after each addition.

When about 2 or 3 tablespoons of the oil have been absorbed, add the oil at a slightly faster rate, beating constantly, until all of it has been worked in. Squeeze and strain the lemon juice, blend it into the mixture and refrigerate, covered, until needed.

Serve this garlic mayonnaise as a dipping sauce. Place in a bowl surrounded by attractively arranged crisp fresh vegetables and let guests help themselves.

Caribbean Hot Sauce

Any meat tastes marvelous when it is served with this authentic Jamaican sweet and hot barbecue sauce.

1/3 cup butter	2 tablespoons Worcestershire sauce
2 medium-sized onions, finely chopped	1/2 cup mild yellow mustard
2 medium-sized green peppers, finely chopped	1 tablespoon lemon juice
1 cup catsup	1/4 teaspoon hot sauce
1 cup brown sugar	1 1/2 teaspoons salt

(Makes about 3 1/2 cups)

Melt the butter in a skillet over medium coals and add remaining ingredients. Cook for 5 minutes, stirring constantly. Serve piping hot.

Fresh-Cooked Horseradish Sauce for Game

Fresh horseradish is often available in fruit and vegetable stores or farmer's markets in the summer and early fall. If you can find some, make this wonderfully fresh-tasting sauce.

1 1/4 cups fresh horseradish, grated	Salt to taste
1 1/2 cups red wine	Freshly ground black pepper to taste
1/2 teaspoon cinnamon	1 cup red currant jelly
1/8 teaspoon each nutmeg and allspice	

26

(Makes 1 cup)

Use a blender or a mortar and pestle to pulverize the horse-radish root. Drain well and set aside. Bring the wine and spices to a boil in a saucepan, lower the heat, and continue to cook until the liquid is reduced to about 1 cup. Remove from the heat and stir in the horseradish and currant jelly. Serve hot with game.

Spicy Chili Barbecue Sauce

Use this with pork, chicken or lamb.

1 medium-sized onion, finely chopped	1/2 cup vegetable oil
1 small green pepper, coarsely chopped	1/3 cup wine vinegar
	1/4 cup water
3 cloves garlic, crushed	1 tablespoon salt
1/2 cup catsup	1 tablespoon chili powder
	1 teaspoon oregano

(Makes 2 1/2 cups)

Place the onion, green pepper and garlic in a saucepan and stir in the remaining ingredients. Cook for 10 to 12 minutes over low heat, stirring occasionally. Serve hot or cold. This barbecue sauce stores very well in the refrigerator.

Frozen Sweet and Sour Horseradish Cream

Any platter of cold meat or fish becomes company fare when served with this frozen horseradish cream.

1 horseradish root	2 cups yoghurt
4 apples, cored	1/4 teaspoon salt
3 tablespoons honey	

(Makes about 4 cups)

Grate the horseradish and apples. Mix with the honey, yoghurt and salt. Freeze the mixture until mushy in a fairly deep glass bowl. Stir the horseradish cream with a fork and refreeze. To serve, arrange cold meat or fish on a platter and decorate with watercress. Allow the cream to soften slightly. Scoop out balls of the frozen cream, place on the meat or fish, and serve immediately.

SAUCES FOR SEAFOOD

Avocado-Sour Cream Sauce

Serve with shellfish.

1 large avocado
2 teaspoons lime juice
1 teaspoon Worcestershire sauce

Dash cayenne pepper
1 cup sour cream

(Makes about 2 cups)

Force the avocado pulp through a fine sieve and mix all ingredients.

Capered Egg Sauce

For hot or cold fish.

8 hard-cooked eggs
1/3 cup capers
2 large cloves garlic, crushed
1 tablespoon anchovy paste

2 teaspoons dry mustard
Salt and freshly ground black pepper to taste
1 cup mayonnaise
1/2 cup sour cream

(Makes about 4 cups)

Shell the eggs and rub them through a fine sieve into a large bowl. Add the drained capers to the sieved eggs, along with the garlic, anchovy paste, dry mustard, salt and pepper. Bind the mixture together with the mayonnaise and sour cream. Chill thoroughly before using.

Green Sauce

Use as a dip for cold lobster or shrimp.

1/4 cup fresh chervil
1/4 cup parsley
1/2 cup watercress
  2 scallions, minced
1/3 cup boiling water
  1 large clove garlic,
    crushed

3/4 cup mayonnaise
  1 teaspoon lemon juice
   Salt to taste
1/2 cup yoghurt

(Makes about 2 1/2 cups)

Wash the greens thoroughly, shake off any excess water and place in a small saucepan. Combine the greens with the scallions, cover with boiling water and allow them to steep for several minutes. Place the undrained greens, scallions, garlic and mayonnaise in the container of your blender. Blend 1/2 minute; then add the lemon juice, salt and yoghurt. Blend 10 seconds. Chill thoroughly.

Goldenrod Sauce

Use as a sauce for cold fish.

1/4 cup scallions, minced
  7 hard-cooked egg yolks
1/4 cup lemon juice
  1 teaspoon fresh horse-

radish, grated (or
  bottled, well drained)
1 1/2 cups heavy cream,
  whipped

(Makes about 2 1/2 cups)

Press the hard-cooked egg yolks through a fine sieve. Combine with the scallions, lemon juice and horseradish and blend in the whipped cream.

Chili-Mayonnaise Sauce

This sauce, which should be prepared in advance and then refrigerated, gives a delightful zest to seafood salads.

3 tablespoons minced scallions	3 cups mayonnaise
3 tablespoons minced fresh parsley	3/4 cup sour cream
3/4 cup chili sauce	Salt and cayenne pepper to taste

(Makes about 4 1/2 cups)

Combine the scallions, parsley, chili sauce and mayonnaise in a bowl. Stir in the sour cream and season with salt and cayenne pepper.

Whipped Mustard Sauce

2 tablespoons French-style mustard	2 cups heavy cream, whipped
1 teaspoon onion juice	Salt to taste
1 tablespoon chives, minced	

(Makes about 2 cups)

Gently fold the mustard, onion juice and chives into the whipped cream. Season with salt and refrigerate (for not more than 1 hour) before serving.

Niçoise Sauce

1 medium-sized green pepper, finely chopped	2 1/2 teaspoons fresh tarragon, finely chopped
2 1/2 teaspoons fresh chives, finely chopped	3 cups mayonnaise
	1 1/2 tablespoons tomato paste

(Makes about 3 cups)

Place chopped pepper in a bowl with chives and tarragon, add the mayonnaise and blend in the tomato paste. Serve as a dressing for cold fish or shellfish.

Red Cocktail Sauce

Prepare in advance and serve as a sauce for seafood.

2 cups catsup	2 tablespoons vinegar
3/4 cup chili sauce	3 tablespoons lemon juice
2 teaspoons fresh horse-radish, grated (or bottled but well drained)	2 teaspoons Worcester-shire sauce
	1/2 teaspoon Tabasco sauce

(Makes about 3 cups)

Place the catsup and chili sauce in a bowl. Stir in the remaining ingredients. Refrigerate.

Egg and Anchovy Sauce

Prepare in advance and use to bind fish salads.

5 hard-cooked eggs	3 tablespoons Russian dressing
15 scallions	
10 tablespoons minced anchovy fillets	2 tablespoons vinegar
	Dash of Tabasco sauce
1 1/2 cups sour cream	

(Makes about 4 cups)

Rub the hard-cooked eggs through a fine sieve. Trim the scallions, keeping at least 3 inches green tip, and chop finely. Mix together the sour cream and Russian dressing, then add the eggs, scallions, anchovies, vinegar and Tabasco sauce. Refrigerate.

Salsa Piquante

Serve this peppery sauce with cold cooked fish or shellfish for a sit-up-and-take-notice first course or entrée.

2 large onions, peeled and finely chopped

4 large ripe tomatoes, peeled, seeded, and cut into quarters

1 small green chili pepper, peeled and finely chopped

Salt to taste

wine vinegar to cover

1 cup catsup

(Makes about 6 cups)

Combine these vegetables in a bowl, add salt to taste and pour in just enough vinegar to cover the mixture. Mix in the catsup. Bring the sauce to a boil. Serve hot or cold.

Tartare Sauce with French-style Mustard

Use a French-style mustard. Delicious with shellfish!

4 scallions, finely chopped

2 small dill pickles, finely chopped

2 tablespoons capers, drained and finely chopped

2 small flat anchovy fillets, finely chopped

1 tablespoon French-style mustard

2 1/4 cups mayonnaise

1 teaspoon lime juice

1/2 teaspoon sugar

Salt and freshly ground black pepper to taste

(Makes about 3 cups)

Combine the scallions, pickles, capers, anchovies and mustard with the mayonnaise and mix thoroughly. Add the lime juice, sugar and seasonings. Chill well.

Ritz Sauce

Serve with fish—delicious!

1 cup chili sauce
1 1/2 cups catsup
2 teaspoons Worcester-
shire sauce

1/2 teaspoon Tabasco
sauce
1/4 cup fresh lemon juice

(Makes 2 1/2 cups)

Combine all ingredients thoroughly and refrigerate at least 3 hours before serving.

Hot Ravigote Sauce

Serve hot with fish.

8 scallions, finely chopped
1/3 cup tarragon vinegar
1/4 cup dry white wine
2 cups Easy White Sauce
(page 35)

2 tablespoons butter
1 teaspoon mixed chervil,
chives and tarragon,
minced

(Makes about 3 cups)

Place scallions in a saucepan with the vinegar and wine and cook over medium heat until the liquid boils down to 1/3 its original quantity. Blend in the white sauce and continue to cook for 5 minutes, stirring constantly. Remove from the flame and quickly mix in the butter and herbs.

Sauce Bercy

Serve over seafood brochettes or fish fillets.

3 tablespoons finely
chopped scallions
3 tablespoons butter
1/3 cup fish stock or bottled
clam juice

1/3 cup dry white wine
3/4 cup mayonnaise
2 tablespoons finely
chopped fresh parsley
2 tablespoons butter

(Makes about 4 cups)

Heat the butter in a small saucepan and gently cook the scallions until they are wilted but not brown. Stir in the fish stock and wine and continue to cook, stirring occasionally, allowing the amount of liquid to be reduced until only half is left. Thicken the sauce by blending in the mayonnaise, parsley and additional butter.

Fish Velouté

2 tablespoons butter
2 tablespoons flour
2 cups fish stock or bottled clam juice

Salt and freshly ground black pepper to taste

(Makes 2 cups)

Melt the butter in a small saucepan over low heat. Blend in the flour to form a smooth paste, and as it darkens, stir in the fish stock a little at a time, mixing well after each addition. Continue to stir the sauce until it thickens, pressing out all lumps with the back of a spoon. Allow the sauce to cook over low heat for 15 or 20 minutes. Add salt and pepper to taste and strain the sauce if necessary.

Caper Sauce

Try this with fried fish or boiled or fried potatoes.

3 tablespoons finely chopped white or wild onions
1 small jar capers, finely chopped

3/4 cup butter
1/4 cup lemon juice
2 tablespoons minced parsley

(Makes about 1 1/2 cups)

Heat the butter over low heat, using a slotted spoon to remove the foam as it rises to the top. Stir in the lemon juice, the chopped onions, the capers and the minced parsley. Serve hot.

Maitre D'Hotel Butter

*Spoon a tablespoon of this tasty butter over
broiled fish.*

3/4 cup butter
3 tablespoons lemon juice
1 tablespoon chopped
fresh parsley

Salt and freshly ground
black pepper to taste

(Makes about 3/4 cup)

Blend all ingredients together thoroughly. Serve hot.

Easy White Sauce

*This recipe makes a medium sauce. If you want a
thicker sauce, reduce the amount of milk by 1/2 cup.
For a thinner sauce, increase the milk by 1/2 cup.*

1/4 cup butter
1/4 cup flour
1 cup cold milk
1 cup heavy cream; or
3/4 cup milk

1/2 teaspoon salt
White pepper to taste
(optional)

(Makes 2 cups)

Melt the butter in a heavy skillet over medium heat, add the
flour and stir until the mixture forms a smooth paste. Remove
the skillet from the heat and add the cold milk all at once,
stirring well. Mix in the cream and stir with a fork until the
sauce is smooth and free from lumps. Return the skillet to
medium coals and cook the white sauce, stirring constantly,
until it thickens. Season with the salt and white pepper.

Entrées from the Grill

Stuffed Beefburgers

1 large onion, finely
  chopped
4 pounds fairly lean ground
  chuck

1 tablespoon flour
1 egg
  Freshly ground black
  pepper to taste

(Serves 8)

Mix the onion, meat, flour, egg and pepper, in a large bowl. Flatten the meat mixture on a large sheet of waxed paper to a thickness of 3/4 inch. Cut into 16 patties with a 3-inch cookie cutter. Place the filling of your choice by teaspoons on 8 of the patties and top each with a second patty. Pinch the edges to secure the filling. Broil over hot coals until done as desired, turning only once. Baste frequently with a sauce made of equal parts of vegetable oil, catsup and mustard; or use a sauce made of equal parts of soy sauce, mustard and molasses; or any other burger sauce. Season with salt to taste before serving.

Fillings for Beefburgers

(Serves 8)

MUSHROOMS AND ONIONS

16 Stuffed Beefburger
   patties (above)
1 large onion, finely
  chopped

1/2 pound mushrooms, very
    thinly sliced
    Salt and freshly ground
    pepper to taste

Prepare the Stuffed Beefburger patties. Combine the chopped onion and sliced mushrooms, season with salt and pepper to taste, and place a rounded teaspoon in the center of each of 8 patties. Cover with the remaining patties and proceed as directed.

36

MUSHROOMS AND WATER CHESTNUTS

16 **Stuffed Beefburger
patties (page 36)**
1/2 **pound mushrooms,
finely chopped**
3 **tablespoons butter**

1 **8-ounce can water
chestnuts**
**Salt and freshly ground
pepper to taste**

Prepare the Stuffed Beefburger patties. Sauté the mushrooms in butter. Drain the water chestnuts and chop them. Add salt and pepper to taste and place a rounded teaspoon of the mixture in the center of each of the 8 patties. Cover with the remaining patties and proceed as directed.

PICKLED MUSHROOM FILLING

16 **Stuffed Beefburger patties
(page 36)**

2 **6-ounce jars pickled
mushrooms**

Prepare the patties. Drain the mushrooms and chop finely. Top 8 of the patties with a rounded teaspoon of the chopped mushrooms. Cover with the remaining patties and proceed as directed.

CAPER FILLING

16 **Stuffed Beefburger patties
(page 36)**

1 **2 1/4-ounce jar whole
capers**

Prepare the patties. Place a teaspoon of whole capers in the center of each of 8 patties, seal with the remaining 8, and proceed to broil as directed.

GHERKIN FILLING

16 **Stuffed Beefburger patties
(page 36)**

1 **10-ounce jar midget
gherkins**

Prepare the patties. Drain the gherkins and finely chop them. Divide evenly among 8 patties. Top with the other 8 patties and proceed as directed.

OLIVE FILLING

**16 Stuffed Beefburger patties
(page 36)**

**1 12-ounce jar green
olives, pimiento-stuffed**

Prepare the patties. Drain the olives and finely chop them. Place a rounded teaspoonful in the center of each of 8 patties and top with the remaining 8. Proceed as directed.

MARINATED ARTICHOKE FILLING

**16 Stuffed Beefburger patties
(page 36)**

**1 7-ounce can marinated
artichoke bottoms**

Prepare the patties. Drain the artichokes, chop them finely and divide among 8 patties. Cover with the remaining patties, seal and broil as directed.

EGGPLANT AND CHEESE FILLING

**16 Stuffed Beefburger patties
(page 36)
1 small eggplant**

**1 tablespoon butter
2 slices American cheese**

Peel the eggplant and cut into 1/2-inch cubes. Heat the butter in a skillet and sauté the eggplant until tender. Prepare the patties as directed. Place 1 teaspoon of sautéed eggplant in the center of each of 8 patties. Cut the American cheese slices into quarters and place over the eggplant. Top with the remaining patties, pinch to seal and broil as directed.

CHERRY TOMATO FILLING

**16 Stuffed Beefburger patties
(page 36)
8 cherry tomatoes**

**Salt, freshly ground black
pepper and oregano to
taste**

Prepare the patties. Wash the tomatoes, pat dry and remove any stems. Set 1 tomato in the center of each of 8 patties and sprinkle with the seasonings. Cover with the remaining patties, molding the meat well around the tomatoes. Broil as directed.

AVOCADO AND ONION FILLING

**16 Stuffed Beefburger patties
(page 36)**

1 small avocado

**1 medium-sized onion,
chopped**

Salt and pepper to taste

Prepare the patties as directed. Peel and seed the avocado, chop it and mix together with the onion. Season with salt and pepper to taste and place a spoonful in the center of each of 8 patties. Cover with the remaining 8 patties and seal by pinching the edges together. Broil as directed.

CHICKEN LIVER FILLING

**16 Stuffed Beefburger patties
(page 36)**

8 chicken livers

1 tablespoon butter

Salt and pepper to taste

Sauté the chicken livers in butter until slightly pink in the centers. Prepare the patties. Chop the livers coarsely, season with salt and pepper to taste and divide among 8 of the patties. Top with the remaining patties, pinch the edges to seal and broil as directed.

BACON FILLING

**16 Stuffed Beefburger patties
(page 36)**

8 slices lean bacon

Fry the bacon until crisp. Drain it thoroughly and crumble into bits. Prepare the patties as directed. Place a spoonful of bacon bits on top of 8 patties. Seal the edges of the patties after topping with the other 8 and broil as directed.

HAM AND PINEAPPLE FILLING

**16 Stuffed Beefburger
patties (page 36)**

**1/2 cup finely chopped
cooked ham**

**8 pineapple chunks,
drained and chopped**

Prepare the patties. Combine the ham and pineapple chunks and place a rounded spoonful in the center of 8 patties. Top

39

with the remaining patties, pinch to seal the edges and proceed as directed.

SMOKED SAUSAGE FILLING

16 Stuffed Beefburger patties (page 36)

1/2 cup ready-to-eat smoked sausage, finely chopped

Prepare the Beefburger patties. Sauté the sausage for 1 minute. Arrange a spoonful of the chopped sausage on 8 patties, top with the remaining patties and seal the edges. Broil as directed.

REFRIED BEAN AND SCALLION FILLING

16 Stuffed Beefburger patties (page 36)

1/2 cup Refried Beans (page 88)

4 scallions, including 3 inches green top, finely chopped

Prepare the patties as directed. Combine the scallions with the Refried Beans. Place a spoonful of this mixture on top of each of 8 patties. Cover with the remaining patties, pinch the edges to seal and broil as directed.

CHEDDAR CHEESE AND ONION FILLING

16 Stuffed Beefburger patties page 36)

3/4 cup Cheddar cheese, cut into 1/4-inch cubes

1 small onion, coarsely chopped

Mustard

Prepare the patties. Place the cubed Cheddar cheese in a bowl. Add the onions and mix together. Place a spoonful of this mixture in the center of 8 patties and dab with a little mustard. Cover with the remaining patties, seal the edges and broil as directed.

BLEU CHEESE AND CHOPPED NUT FILLING

16 Stuffed Beefburger patties (page 36)

4 ounces bleu cheese

1/4 cup walnuts, coarsely chopped

Allow the bleu cheese to soften slightly, then blend with the chopped nuts. Prepare the patties. Spread the top of 8 patties with the cheese-nut mixture. Place the other 8 patties on top and seal the edges. Broil as directed.

MOZZARELLA FILLING

16 Stuffed Beefburger patties
   (page 36)

4 ounces Mozzarella
   cheese

Prepare the patties as directed. Cut the Mozzarella into 8 paper-thin slices and set one on top of each of 8 patties. Cover with the remaining patties, seal and broil as directed.

CREAM CHEESE AND HORSERADISH FILLING

16 Stuffed Beefburger patties
   (page 36)
2 teaspoons prepared
   horseradish

3 tablespoons cream
   cheese, at room temperature

Prepare the patties. Drain the horseradish thoroughly and mix with the softened cream cheese. Spread the mixture over 8 patties, top with the remaining 8 patties; seal. Broil as directed.

Tomato-Olive Ice Cube Hamburgers

16 very small olives
1 16-ounce can tomato
   juice
4 pounds ground steak,
   fairly lean
2 small onions, chopped
3 cloves garlic, minced

3 cups white wine
3 tablespoons lemon
   juice
1/4 cup butter
1 1/2 tablespoons fresh
   chives, finely chopped
3 tablespoons mustard

(Serves 8)

Make 16 small tomato-olive ice cubes by placing 1 olive in each compartment of an ice cube tray, covering with tomato juice and freezing. Chill the ground steak, cover and keep cold until serving time.

Place the wine in a small saucepan, add the onions and garlic, and cook over medium coals until only 1/2 of the liquid remains. Quickly mix in the lemon juice, butter, chives and mustard. Stir the sauce only long enough to melt the butter, then set the sauce aside to keep warm.

Shape the ground steak into 16 patties, inserting 1 tomato-olive ice cube into the center of each. The ice cubes will keep the centers of the hamburgers rare. Broil the hamburgers to your liking over medium coals, turning once. Place each burger on half a roll, top with sauce and serve immediately.

Hamburgers Au Poivre

3 to 4 tablespoons pepper-corns	1 teaspoon lemon juice
4 pounds fairly lean chuck, chopped	6 drops tabasco sauce
	4 tablespoons cognac
2 1/2 tablespoons butter	Salt to taste
2 tablespoons Worcestershire sauce	3 tablespoons fresh chives, minced

(Serves 8)

Crush the peppercorns with a rolling pin. Spread the pepper on a flat dish or pastry board. Divide the chopped chuck into 8 portions and pat all sides smooth with your hands. Press the hamburgers, one side at a time, into the pepper, making sure that the sides are well coated. Refrigerate the hamburgers and allow them to season for 30 minutes. Broil over hot coals, turning frequently, until the meat is cooked as desired. Just before the hamburgers are turned for the last time, put the butter in a small skillet and place over the coals. When the butter melts, stir in the Worcestershire, lemon juice and tabasco. Remove the hamburgers to serving plates and sprinkle with salt to taste. Stir the Cognac into the butter mixture and set aflame. Pour the flaming sauce over the hamburgers, sprinkle each with chives and serve immediately.

Stuffed Lamb-Burgers

1 large onion, finely
  chopped
4 pounds lean ground lamb
1 tablespoon flour

1 egg
Freshly ground black
  pepper to taste

(Serves 8)

In the kitchen, combine onions with the ground lamb, flour, egg and pepper to taste. Roll out to 3/4 inch thickness on a large sheet of waxed paper. Cut into 16 3-inch round patties.

Outdoors top 8 of these patties with your choice of fillings and cover with the other 8. Seal the edges by pinching all around. Broil over hot coals to the desired degree of doneness, turning once. Brush the burgers occasionally with olive oil while cooking. Sprinkle with salt to taste before serving.

Fillings for Stuffed Lamb-Burgers

(Serves 8)

RICE FILLING

16 Stuffed Lamb-Burger
   patties (above)
 1 cup cooked rice
1/3 cup pine nuts, chopped

1/4 cup raisins
 2 cloves garlic, minced
1/4 teaspoon nutmeg
1/4 teaspoon allspice

Prepare 16 patties from the Stuffed Lamb-Burger mixture. Combine the rice, pine nuts, raisins, garlic and spices. Place 1 rounded teaspoonful on each of 8 of the patties. Top with remaining 8, pinch the edges to seal, and broil as desired.

CREAM CHEESE AND FRESH MINT FILLING

16 Stuffed Lamb-Burger
   patties (above)
 1 3-ounce package cream
   cheese, at room
   temperature
 2 tablespoons undiluted
   frozen orange juice

2 tablespoons finely
  chopped fresh mint
3/4 cup cooked rice
   Salt and freshly ground
   black pepper to taste

Prepare the Stuffed Lamb-Burger patties. Mash the cream cheese slightly with a fork, add the orange juice, mint leaves, rice, salt and pepper. Mix well to blend all ingredients. Spread a spoonful of the mixture on top of 8 patties, cover with the remaining patties and seal the edges. Broil as directed.

CREAM CHEESE AND CURRY FILLING

16 Stuffed Lamb-Burger patties (page 43)

1 3-ounce package cream cheese

1/4 teaspoon curry powder

Let the cream cheese soften slightly while you prepare the Lamb-Burger patties. Blend the curry with the cream cheese and divide the spread over the tops of 8 patties. Cover with the remaining 8 and pinch the edges to seal the burgers. Broil as directed.

APPLE AND JACK CHEESE FILLING

16 Stuffed Lamb-Burger patties (page 43)

1 medium-sized onion, coarsely chopped

1 medium-sized apple,

peeled, cored and chopped

1/4 cup cubed Jack cheese

1/4 teaspoon curry powder

Cut 16 patties out of the Lamb-Burger mixture. Mix the onion and apple with the cubed jack cheese and curry powder. Top 8 Lamb-Burgers with the filling. Place the remaining 8 patties over the filling and seal all around the edges. Broil as directed.

ONION AND DILL FILLING

16 Stuffed Lamb-Burger patties (page 43)

1 medium-sized onion, finely chopped

2 1/2 tablespoons finely chopped fresh dill

Prepare the Lamb-Burger patties as directed. Mix together the onion and dill, and place a spoonful in the center of each of 8 patties; cover with the other 8. Seal and broil as directed.

44

RECIPES FOR THE OPEN GRILL

GARLIC SALT AND ROSEMARY FILLING

16 Stuffed Lamb-Burger
patties (page 43)

2 teaspoons minced fresh
rosemary
1/2 teaspoon garlic salt

Cut 16 patties out of the Lamb-Burger mixture. Combine the rosemary and garlic salt and divide the filling over the tops of 8 patties. Cover with the remaining patties, pinch the edges to seal and broil as directed.

Meat Loaf Pickle Roll

2 pounds fairly lean
chopped chuck
1 onion, finely chopped
2 eggs
1 teaspoon salt
1/8 teaspoon freshly
ground black pepper

1/2 cup heavy cream
2 cups soft breadcrumbs
2 or 3 large sweet pickles
1/2 cup catsup
1/2 cup yellow mustard
4 teaspoons maple syrup

Combine the chopped chuck with the onion, the eggs, the salt and pepper in a large bowl. Stir in the cream and the bread-crumbs; mix thoroughly. Lay out a sheet of wide (18-inch) aluminum foil. Turn the mixture out onto it and shape into a wide 12-inch-long loaf. Arrange the whole pickles in a straight line down the center of the loaf and bring both sides of the loaf up to cover the pickles completely. Fold up the foil all around the meat to enclose the loaf. Place the loaf package over *hot* coals for approximately 50 minutes, turning it partially every 10 minutes until it has made a complete circle. Open and flatten the foil around the loaf. Combine the catsup, mustard and maple syrup. Brush the loaf lightly with the sauce while it cooks for 15 minutes longer. To serve, slice into individual por-tions and insert in warmed hamburger rolls. Top with the re-maining sauce. This loaf is also tasty when made ahead and served cold.

Beef Stuffed Franks

1 pound fairly lean
chopped chuck
2 medium-sized onions,
finely chopped
2 medium-sized green
peppers, finely chopped
1/4 cup maple syrup
2 tablespoons yellow
mustard

1 cup catsup
1/4 teaspoon celery seed
1 teaspoon bottled steak
sauce
8 frankfurters
8 frankfurter rolls

(Serves 8)

Prepare the sauce by first browning the chopped chuck in a heavy skillet over medium heat. Reserve 1/4 cup of the chopped onions. Mix the rest of the onion and green pepper into the meat and sauté until the onion is soft. Remove the skillet from the coals and carefully drain off any fat from the meat. Mix together the maple syrup, mustard, catsup, celery seed and steak sauce. Blend thoroughly into the meat mixture. Cook until bubbling hot. Meanwhile, butterfly the frankfurters by splitting them lengthwise about 2/3 of the way through. Broil them split-side down, until nicely browned. Turn once to brown the bottoms. Remove the franks from the grill, place each in a roll, spread each with mustard, a sprinkling of the reserved chopped onion and several spoons of barbecued chopped meat.

Pickle Pups

8 frankfurters
2 dill pickles

3 tablespoons minced onion
8 strips lean bacon

(Serves 8)

Use a sharp knife to gash a slit lengthwise in the frankfurters. Do not cut all the way through. Cut the dill pickles in quarters lengthwise. Stuff each frank with a pickle quarter and a little minced onion. Wrap a bacon strip around each frank, secure the ends with thin metal skewers and broil over medium-hot coals until the bacon is brown on all sides. Serve with mustard and catsup.

Pizza Franks

2 medium-sized tomatoes	Pinch each of thyme, sage
1 clove garlic, crushed	and oregano
6 tablespoons shredded	8 frankfurters
sharp Mozzarella cheese	8 strips lean bacon
	8 frankfurter rolls

(Serves 8)

Peel the tomatoes and cut into eighths. Shake out the seeds and chop the tomatoes finely. Mix the tomatoes and garlic with the cheese and the spices. Make a lengthwise slit in the frankfurters without cutting through the bottoms or ends. Spoon the tomato and cheese mixture into the slits. Wrap the franks tightly with the bacon strips, holding the ends of the bacon fast with short skewers. Place the frankfurters over medium-hot coals and grill until the bacon is crisp on all sides. Remove the skewers, place the franks in rolls, and serve them immediately.

Franks with Sauerkraut

1 1/2 cups sauerkraut	1 teaspoon caraway
1 large onion, cut into	seed
thin slivers	8 frankfurters
1/4 cup honey	8 strips lean bacon
3 tablespoons tarragon	8 frankfurter rolls
vinegar	

(Serves 8)

Rinse the sauerkraut and drain thoroughly. Mix together the onion, honey, vinegar, caraway seed and drained sauerkraut. Use a sharp knife to slit the frankfurters lengthwise without cutting through the tips. Stuff the franks with the sauerkraut, packing it well into the slits. Secure the sauerkraut stuffing in the frankfurters by binding each frank with a strip of bacon. Skewer the bacon ends with thin metal skewers. Place franks over hot coals, turning frequently until the bacon is crisp. Brown the rolls if desired. Remove the skewers and place a frankfurter in each roll. Serve immediately.

Ham and Cheese Dogs

8 frankfurters

1 cup cooked or canned ham, finely chopped

3 tablespoons Jack cheese, finely chopped

3 tablespoons minced onion

3 tablespoons minced sweet pickle

1 tablespoon cream

2 tablespoons mustard

8 strips bacon

3 tablespoons catsup

2 tablespoons grape (or other) jelly

(Serves 8)

Use a sharp knife to split the frankfurters lengthwise, almost to the ends and about 3/4 of the way through. Combine the ham, cheese, onion and pickle, and bind them together with the cream and mustard. Divide this mixture among the frankfurters, allowing about 2 tablespoons each. Wind a bacon strip around each frankfurter, securing the ends with short metal skewers. Grill the frankfurters until browned and nicely crisp over hot coals, turning frequently and basting often with a mixture of catsup and jelly. Remove the skewers. Place frankfurters in rolls and serve piping hot.

Nutty Cheese Franks

8 frankfurters

1/4 cup Cheddar cheese spread

1/4 cup finely diced Cheddar cheese

3 tablespoons chopped pecans

8 strips bacon

8 frankfurter rolls

(Serves 8)

Split the frankfurters lengthwise, taking care not to cut through to the bottoms or ends. Mix together the cheese spread, chopped cheese and nuts. Stuff about 1 tablespoon of the mixture into each frankfurter slit. Wrap a bacon strip tightly around each frankfurter, securing the ends with short metal skewers. Grill over hot coals until the bacon is browned. Remove the skewers. Place in frankfurter rolls and serve immediately with catsup or mustard, or both.

Broiled Steak with Bleu Cheese

4 2-pound porterhouse steaks

8 ounces bleu cheese, at room temperature

2 tablespoons sour cream

2 tablespoons milk

2 cloves garlic, crushed

(Serves 8)

Trim the fat from the steaks and score the edges. Mix together the softened bleu cheese, the sour cream and the milk. Add the garlic and blend thoroughly.

Broil the steaks over hot glowing coals to the desired degree of doneness, brushing from time to time with the cheese mixture. Turn the steaks for the last time and coat the top evenly with the remaining bleu cheese mixture. Remove the steaks from the heat, slice and serve immediately.

Broiled Marinated Steak

4 2-pound porterhouse steaks (or 2 large sirloin)

1 medium-sized onion, finely chopped

2 cloves garlic, crushed

2 cups red wine

1 tablespoon bottled horseradish

1/2 teaspoon freshly ground black pepper

2 tablespoons butter

49

(Serves 8)

Trim the fat from the steak and score the sides with a sharp knife. To prepare the marinade, place the onion and garlic in a dish large enough to hold the steak, pour in the red wine and horseradish and season with the pepper. Marinate the steak in this mixture for at least 2 hours, turning occasionally. When the coals are ready, lift the steak from the marinade and pat dry. Spread both sides with the butter. Broil over hot coals, turning once. Boil the marinade to reduce to 1/3 its original volume, and serve over the steak.

Steak au Poivre

Your favorite steak to feed 8 (at least 2 inches thick)

2–3 tablespoons pepper-corns

Salt to taste

2 1/2 tablespoons sweet butter

1/4 cup red wine

(Serves 8)

To prepare the steak for broiling, spread peppercorns on a pastry board and crush them coarsely with a rolling pin. Use the heel of your hand to press the pepper into the sides of the steak. Allow the steak to season for at least 45 minutes. Broil over hot coals for 1 or 2 minutes on each side to sear the meat. Transfer to a skillet or a folded aluminum foil pan and cook over hot coals to the desired degree of doneness, turning once or twice. Remove to a warm platter, sprinkle with salt to taste, and cover the top with the butter. Add the red wine to the juices remaining in the pan, swirl to blend the mixture, and pour the liquid over the steak before slicing. Serve hot.

Carpetbag Steak

*This is a recipe for a very special occasion. Thick
sirloin steak with a pocketful of oysters, an
expensive but exquisitely satisfying culinary
adventure.*

**2 4-pound sirloin steaks,
cut 3 inches thick (ask
your butcher to cut a
pocket in each)**
24 small raw oysters

Worcestershire sauce
**Freshly ground black
pepper to taste**
**Maitre d'Hotel Butter
(page 35)**

(Serves 8)

Season the oysters with a bit of Worcestershire sauce and a
sprinkle of pepper. Put 12 oysters in each pocket and sew the
sides together. Broil the steaks as you like them (approximately
12 to 14 minutes on each side). Slice the steaks and serve
topped with Maitre d'Hotel Butter.

Sugar-Broiled Steak

If you feel the urge to splurge—try these.

**8 fairly large porter-
house steaks**

**3 1/2 cups Bar Syrup
(page 128)**

(Serves 8)

Choose fairly large steaks, because broiling them in this unique
way results in a good deal of shrinkage. Place the steaks on a
flat surface. Sprinkle each steak with sugar, and press it into
the meat with your fist. Turn the steaks over and repeat the
procedure. No salt is necessary in preparing or broiling these
unusual steaks. Arrange the steaks over hot coals and broil for
5 minutes. Turn the steaks and sear them on the other side for
5 minutes. Searing in this way seals in the juices. Continue to
broil, turning every 5 minutes for 20 minutes more. As the

steaks broil, the sugar will encase the steaks within a thin, hard, dark-brown coating. To serve, carefully cut away this coating from each steak and slice each portion diagonally. The center of the steak will be bright red and very juicy.

Steak à la Mirabeau

8 small steaks, at least
1 inch thick
1/2 cup butter
2 teaspoons anchovy
paste

24 green olives, pimiento-
stuffed
16 flat anchovy fillets

(Serves 8)

Place the steaks in a wire basket and broil over hot coals to the desired degree of doneness, turning several times. Heat the butter in a small saucepan over the coals and mix in the anchovy paste. Keep warm. Slice the olives. Just before the steaks are turned for the last time, arrange the anchovy fillets in a crisscross pattern over the side to be broiled. Cook for a minute or two, then turn the steaks out onto serving plates with the anchovy side up. Arrange the olive slices in the open spaces between the anchovies. Pour the hot anchovy butter over the steaks and serve immediately.

Tournedos with Mushroom Sauce

For an elegant outdoor meal serve tender Tournedos with mushrooms on slices of sautéed bread.

8 slices French bread
1/2 cup butter
16 fresh mushrooms, sliced
8 1-inch-thick tournedos

1 cup port wine
5 tablespoons heavy
cream

(Serves 8)

Over hot coals, sauté the bread slices on both sides in 2 table-spoons of the butter and set aside to keep warm. Sauté the mushrooms in 2 tablespoons of the butter. Heat the remaining butter in a large skillet over the coals and sauté the Tournedos 1 minute on each side. Place the Tournedos in a hinged wire basket and broil over medium heat, brushing frequently with butter until the meat is done to your liking. Meanwhile stir the mushrooms, wine and cream together and simmer for several minutes. Set the bread slices on individual serving plates, top each with a tournedo and several tablespoons of the mush-room sauce.

Broiled Ginger Short Ribs

Marinate overnight.

8 pounds lean short ribs
3 large cloves garlic,
    crushed
3/4 teaspoon powdered
    ginger

1/3 cup honey
    2 tablespoons sesame oil
1/2 cup soy sauce

(Serves 8)

Have your butcher cut the meat through to the bone to form 2-inch lengths. Place the ribs in a large bowl and set them aside. Place the garlic, ginger, honey, oil and soy sauce in a saucepan and cook over medium high flame, stirring con-stantly, until the mixture comes to a boil. Remove the sauce from the stove and when it cools, pour it over the meat. Marinate the ribs in this mixture overnight, turning occasionally. Drain off and reserve the marinade. Broil the marinated ribs over medium-hot coals until they are tender and brown, bast-ing with the reserved marinade during the last 10 minutes of broiling. Serve hot.

Chili Ribs

8 pounds loin back ribs or spareribs	1/4 cup red wine vinegar
1/2 teaspoon black pepper	1/2 cup vegetable oil
1 tablespoon chili powder	1 cup beef broth
1 medium-sized onion, minced	1/4 cup Worcestershire sauce
3 cloves garlic, peeled	1 tablespoon dry mustard
1 medium-sized green pepper	1 tablespoon paprika
2 cups catsup	2 teaspoons dried tarragon
1/4 cup honey	1/2 teaspoon cinnamon
	1/2 teaspoon allspice

(Serves 8)

Trim any fat from the ribs and rub them on both sides with pepper and chili powder. When the coals are reduced to slow, push them to the back and front of your barbecue-smoker, and place the ribs, base side down, on the center of the grill. Close the lid over the ribs, and cook them for about 2 hours or until they are well done. Cook the barbecue sauce indoors or over hot coals. Discard stem, seeds and white pith of the green pepper and mince. Add to garlic and onion. Place in a saucepan along with the catsup, honey, wine vinegar, oil, beef broth, Worcestershire sauce, mustard, paprika, tarragon, cinnamon and allspice. Bring to a boil, lower the heat and simmer, stirring from time to time, about 20 minutes. Baste the ribs frequently with this sauce during the last 30 minutes of broiling. Cut the ribs into serving portions and boil the remaining sauce and serve with the ribs.

Hawaiian Spare Ribs

*These spareribs are enhanced by an unusual
basting sauce prepared with those delicious fruits that
babies love so well.*

8 pounds meaty spareribs
Salt and freshly ground
black pepper
2 cloves garlic
1 cup dark brown sugar
2/3 cup lemon juice
2/3 cup catsup

2 tablespoons molasses
4 teaspoons ginger
1/4 teaspoon tabasco sauce
2 small jars strained
apricots
2 small jars strained
pineapple

Trim any fat from the ribs; sprinkle with salt and pepper. Arrange the ribs with the bone side down over slow coals. Grill for about 20 minutes on the bone side and 10 minutes on the meat side. Prepare the basting sauce. Mix together the garlic, sugar, lemon juice, catsup, molasses, ginger, tabasco sauce and strained fruit. Cook this basting sauce 5 minutes over medium heat. Turn the ribs so that the bone sides are directly over the coals again, and continue to cook the ribs 30 minutes longer, basting frequently with the sauce. Cut into individual portions and serve hot.

Red-Glazed Ham Slices

2 1 1/2-pound slices
pre-cooked ham,
about 1-inch thick
4 scallions with 3 inches
of green top, finely
chopped
3 tablespoons vegetable
oil

1 1/2 tablespoons lemon
juice
3/4 cup catsup
1/2 cup orange marma-
lade
1 1/2 teaspoons dry mustard
1/8 teaspoon tabasco
sauce

(Serves 8)

Use a sharp knife to gash the fat around the edges of the ham slices to prevent curling. Broil the ham slices over low coals

for 8 minutes on each side, turning once. In a saucepan combine the oil, scallions, lemon juice, catsup, marmalade,
mustard and tabasco sauce. Brush the tops of the ham slices
with this mixture, then turn brushed side down and broil for
7 minutes. Brush the other side of the slices, turn them once
more and continue to broil for about 5 minutes. While the
slices finish broiling, heat the remaining sauce over the low
coals. Arrange the ham slices on a platter and top with sauce.
Serve immediately.

Broiled Chicken on Watercress

Marinate for 2 hours.

1/4 cup vegetable oil
1/4 cup lemon juice
1 teaspoon dry mustard
4 young broiling chickens,
  split

40 sprigs watercress
Vinaigrette Dressing
(below)

(Serves 8)

Combine the oil, lemon juice and dry mustard, and pour this
mixture over the chicken. Marinate in the refrigerator for 2
hours, turning occasionally. Broil over hot coals, 5 minutes on
each side, then move the chicken pieces to a cooler place on
the broiler and continue cooking until done. Turn every 2 or 3
minutes and baste with marinade. Meanwhile wash, dry and
refrigerate the watercress. To serve, dip watercress in Vinaigrette Dressing, shake off excess, and arrange 5 sprigs on each
serving plate. Top with the broiled chicken.

VINAIGRETTE DRESSING

1/2 cup olive oil
3 tablespoons lemon juice
1 teaspoon sugar

1/4 teaspoon salt
1/4 teaspoon dry mustard
1/4 teaspoon pepper

Mix all ingredients well. Use to flavor watercress sprigs and
also as a sauce for the chicken if desired.

Pork Dogs

2 1/2 pounds very lean
    ground pork
    Salt and freshly
    ground pepper to
    taste
1/2 cup flour

4 large onions, peeled
    and sliced
4 large green peppers,
    sliced
3 tablespoons oil
16 hot dog rolls

(Serves 8)

Season the ground pork with salt and pepper to taste and shape into 16 "pork dogs" about 4-inches long and 1-inch in diameter. Roll the "pork dogs" in flour and arrange 8 side by side in a 1-inch-deep wire basket. Push the hot coals out toward the sides of the grill to form a rectangle of coals slightly smaller than the wire basket. Place the wire basket over this rectangle and broil until the pork is well done, about 15 minutes on each side. Meanwhile, sauté the sliced onions and the green pepper rings in the oil. Serve the "pork dogs" hot on toasted rolls with sautéed onions and peppers, and top with catsup and/or mustard. Repeat this process with the remaining "pork dogs," rolls, and the sautéed onions and green peppers.

Chicken-Burgers

Pre-fry these scrumptious chicken-burgers so that they will hold together when they're placed over the open fire. Serve on hamburger rolls topped with tomato, grilled bacon slices, small pieces of lettuce and Piquant Mayonnaise (p. 238). These provide a nice change of pace.

8 chicken breasts, boned
    and skinned
4 large onions, minced
1/4 teaspoon thyme

Butter or oil for frying
Salt and freshly ground
    black pepper to taste

(Serves 8)

Cut the chicken into fine mince. Add the onions and thyme and mix well. Form the mixture into 16 burgers and fry for 2 minutes on each side. Chill until serving time. Reheat thoroughly in a wire burger-basket. Season with salt and pepper and serve as described above.

Crab-Stuffed Chicken Breasts

8 whole chicken breasts, boned
6 ounces crabmeat
1/4 cup finely chopped pimiento
1 cup Easy White Sauce (page 35)
1 egg
1 tablespoon sherry

1/4 teaspoon salt
dash pepper
2 tablespoons vegetable oil
1 tablespoon tomato paste
1/2 teaspoon sugar
1/8 teaspoon garlic powder

(Serves 8)

Place the chicken breasts on a table top and pound them lightly to flatten. Drain the crabmeat thoroughly. Place it in a large bowl and flake with a fork. Take care to remove all bits of shell. Add the pimiento and 1/2 of the white sauce to the crabmeat. Lightly beat the egg and stir it into the crabmeat mixture. Add the sherry, salt and pepper. Toss the mixture several times to blend thoroughly. Divide the mixture evenly among the 8 chicken breasts, spreading it over the top of each breast. Carefully fold the breasts into "packages" and sew each package shut.

When coals are very hot, broil the chicken breasts for about 30 minutes. Turn them every 5 minutes or so until they are cooked through. Brush them during the last 15 minutes of broiling with a sauce made by combining the remaining white sauce with the oil, tomato paste, sugar and garlic powder. Serve immediately.

Broiled Ducklings with Lemon Sauce

2 4- to 5-pound ducklings, split in half	1 whole lemon
Salt and freshly ground pepper	1/4 cup lemon juice
	1/2 cup honey

(Serves 8)

Rinse the duckling halves and pat them dry. Rub salt and pepper on the inside of each. Place the birds rib-side down over small drip pans. Broil over slow coals for 25 minutes. Turn the birds and broil for 15 minutes or until the meat is slightly pink. To make the lemon sauce, cut away and discard the peel and white membrane and slice the lemon as thinly as possible. Place the slices in a small saucepan and add the honey and lemon juice. Boil the mixture for 3 minutes. Strain this sauce, pressing some of the pulp through with a spoon. Broil the ducklings 15 minutes longer, brushing frequently with the lemon sauce. Cut the ducklings into quarters and serve garnished with the remaining sauce.

Herb-Broiled Sea Bass Saint Tropez

Try this French technique for the ultimate in broiled fish. Be sure the fish is super-fresh! This method is equally effective for broiling any variety of whole fish.

1 1 1/2 pound cleaned whole sea bass (or other fish) for each person	1/2 cup melted sweet butter branches of fresh herbs according to your taste

Rinse and dry each fish inside and out and brush with melted butter. Cut branches of fresh herbs 6 to 8 inches long. Wrap each fish in 4 of these and place the herb-wrapped fish in an oiled hinged wire basket. Broil about 6 inches above low coals, turning occasionally, until the fish flesh flakes when pricked with a fork. Discard the charred herbs, sprinkle the fish with salt to taste, and serve *immediately*.

Tuna Teriyaki

Marinate several hours.

3 pounds fresh tuna fillets
2 cloves garlic, crushed
1 small onion, grated
3 tablespoons sherry

1 cup soy sauce
1/4 cup light brown sugar
Pinch of powdered ginger

(Serves 8)

Prepare a marinade by mixing together the garlic, onion, sherry, soy sauce, sugar and ginger. Place the tuna fillets in a bowl, pour in the marinade and stir gently once or twice to ensure an even coating. Refrigerate for several hours. At serving time, drain the fish and arrange it in an oiled hinged wire basket. Broil over medium coals, turning the fish and brushing it with the marinade until it flakes easily when pierced with a fork.

Mixed Meats and Squash

An interesting meal is one where foods are cooked partly indoors and partly on your outdoor grill. The ingredients are then combined and served in the open air.

1 3 1/2 pound frying chicken
1 1 1/2 pound piece lamb shoulder
1/2 pound piece cooked ham
1/2 cup bacon fat

3 cups summer squash and zucchini, cubed
3 tablespoons butter
1 1/2 cups rice
3 cups beef consommé
2 teaspoons dried mint
1 cup sour cream

(Serves 8)

In your kitchen remove the skin and bones from the chicken, trim the lamb and the ham and cut the meats into bite-sized pieces, keeping each meat separate. Sauté the squash in the butter. *Do not overcook.* Set aside. Place the rice in a large skillet, add hot consommé, and cook over low heat until the rice is tender when a grain is rubbed between the thumb and forefinger.

Out-of-doors thread each of the meats on a separate skewer, brush with the bacon fat, and broil over low coals until the lamb is slightly pink, the chicken is well-done, and the ham is browned slightly. Stir the squash, the mint, and the rice together in a skillet over medium coals. Top the rice mixture with the grilled meat cubes and a dollop of sour cream. Serve hot.

Falafel

*Falafel is an unusually tasty dish sold in cafés and by street vendors in the Middle East. It lends itself admirably to outdoor eating because it requires neither utensils nor plates. If the round disks of Pita or Sahara bread are available in your area—
do try this.*

(Serves 8)

CHICK-PEA BALLS

These may be made a few hours in advance and reheated while you warm rounds of Pita or Sahara bread on the grill.

3 cups dried chick peas
1 tablespoon salt
2 eggs
3 tablespoons flour
1 teaspoon baking powder
1 teaspoon salt
1 large clove garlic

1 tablespoon ground cumin seed
1 teaspoon oregano
1 teaspoon thyme
1/2 teaspoon cayenne pepper
Oil for deep frying (about 1 1/2 inches deep)

Place dried chick peas in a large bowl, add water to cover and 1 tablespoon of salt. Cover the bowl and allow the peas to stand overnight.

The next day, drain the peas thoroughly and put them through the fine blades of a food grinder. Beat 2 eggs lightly and add to the peas. Blend in the flour and baking powder. Mash the salt and peeled garlic clove together to a fine paste, and add it, along with the spices, to the chick-pea mixture. Mix all ingredients thoroughly. Heat the cooking oil to 390° F. in a deep skillet. Roll the chick-pea mixture between your palms to form 1-inch balls. Test the balls by dropping one in the hot oil. If it falls apart, add a little more flour to the mixture. The deep-fried balls will be brown and crusty on the outside and fluffy and light on the inside.

To serve, cut 8 Pita, or flat Sahara bread, in half. Slice a pocket in each half and insert a spoonful of Green Salad in the bottom. Add 3 or 4 hot fried chick pea balls, another spoonful of Green Salad, and top with a spoonful or two of Tahini Dressing (below). Serve immediately.

GREEN SALAD

1 large tomato, peeled	1/4 cup olive oil
1 large cucumber, peeled	Lemon juice
5 scallions, trimmed	Salt and pepper to taste
1 small green pepper	

Cut the tomato into quarters and shake out the seeds. Remove the pith and seeds from the green pepper. Finely chop all the vegetables and mix together well. Refrigerate. Just before serving, sprinkle with the olive oil. Add lemon juice, salt and pepper to taste, and toss vegetables lightly.

TAHINI DRESSING

(Sesame Dressing)

1/2 cup sesame oil (Tahini)	2 teaspoons salt
1/2 cup water	3 tablespoons lemon juice
2 cloves garlic, peeled	

Mix the sesame oil and water together thoroughly. Crush the garlic and salt together, using a mortar and pestle. Beat this garlic paste and the lemon juice into the oil and water mixture.

Hot and Cold Tartare Sandwiches

3 3/4 pounds coarsely ground lean steak*— tartare steak should be packed and wrapped loosely to prevent discoloration

32 thin slices pumpernickel bread

French-style (or other) mustard

2 medium-sized sweet onions, chopped

1/2 cup capers, drained

8 tablespoons butter

16 flat anchovy fillets (optional)

4 tablespoons cooking oil

Salt and freshly ground black pepper to taste

(Serves 8)

Keep the steak well chilled until just before cooking. Trim the crusts and spread one side of the bread slices with mustard. Rinse and dry the capers. Heat 2 tablespoons butter and 2 tablespoons oil in each of 2 skillets. Quickly assemble the sandwiches by spreading the *cold* steak tartare on 8 of the slices spread with mustard. Top the meat with the onions, capers, 2 anchovy fillets, and a second slice of bread. Place the sandwiches in the sizzling fat. Turn each *immediately!* Fry each side just long enough to brown the bread. Serve directly from the pan. The bread should be hot and the chopped steak cold. Repeat the process with the remaining ingredients.

* *Important:* Ask your butcher to grind the steak in a machine that hasn't been used to grind pork. This is important since raw pork can cause trichinosis. Better forego this one if your butcher can not give you this guarantee.

Hot Tartare Sandwiches with Fresh Horseradish

*Corn on the cob and broccoli wrapped in foil
complement this delicious sandwich.*

1/4 cup horseradish, grated (or bottled, well drained)	1 1/2 pounds very lean ground beef
1 cup butter at room temperature	Onion slices
	Capers
16 slices rye bread	

(Serves 8)

Mix the horseradish with 1/2 cup of the butter to spreading consistency. Spread the mixture over 8 slices of bread. Top each slice with ground steak, making sure that the meat reaches the edges of the bread. Finish by placing a bread slice on top of the meat. Melt the remaining butter. Brush the outside surfaces of the sandwiches with the melted butter. Place the sandwiches securely in a long-handled shallow wire basket, and toast over medium coals, turning once, only long enough to brown the bread. Garnish the sandwiches with sliced onion rings and capers. Serve immediately.

Lamb and Pistachio Nut Squares

*This Near-Eastern make-ahead meat pie need only
be baked for 30 minutes over medium coals. Plan an
outdoor meal where everything is placed on the grill,
the hood is lowered and baking takes place very
nearly unattended, leaving you free to enjoy a cold
soup or hors d'oeuvre, a drink, and your family
and friends.*

INGREDIENTS FOR STEP 1

1/4 cup butter	1/4 teaspoon freshly ground black pepper
1/2 pound lamb, ground twice	1/2 teaspoon allspice
2 onions	1 cup pistachio nuts, shelled
1/2 teaspoon salt	

(Serves 8)

RECIPES FOR THE OPEN GRILL

DIRECTIONS FOR STEP 1

Melt the butter in a skillet and sauté the lamb for about 5 minutes over medium heat. Peel and chop the onions finely. Add the onions and the salt to the lamb in the skillet and cook gently for about 25 minutes. Drain off and discard any excess fat. Stir the pepper, the allspice and the pistachio nuts into the meat mixture. Cool to room temperature and chill in the refrigerator for 1 hour.

INGREDIENTS FOR STEP 2

1 onion	1 package dried onion soup mix
3/4 pound lamb, ground twice	1 1/4 cups bulghour (avaiable at most health-food stores)
3 tablespoons sesame seeds	1 cup cold water
1 large egg	2 tablespoons butter
1 1/2 teaspoons sugar	1 teaspoon liquid meat concentrate
1/4 teaspoon cayenne pepper	

DIRECTIONS FOR STEP 2

Peel and mince the onion. Place the onion, 3/4 pound of the ground lamb, the sesame seeds, the egg, the sugar, the cayenne pepper and the onion soup mix into a large bowl. Soak the bulghour in water for 10 minutes, drain it through cheesecloth and squeeze out all the water. Add the well-drained bulghour to the meat mixture and knead for about 15 minutes or until the ingredients are blended and the filling is soft. Add 2 tablespoons melted butter if the mixture seems too dry. Grease an 8-inch pan and spread half the lamb and bulghour mixture over the bottom of the pan. Carefully spread the chilled pistachio mixture on top. Spread the remaining lamb and bulghour evenly over the pistachio layer and press down very firmly with the heel of your hand. Brush the top with meat concentrate. Spread the softened butter evenly over the top of the meat pie. Cut the pie into 3-inch squares and bake on the back of the grill with the hood down for 30 minutes.

Deep Fried Sausage Pies

Reheat these tasty meat pies on the grill and serve them to add variety to a 'burger meal.

THE CRUST

8 teaspoons butter
1/2 cup cold water

2 boxes prepared pie crust mix
1 1/2 cups vegetable oil

(Makes 16 little pies)

Melt the butter over hot water; then combine with the cold water and blend into both packages of pie crust mix. Use a fork to stir the mixture until the dough comes clean from the bowl. Dust a pastry board and your rolling pin with flour. Shape the dough into a ball, roll it out to 1/4-inch thickness, and cut the dough into 4-inch squares. Place 1 heaping table-spoon of Sausage Filling on each square, slightly off center to one side. Moisten the 2 inside edges of each square. Fold the edge of the side without the filling over to meet the edge of the other side and press gently to seal, fluting the 2 together. Heat the oil to sizzling in a large skillet, and fry each pie until crispy golden brown, turning once. Cool. Wrap the pies in foil. Reheat on the grill over low coals.

THE SAUSAGE FILLING

1 large onion
16 ready-cooked sausages
1/2 teaspoon oregano
1/8 teaspoon powdered cloves
1/4 cup catsup

2 tablespoons mild mustard
2 tablespoons dried beef broth mix (with no water added)

Peel the onion and chop it finely. Cut the sausages into 1/4-inch slices. Place the onion and the sausages in a skillet, sprinkle with the oregano and powdered cloves, and cook the mixture, stirring occasionally, until the onion is golden. Add the catsup and the mustard, stir in the beef broth mix, and continue to cook and stir over low heat for 3 minutes. Cool the filling, and place by heaping tablespoons on the rolled out squares of crust.

ON A SKEWER

Skewered foods are ideally suited to cooking over charcoal and are great favorites with guests. You can use metal skewers (available at hardware stores) or disposable bamboo skewers.

Broiled Bits of Beef Lisbon

Marinate overnight.

6 pounds top sirloin roast, cut into 2-inch cubes

3 medium-sized onions, quartered

4 medium-sized tomatoes, quartered

3 cloves garlic, finely chopped

1 cup tomato juice

2 1/4 cups tarragon or wine vinegar

1 1/2 teaspoons salt

3/4 teaspoon freshly ground black pepper

1 1/4 teaspoons ground cuminseed

2 1/2 teaspoons powdered allspice

3/4 teaspoon liquid meat concentrate

(Serves 8)

Arrange the meat in the bottom of a large bowl. Mix together the tomato juice, vinegar, spices, onions, tomatoes and garlic; pour over the meat. Marinate overnight, stirring from time to time.

Thread the beef cubes on skewers alternately with the tomato and onion quarters. Broil over hot coals until the beef is brown on the outside, and pink on the inside.

67

While the meat and vegetables are cooking, add the meat concentrate to the marinade and boil over medium heat until the sauce has thickened slightly. Serve the hot sauce spooned over the meat and vegetables.

Hawaiian Chicken Kebabs

Marinate 2 hours.

10 chicken breasts, boned and cut into 1-inch cubes

5 green peppers, cut into eighths

16 small white onions, peeled and halved

24 pineapple chunks

3/4 cup soy sauce

1/2 cup pineapple juice

1/2 cup Benedictine

2 garlic cloves, crushed

1 teaspoon dry mustard

1 teaspoon cardamom

1/2 teaspoon freshly ground black pepper

(Serves 8)

Drain the pineapple chunks, reserving 1/2 cup of the juice. Place chicken, peppers, onions and pineapple chunks in a bowl. Make a marinade by combining the soy sauce, reserved pineapple juice, Benedictine, garlic and spices. Pour this mixture over the chicken, etc., in the bowl and marinate for 2 hours or more.

Alternate the chicken on skewers with pieces of pepper, onion and pineapple. Broil over medium hot coals approximately 15 minutes, turning the skewers, frequently only until the chicken is white clear through. Do not overcook. Serve hot.

Skewered Chicken Livers and Apple with Honey

2 1/2 pounds chicken livers

1/2 cup honey

1/2 cup soy sauce

1/2 teaspoon nutmeg

1/8 teaspoon powdered anise

8 MacIntosh apples, unpeeled, cored and cut into 1-inch chunks

(Serves 8)

Wash the livers, drain on paper towels, then place in a bowl. Mix together the honey, soy sauce and spices, and pour this over the livers. Marinate for 15 minutes; remove the livers. Dip the apple chunks in the marinade. Thread the fruit and livers alternately on a skewer, beginning and ending with an apple chunk. Broil, turning the skewer several times, until the livers are cooked but still slightly pink in the centers. Serve immediately.

Skewered Chicken Livers and Shrimp with Water Chestnuts

16 fresh chicken livers
32 shrimp, shelled and de-veined
1 pound sliced lean bacon
1 can water chestnuts, drained

1/4 cup maple syrup
3 tablespoons mild yellow mustard

(Serves 8)

Clean the chicken livers, cut them in half and couple each half with a cooked shrimp. Cut each bacon strip into 4 pieces; wrap 1 piece around each liver-shrimp pair. Thread the bacon-wrapped liver and shrimp alternately with water chestnuts on 8 skewers. Mix together the maple syrup and mustard. Place skewers over medium coals and broil, brushing frequently with the mustard mixture, until the bacon is crisp and brown on all sides. Serve immediately.

Skewered Peanut Pork

This unlikely sounding combination is a classic and delicious Indonesian dish well worth trying.

5 pounds boned pork loin, cut into 1 1/2-inch cubes

Pepper to taste

1/4 cup chunky peanut butter

1/2 cup frozen orange juice concentrate

2 tablespoons soy sauce

Grilled Peaches (page 97)

(Serves 8)

Remove most of the pork fat. Sprinkle pork with pepper and thread on skewers. When the coals are medium hot, make 2 long, narrow aluminum foil drip pans. Push the coals to the side and in between the drip pans. Position the skewers directly over the drip pans. Cook the pork over medium-hot coals, turning frequently until the meat is nearly done (about 25 minutes).

Meanwhile, thin the peanut butter with the orange juice and soy sauce and brush the pork with this mixture, rotating the skewer over the coals an additional 15 minutes. Serve hot with Grilled Peaches.

Skewered Chicken Teriyaki

Marinate several hours or overnight.

6 large chicken breasts, boned and cut into 1 1/2-inch squares

2 cloves garlic, crushed

1 cup brown sugar

1/2 cup soy sauce

1/3 cup dark rum

1/8 teaspoon coarsely ground black pepper

2 green peppers, cut into 1-inch squares

2 cups canned pineapple chunks, drained

2 cups very small white onions, peeled

(Serves 8)

70

Arrange the chicken pieces in a single layer in a shallow glass baking dish. Place the garlic in a small bowl, and add brown sugar, soy sauce, rum and pepper. Mix this marinade thoroughly and pour it over the chicken pieces. Refrigerate and allow the chicken to marinate for several hours or overnight, turning the pieces once.

Before cooking, while your coals are heating, prepare the green peppers, the pineapple chunks and the onions. Thread the chicken, pepper squares, pineapple chunks and onion alternately on skewers. Broil over medium coals for 15 minutes, turning frequently and basting from time to time with the marinade, until the chicken is pearly-white inside and golden-brown on the outside. Do not overcook.

Cook-Ahead Pork Kebabs

Marinate 5 hours or overnight.

3 pounds fillet of pork, cut into 1 1/2-inch cubes

1 large onion, crushed

5 garlic cloves, crushed

Juice of 2 oranges

Juice of 1 lime

3 tablespoons melted butter

2 tablespoons flour

3 tablespoons sugar

3 ripe bananas

1/2 cup shredded coconut

(Serves 8)

Place the meat in a large bowl. Mix the orange and lime juice with the crushed onions and garlic. Pour this marinade over the pork pieces and marinate them for 5 hours, or overnight.

Heat the butter in a skillet over medium coals. Drain the pork, reserving the marinade, pat the cubes dry, and sauté them in the butter until they are no longer pink inside. Remove the pork from the skillet. Sprinkle the flour over the butter, letting it brown slightly. Stir in the reserved marinade and the sugar, and continue to stir until the mixture boils and thickens. Set the sauce aside to keep warm.

Peel and cut the bananas into 1 1/2-inch pieces. Coat each banana section with shredded coconut. Alternately thread pieces of pork and pieces of banana on 8 individual skewers. Place over slow coals, turning frequently, until the pork is hot and the coconut is brown. Serve with the warm sauce.

Seafood Brochettes with Bacon

16 sea scallops
4 dozen shrimp, peeled and deveined
2 dozen frozen oysters, thawed
1 pound sliced lean bacon
1/2 cup butter
Freshly ground black pepper to taste

1 tablespoon minced chives
2 teaspoons minced fresh tarragon (or 1/2 teaspoon dried)
2 teaspoons minced fresh thyme (or 1/2 teaspoon dried)

(Serves 8)

Slice the sea scallops in half. Beginning with a shrimp, thread each skewer with the end of one slice of bacon, next thread 1/2 a scallop. Thread the skewer through the middle of the bacon slice, a shrimp and then the other end of the bacon. Start once more with the end of another piece of bacon and alternate scallops, shrimp and oysters with threaded bacon. Season the seafood with pepper to taste. Melt the butter in a saucepan on top of the grill and add the fresh herbs. Set the sauce to one side to keep it warm, brush all sides of the skewered seafood with the butter sauce and allow the seafood to broil over hot coals for several minutes on each side, continuing to brush with butter until the bacon is fairly crisp. Serve immediately with the remaining sauce.

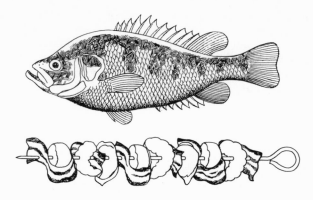

Shish Kebab or Shaslik

Marinate for 2 days.
These renowned meat dishes are one and the same—
Shish Kebab being the Armenian and Shaslik the
Russian version of broiled, skewered bits of meat.
Lamb or mutton is traditional but veal or beef
may be used.

1 medium size leg of lamb	16 cherry tomatoes
1/2 cup olive oil	3 green peppers, with pith and seeds removed
1/4 cup lemon juice	16 mushroom caps
1 cup red wine	16 small onions, parboiled for 3 minutes
3 cloves garlic, crushed	
1/4 teaspoon black pepper	1 large eggplant, cut into 2-inch cubes
4 bay leaves, broken into 1/4-inch pieces	

(Serves 8)

Trim the lamb of all gristle, bone and fat. Cut the meat into 2-inch cubes and place it in a large plastic, glass or enamel receptacle. Mix the olive oil, lemon juice, wine, garlic, pepper, and bay leaves and pour this marinade over the meat. Marinate for 2 days in the refrigerator. One hour before cooking time place the cherry tomatoes, the green peppers (cut into 2-inch squares), the mushroom caps, the parboiled onions and the cubed eggplant in the bowl with the meat and the marinade. Stir. Refrigerate for one hour longer. At cooking time thread the vegetables and the meat alternately on 8 skewers. Broil over medium coals until the meat is brown on the outside but still pink on the inside . . . or about 8 minutes on each side. Serve hot.

SPIT-ROASTED MEATS

If you are fortunate enough to have a rotisserie attachment for your grill, you can serve these delicious treats to your family and friends. There are portable rotisseries on the market which can be placed over a basic grill and used over the fireplace in the winter.

Try to keep the spit centered as much as possible in attaching the meat to the spit, so that the weight is equally distributed. When the food is not in a compact form, such as is the case with ribs or poultry, use string to tie up loose ends and keep it all together.

Charcoal-Roasted Spiced Beef

1 tablespoon Chinese Five Spice Powder; or 3/4 teaspoon each powdered ginger, anise, nutmeg and cloves

1 teaspoon white pepper

2 tablespoons salt

5 1/2 pounds sirloin tip of beef

8 tablespoons butter, melted

1 tablespoon Worcestershire sauce

2 teaspoons onion juice

74

(Serves 8)

Prepare the fire well ahead of time so that the coals will be gray when you are ready to cook the roast. Combine the spices, and work thoroughly into the meat. Brush aside the ash from the coals and place the meat on a spit about 8 inches above the hot coals. Cook 60 to 90 minutes, allowing the meat to turn continually. Don't worry if some of the fat catches on fire. The roast should be charred on the outside and rare on the inside.

Cut the meat into 1/2-inch-thick slices and serve with a mixture of hot melted butter, Worcestershire sauce and onion juice.

Broiled Peppered Rib Eye of Beef

Marinate overnight.

1 8-pound boneless rib eye of beef	3/4 cup lemon juice
1/3 cup black peppercorns, coarsely cracked	3/4 cup soy sauce
	1/4 cup catsup
1/2 teaspoon ground cardamom	4 garlic cloves, crushed

(Serves 8)

Trim all fat from the beef. Combine the cracked peppercorns with the ground cardamom, and press this mixture against all sides of the beef, making sure that as much adheres as possible. Prepare a marinade by blending the lemon juice, soy sauce, catsup and garlic. Allow the beef to marinate overnight in this mixture. Turn occasionally. Balance the roast evenly on a spit and rotate over medium coals until the meat is as well done as you like it (about 2 hours for medium rare).

Barbecued Ribs with Tomato Glaze

8 pounds lean back ribs
or spareribs
Salt and freshly ground
black pepper to taste
3 medium-sized onions,
coarsely chopped
1/2 cup salad oil

1/2 cup lime juice
1/2 cup orange juice
2 cups spaghetti sauce
1/2 cup bottled steak sauce
2 teaspoons sage
1/2 teaspoon freshly ground
black pepper

(Serves 8)

Trim as much fat as possible from the ribs and season with salt and pepper. Secure ribs to the spit by interlacing between the bones at several points in each rack of ribs. Set over an aluminum foil drip pan surrounded by hot coals, and rotate spit slowly until the ribs are thoroughly cooked, approximately 75 minutes.

While the ribs are cooking, prepare the barbecue sauce. Heat the oil in a skillet over the coals and gently sauté the onions until they are transparent. Add the lime juice, orange juice, spaghetti sauce, steak sauce, sage and pepper; mix thoroughly. Cook the sauce over low coals for 15 minutes, stirring occasionally, until the original quantity is reduced and starts to thicken. Brush the ribs frequently with the sauce during the last 30 minutes of cooking to give the meat a mouth-watering glaze.

Cut into serving pieces before passing to your guests.

Spitted Turkey with Tarragon

2 6-pound turkeys
Juice of 1 lemon
Salt and freshly ground
black pepper to taste
1 bunch fresh tarragon,

chopped; or 2 1/2 tea-
spoons dried tarragon
1 cup white wine vinegar
3/4 cup vegetable oil
1/4 cup sugar

(Serves 8 to 10)

Rub the insides and outsides of the turkeys with lemon juice. Rinse and dry a bunch of tarragon sprigs, chop and use to rub the inside of the turkeys. Reserve at least 1/4 cup of chopped fresh tarragon or 1 teaspoon dried tarragon for the sauce. Truss the turkeys and secure them so that they balance evenly on a revolving spit. Roast over slow coals for 2 hours or until the drumsticks no longer run pink when pierced with a fork.

Prepare the sauce while the birds revolve. Place remainder of tarragon with the vinegar, oil and sugar in a small saucepan. Bring to a boil and cook for 5 minutes over low heat. Refrigerate until serving time.

To serve, remove the trussing string and allow the turkeys to cool a bit before carving. Top each serving with a spoonful or two of the tarragon sauce, either cold or at room temperature.

Spit-Roasted Turkey

*If Thanksgiving Day is fair and dry, it might be a
nice idea to spit-roast the holiday turkeys.*

2 6-pound turkeys	1/2 teaspoon sage
4 onions, chopped	Freshly ground black
1/2 pound sausage meat	pepper to taste
30 prunes, soaked over-	1/3 cup fresh mint, minced
night	1/2 cup honey
5 cups breadcrumbs	1/2 cup soy sauce
1/2 teaspoon salt	10 strips bacon
1/2 teaspoon thyme	

(Serves 10)

Rinse the turkeys and dry well inside and out. Set aside. Prepare the fire well ahead of time so that the coals will be gray when the turkey is ready to cook.

Fry the sausage until it is crumbled and brown. Pour off all but 1/2 cup of the sausage fat and sauté the onions until they are golden and transparent. Add the pitted prunes to the sausage along with breadcrumbs, salt, thyme, sage, pepper and 2 tablespoons of the mint. Allow stuffing to cool.

Fill the body and neck cavities of the turkeys with the stuffing and sew up the openings. Use thin metal pins to secure the bacon strips across the breasts. Truss the birds by tying the legs and wings securely to the body. Crisscross the string across the breasts to help secure the bacon strips. Push the spit rod through the birds so that the birds will be evenly balanced. Place the turkeys about 8 inches above the coals. Use small aluminum foil pans to catch the drippings. Roast the birds for about 2 hours or until the juice no longer runs pink when the thighs are probed with a fork.

Meanwhile, combine the honey, the rest of the mint and the soy sauce. Baste the bird with this mixture every 5 minutes for the last 1/2 hour of roasting. Serve hot.

Spit-Broiled Ducklings with Lichees

2 4- to 5-pound ducklings	Freshly ground black pepper to taste
1/4 cup honey	1 can lichees; or peach slices if lichees are not available
3/4 cup soy sauce	
1 cup orange juice	
1/4 teaspoon powdered anise	

(Serves 8)

Prepare the fire ahead of time so that the ducklings will be cooked over medium-hot coals. Tie the wings and legs securely and balance the birds evenly on the spit rods.

Combine the honey, soy sauce, orange juice, anise and pepper in a small saucepan. Simmer over low coals for 5 minutes; set aside.

Place the spit rod with the ducklings over the coals with a drip pan underneath to catch the juices. Broil the birds for about 1 1/2 hours, basting every 15 minutes with the pan drippings. During that last 1/2 hour of broiling, baste with the honey-orange mixture.

Heat the lichees in the remaining basting sauce. Serve with the hot ducklings.

Roast Duckling with Bing Cherry Sauce

2 6-pound ducklings
1/2 teaspoon onion
powder
1 teaspoon marjoram
1/4 teaspoon pepper
Vegetable oil

3 cups canned Bing
cherries with juice
1 tablespoon orange
zest (grated outer
rind)
1 1/2 tablespoons corn-
starch

(Serves 8)

Use your fingers to press a mixture of onion powder, marjoram and pepper into the cavities and skin of the ducklings. Place ducklings in the refrigerator for an hour at least.

Remove from the refrigerator and brush with vegetable oil; truss securely with string and refrigerate overnight.

When ready to roast, balance the ducklings evenly on a spit and allow them to rotate over a circle of medium coals for 1 hour, or until the meat of the breast is still slightly pink. Remove the ducks from the spit; cut the trussing cord and split ducks in half. Broil each half over medium coals, skin side down, until the skin is crispy brown. Allow about 10 minutes for each half. Serve immediately with hot Bing Cherry Sauce on the side.

BING CHERRY SAUCE

Mix the cherries with their juice, the orange zest and the corn-starch. Bring to a boil over medium heat, stirring constantly.

Canadian Bacon with Ginger-Mustard Glaze

Serve this succulent bacon roast with fried eggs.
Breakfast has never tasted so good!

2 1/2 pounds fully cooked
    Canadian bacon
1/2 teaspoon powdered
    ginger

1/2 cup currant jelly
2 tablespoons mild
    yellow mustard

(Serves 8)

With a sharp knife, score the sides of the bacon, making diagonal crisscross slashes about 1/2-inch deep. Secure the bacon evenly on a spit over an aluminum foil drip pan. Allow the bacon to rotate over the coals for 1 hour.

    Mix together the ginger, jelly and mustard. Brush the bacon frequently with this mixture as it continues to cook for about 15 minutes more. Cut into 1/3-inch slices and serve with fried eggs, orange juice, biscuits and coffee.

Grilled Bologna with Sweet and Hot Sauce

This may sound very "unspecial," but it is tasty as
well as attractive.

1 4-pound whole bologna
1/2 cup currant jelly
2 tablespoons soy sauce
1 tablespoon brown
    mustard

1/4 teaspoon tabasco sauce
1 clove garlic, crushed
1 cup catsup
16 hamburger rolls

(Serves 8)

With a sharp knife, make lengthwise cuts 1/4-inch deep in the bologna at 1/3-inch intervals. Balance the bologna on a spit and rotate it, covered with a hood, over medium coals for about 75 minutes. Use an aluminum foil pan to catch the drippings.

    While the bologna is grilling, mix together the currant jelly, soy sauce, mustard, Tabasco sauce, garlic and catsup. Brush the bologna frequently with this mixture during the last 15 minutes of cooking.

To serve, lightly brown the hamburger rolls, heat the remaining sauce to bubbling, slice the bologna into thin slivers and place the meat on the bottom halves of hamburger rolls. Spoon the hot sauce over the meat, cover with the tops of the rolls and serve immediately.

Spit-Broiled Canadian Bacon Roll

1/2 cup sherry
2 tablespoons molasses
1 cup orange marmalade

1 2 1/2-pound piece fully cooked Canadian bacon

(Serves 8)

Combine the sherry, molasses and marmalade in a small saucepan. Over low heat, bring the mixture to a boil, stirring occasionally. Remove to the back of the grill.

Insert the spit securely through the bacon and broil over medium-hot coals for 60 minutes. Brush the meat with the marmalade mixture and continue to baste every few minutes for 15 minutes more. When the outside is browned and glossy, slice and serve.

Spit-Roasted Venison

Marinate overnight.
A gift of a saddle of venison from a relative who hunts with bow and arrow, "one deer for table"
each year, produced this recipe and a
marvelous dinner.

1 8-pound saddle of venison
Salt and pepper
3/4 cup vinegar
1 1/2 cups red wine
Juice of 2 lemons
1/4 cup Worcestershire sauce

1/4 teaspoon allspice
1/2 cup butter
Game Sauce (for example Fresh-Cooked Horseradish Sauce For Game (page 26)

(Serves 8)

81

Sprinkle the saddle of venison generously with salt and pepper, pressing in as much of the seasoning as possible. Mix together the vinegar, red wine, lemon juice, Worcestershire sauce and allspice. Marinate the venison in this mixture overnight.

Melt the butter. Spit-roast the venison over high heat for 30 minutes, basting often with a mixture of the melted butter and marinade. Lower the coals and continue to roast the venison 45 to 60 minutes for rare meat. Remove from heat and serve with Game Sauce.

NOTE: Most game should be hung in a cool place for three days to a week and marinated for several days before preparing.

Barbecued Suckling Pig

1 25-pound suckling pig, cleaned and dressed	2 teaspoons freshly ground black pepper
Juice of 2 oranges	2 tablespoons thyme
Juice of 1 lime	4 tablespoons butter
8 garlic cloves, crushed	1/4 teaspoon saffron
1/4 cup salt	

(Serves 15)

Use a sharp knife to gash the pig lightly on all sides. Combine the juices with the garlic, salt, pepper and thyme. Rub in this mixture over the cavity and outside surfaces of the pig. Refrigerate the pig overnight, covered with a dish towel. Secure the pig so that it balances evenly on a revolving spit, place a drip pan under it and slowly roast it over medium coals for 5 to 6 hours. Make a mixture of melted butter and saffron and use to baste the pig frequently. To serve, carve into chops and slices, and accompany each serving with a sweet, hot barbecue sauce. WARNING: Be very sure that the meat is thoroughly cooked. Pork should never be pink when eaten.

Ham on a Spit with Pineapple Marinade

6 pounds fully cooked
boneless ham

1 1-pound can crushed
pineapple

1/2 cup maple syrup

1/4 cup mild yellow
mustard

1/2 teaspoon powdered
cloves

(Serves 10)

Cut away any rind from the ham. When the coals in the grill
are hot, push them to the back and set an aluminum foil drip
pan under the spot where the ham will cook. Balance the ham
on the spit evenly and allow it to rotate, with the grill lid down,
for 90 minutes.

Meanwhile, in a small saucepan, mix the pineapple, maple
syrup, mustard and cloves and bring to a low boil over
medium heat. Remove the spit from the heat and score the ham
with crisscross diagonal lines. Return the ham to cooking position. Discard all fat from the foil drip pan and replace the pan
under the ham. Brush the meat frequently with the sauce
while it continues to cook for another 30 minutes. A
meat thermometer should register 130° F. when the ham is
ready to serve. Cut the ham into thin slices, arrange on a serving platter, and garnish with the remaining sauce.

Spit-Roasted Small Game Birds

*When small game birds are in season and plentiful,
this is the recipe you'll need. Partridge are fabulous
cooked this way! If you're adventurous, try this
one on a camping trip, using a spit supported by
forked sticks.*

2 small young game birds,
dressed

1/4 teaspoon thyme powder
Freshly ground black
pepper to taste
Butter

4 slices bacon

4 tablespoons butter or
oil

2 scallions, white part
only; or 8 wild onions

1/2 cup sherry or any other
alcoholic beverage

4 slices toast

(Serves 4)

Clean the birds inside and out, rinse with cold water, pat dry, and rub with thyme. Wash the livers, cut in half, and set aside. Sprinkle pepper over the inside of each bird; rub butter over the skins. Crisscross 2 slices of bacon over each breast and truss the legs of each bird close to its body. Use extra string to secure the bacon slices.

Spit-roast the birds over high heat for approximately 35 to 45 minutes, basting frequently with 2 tablespoons of butter or oil. The birds are ready to eat when the thigh is fully cooked but the breast is still pink. Do not overcook!

While the partridge are being roasted, heat the other 2 tablespoons of butter or oil in a skillet. Trim and finely chop the scallions, and sauté them in the butter or oil for 3 minutes, stirring frequently. Sauté the reserved liver halves until they are browned, with only a pinkish tinge in their centers. Remove from heat, mash the livers, and season with salt and pepper to taste. When the partridge juices no longer run pink, remove the birds from the spit and set them aside to keep warm. Untie and remove string. Make a sauce by adding 2 tablespoons of butter and 1/2 cup of sherry to the mashed liver. Reduce the liquid by cooking it over medium heat, stirring frequently.

To serve, cut the partridge in half. Spread 4 slices of toast with the seasoned liver-sherry mixture. Place a partridge half on each slice and garnish with any remaining sauce. Serve hot.

Charcoal-Cooked Vegetables

One standard barbecue recipe covers nearly every summertime vegetable. Rinse, peel and/or seed the vegetable as you would for indoor cooking.

Cut as follows:

Carrots, squash, celery—bite size pieces
Broccoli spears, eggplant fingers—serving size pieces
Eggplant, potatoes, squash—slice

Acorn squash—cut in half

Tomatoes, squash, onions, etc. may be halved, brushed with butter and grilled in a fairly wide wire barbecue basket.

Corn, new potatoes, onions—leave whole

Wrap and season as follows: Place the vegetables on a double thickness of aluminum foil with the water that clings to them after washing, sprinkle with salt or other spices and dot generously with butter.

To steam vegetables, fold the foil tightly so that no steam will escape; to bake them (as for acorn squash and potatoes), leave a small hole in the top for the steam to escape.

Broil over medium coals until the package and the vegetable may be pierced easily with a skewer or fork, (from 15 minutes to 1/2 hour for cut vegetables—1/2 to 1 hour for whole vegetables). Be careful not to overcook vegetables.

Vegetables may also be broiled as described in Broiled Zucchini with Parmesan and Broiled Eggplant Slices on the following pages.

Sweet and Salty Corn on the Cob

16 small ears of corn	2 1/2 teaspoons salt
1/2 cup honey	1/4 cup water

(Serves 8)

Gently pull the husks down from the corn but do not tear them off. Remove the corn silk. Place the honey, salt and water in a small saucepan, bring to a boil and boil gently for 3 minutes. Brush the corn with this syrup, pull the husks up around the ears and wrap each ear with aluminum foil. Place the wrapped corn in the coals. Turn frequently until the corn is tender, about 20 minutes.

Onions Stuffed with Ham

8 large onions
2 cloves garlic
3 tablespoons olive oil
5 tablespoons minced boiled ham

1 tablespoon catsup
Freshly ground black pepper to taste

(Serves 8)

Place the onions in a large saucepan, cover them with water and cook over medium-high heat until they are barely tender. Simmer the garlic cloves with enough water to cover until soft. Remove the centers from the onions with a teaspoon. Put the onion centers in a mortar along with the garlic cloves, the olive oil, the ham, the catsup and the pepper. Using the pestle, pound the ingredients into a smooth paste. Stuff the onions with the onion-garlic mixture, wrap them in foil without completely closing the top, and place over medium coals for 15–20 minutes. Serve hot.

Broiled Zucchini with Parmesan

16 small zucchini
1/4 cup melted butter or vegetable oil

3 tablespoons soy sauce
3 tablespoons Parmesan cheese

(Serves 8)

Wash the zucchini well and cut off the ends. Peel two 1/2-inch strips of skin from each zucchini. Cut the vegetables into 2-inch sections. Mix the butter or oil and the soy sauce. Thread the zucchini sections onto skewers, brush with the butter-soy sauce mixture, and broil over medium coals. When the zucchini is nearly tender, brush once again with the mixed butter and soy sauce, sprinkle generously with Parmesan cheese and continue to broil until the cheese is brown. Serve hot.

Broiled Eggplant Slices

2 large eggplants

3 large cloves garlic

1 tablespoon salt

1/3 cup olive oil

1/4 teaspoon oregano

1 tablespoon wine vinegar

(Serves 8)

Remove stem ends from both eggplants. Cut each eggplant lengthwise into 4 slices of equal thickness. Cut the peel from the rounded outer eggplant slices. Peel the garlic cloves, place them in a mortar and use the pestle to crush them with the salt. Pour the oil over the garlic–salt mixture, season with the oregano and stir in the vinegar. Brush both sides of each eggplant slice with this marinade. Broil over slow coals until the eggplant slices are golden brown, turning the slices frequently and brushing often with the marinade. Serve hot.

Eggplant Parmesan

If you have a grill with a hood, you can make Eggplant Parmesan. A few minutes before serving, top each eggplant slice with 2 tablespoons Parmesan cheese, 1 tomato slice and a sprinkle of oregano. Lower the hood and cook for 4 minutes.

Broiled Sweet Potato

Sweet potatoes appear in the early fall. Watch for them. They are particularly good broiled this way.

8 sweet potatoes

2 tablespoons vegetable oil

(Serves 8)

Wash the potatoes and remove 1/2 inch from each end. Rub with oil. Place over low coals. Turn frequently. Broil until soft— about 1 hour. Serve hot.

Garlic Potatoes

8 large all purpose
potatoes, peeled

10 cloves garlic, chopped
1/3 cup vegetable oil

(Serves 8)

Cut potatoes into 1/2-inch-thick slices. Heat the oil in a large heavy skillet and fry the garlic for several minutes. Remove garlic. Fry the potatoes until they are browned on one side, then turn and brown on the other side. Remove the slices with a slotted spoon and drain on paper toweling. Serve very hot.

Breaded Tomato Slices

3 eggs
3/4 cup milk
1 1/2 teaspoons salt
3 tablespoons melted
butter
1/4 teaspoon sage

9 tomatoes
Salt, flour
1 cup fine, dry bread-
crumbs
Butter for frying

(Serves 8)

Beat the eggs. Add the milk, salt, melted butter and sage; mix well. Cut each tomato into 4 slices, discarding the end pieces. Sprinkle each slice with salt and dust both sides with flour. Dip each floured slice first in the egg mixture and then in the breadcrumbs. Melt a little butter in a skillet and fry the tomato slices, turning once, until they are golden and crispy. Serve hot.

Refried Beans

*Soak overnight and prepare your basic bean recipe
ahead of time and finish the cooking outdoors.
This easy, economical and utterly delicious dish
makes a perfect "go-with" to accompany almost any
outdoor meal. These versatile beans, which team up
with other ingredients to produce a number of*

tempting recipes, may be cooked a day or two in advance and refrigerated until serving time. Beans may be reheated by adding a few tablespoons of bacon fat (or butter) to a skillet and stirring until the beans are soft and hot.

1 1/2 **pounds dried pinto beans***
8 **cups cold water**
2 **medium-sized onions, chopped**

3/4 **cup bacon fat**
Salt to taste

(Serves 8)

In your kitchen—soak the beans overnight in the cold water. The following day, bring the beans to a boil, then lower the heat and simmer partially covered for 2 1/2 to 3 hours, or until beans are very tender, adding a bit of hot water from time to time if necessary to keep the beans from boiling dry. Drain well and mash the beans with a potato masher.

Outdoors—sauté the onions in the bacon fat until soft and transparent but not browned. Mix the onions and fat into the mashed beans and stir over medium-low heat until the beans are hot and the fat has been absorbed. Serve hot as a potato substitute.

* Available at Mexican grocery stores, large supermarkets or health food stores.

New Potatoes with Lemon Butter Sauce

32 **very small new potatoes**
5 **scallions with 3 inches green top**
1/3 **cup butter**
2 **teaspoons lemon zest (thinly grated outer skin**

of the lemon with no white underskin)
Coarse salt and freshly ground black pepper, to taste

(Serves 8)

89

Wash the potatoes well and cook them in their skins until they are *just* tender. Do not overcook. Wash, trim and finely chop the scallions. Melt the butter in a heavy skillet, add the lemon zest and the scallions and sauté for 2 minutes. Cut a crisscross gash in each potato and serve with the hot lemon-butter sauce in a separate pitcher or bowl.

Hot Green Beans with Bacon

6 slices bacon, chopped	3/4 teaspoon salt
2 pounds fresh green beans	3/4 teaspoon freshly ground black pepper
1/3 cup bacon fat	4 tablespoons wine vinegar
3 scallions with 3 inches green top, chopped	
2 teaspoons parsley, chopped	

(Serves 8)

Sauté the bacon until crisp. Drain the bacon pieces and reserve the fat. Rinse the beans and snap off the tips. Bring about 2 inches of salted water to a boil in a large saucepan. Add the beans, bring to a boil again, and cook for 5 minutes. Reduce the heat, cover, and cook for 8 minutes longer, or until the beans are tender but still firm. Drain the beans and sauté them in the bacon fat for 3 minutes. Place the scallions, parsley, salt, pepper and vinegar in a small jar. Cover and shake thoroughly. Pour this mixture over the hot beans and toss quickly. Serve immediately.

Asparagus with Sesame Seeds

8 cups diagonally cut, scraped asparagus spears	4 teaspoons hulled white sesame seeds
4 teaspoons olive or safflower oil	3 tablespoons vinegar
	1 1/2 tablespoons sugar
	1 1/2 tablespoons soy sauce

(Serves 8)

Steam the asparagus pieces and set aside. Heat the oil in a skillet and lightly brown the sesame seeds. Mix together all ingredients and refrigerate. Serve cold.

Ratatouille

3 large onions
1/2 cup olive oil
3 small eggplants, peeled and cut into 1/2-inch cubes
4 green peppers, coarsely chopped
6 medium-sized tomatoes

6 small zucchini
2 cups celery, chopped
1 clove garlic, crushed
Salt and freshly ground black pepper to taste
1/4 teaspoon each of dried marjoram and basil

(Serves 8)

Peel the onions, slice them into thin rings and sauté them gently in the oil in a large skillet until they are soft but not browned. Stir the eggplant and pepper into the onions and sauté over low heat for 5 minutes. Peel the tomatoes, seed them by cutting them into quarters and shaking out the seeds, then chop them coarsely. Cut the zucchini into 1/2-inch slices. Combine the tomatoes, zucchini and celery with the other vegetables in the skillet and allow the mixture to simmer, covered, for about 50 minutes. Add the garlic, pepper, marjoram and basil during the last 5 minutes of cooking. Serve the *ratatouille* hot, or chill it and serve with cold meat.

Breads and Desserts

If you have a grill with a hood, it is great fun to surprise your family and guests with a treat or two not generally prepared out-of-doors.

Burger Buns

Any burger or sandwich tastes better on a
"home-baked" bun.

1/3 cup powdered milk
    solids
1/4 cup sugar
  2 packages dry active
    yeast

1 tablespoon salt
6 cups flour, unsifted
1/3 cup butter, softened
2 cups lukewarm tap
   water

(Makes 20 buns)

In a large mixing bowl, combine the powdered milk solids, sugar, yeast and salt with 2 cups of flour. Cut in the softened butter. Slowly stir in 2 cups of warm tap water, blending well. Use an electric mixer and beat at medium speed for 2 minutes, scraping the sides of the bowl from time to time. Blend in 3/4 cup of flour and beat for 2 minutes at high speed, stopping occasionally to scrape the bowl.

Make a stiff dough by blending in as much of the remaining flour as necessary. Knead the dough on a lightly floured board 10–12 minutes, or until it becomes elastic and smooth. Grease a large bowl and put the dough in it; turn the dough upside down once to grease the top. Allow the dough to rise, covered, in a warm, draft-free place until it doubles in volume, approximately 55 minutes.

Using your fist, punch the dough down. Cover and allow to rise again for only 25 minutes. Before it doubles in size, cut the dough into 2 equal portions and divide each portion into 10 pieces of equal size. Shape these pieces into balls. Position about 2 inches apart on a baking sheet or 4 thicknesses of aluminum foil and press into bun shapes. Allow to rise once more, covered, in a warm, draft-free place, until doubled in volume. This should take approximately 60 to 70 minutes. Place the risen rolls on 3 more aluminum sheets about 6 inches from the hot ashy coals. Lower the hood of the grill and bake for 60 minutes. Turn the rolls and bake until the tops are fairly brown, approximately 20 minutes more. Cool on wire racks.

Sesame Pretzels

2 cups warm water
2 packages active
  dry yeast
1/2 cup granulated
  sugar
2 1/4 teaspoons salt

4 tablespoons
  butter, softened
1 egg
7 to 7 1/2 cups flour
1 egg yolk
Sesame seeds

(Makes 30 pretzels)

Place water and yeast in the large bowl of electric mixer. Stir until yeast is dissolved. Add the sugar, salt, butter, egg and 3 cups of flour. Beat at medium speed to make a smooth batter. Add enough additional flour to make a stiff dough. Cover the bowl tightly with aluminum foil and refrigerate 4 to 6 hours.

Turn out the cold dough on a lightly floured breadboard, and divide in half. Cut each half into 15 pieces. Roll each piece between your hands to form pencil shapes about 18-inches long. Work fast because the dough is springy and tends to shrink up into shorter lengths. Give each piece a final stretch before shaping it, form into a pretzel and pinch the ends together. Beat the egg yolk and brush each pretzel generously with the mixture. Dip the side glazed with egg yolk into the sesame seeds and arrange on lightly greased baking sheets. Cover and let rise in a warm, draft-free place for 30 minutes. Bake on a hooded grill at 400° F. When golden brown, after approximately 15 minutes, remove from baking sheets and cool on wire racks.

New Orleans Yam Cake

This smooth, spicy Yam Cake is particularly nice when served with vanilla ice cream. Bake it over the coals that remain after you grill a meat or fish dish.

2 pounds yams
1 large, ripe banana
3 tablespoons butter, melted
3 eggs
1 cup milk
6 tablespoons molasses
1 cup sugar

1/2 teaspoon almond extract
1/4 teaspoon allspice
1/4 teaspoon powdered anise
1/4 teaspoon nutmeg
1 cup buttered graham-cracker crumbs

(Serves 8)

Scrub the yams, cover them with water and boil them until soft. Drain off the water, and when they are cool enough to handle, peel and mash them. Peel and mash the banana. Place the mashed yams in the large bowl of your electric mixer. Beat in the melted butter, the banana and the eggs. Stir in the milk, molasses, sugar, almond extract, allspice, anise and nutmeg and beat until the batter is smooth. Spread the graham-cracker crumbs on the bottom of a large, well-greased, heavy skillet. Spoon the batter over the crumbs. Cover the pan and place under it 4 thicknesses of aluminum foil. Cook on grill over slow coals for 1 hour and 15 minutes, or until a toothpick comes out clean when inserted into the center of the cake. Turn this spicy cake onto a plate, cut into wedges and serve hot or cold with vanilla ice cream.

Skillet Apple Gingerbread

2 cups all-purpose flour
1 1/2 teaspoons ground ginger
1 1/4 teaspoons ground cinnamon
1/4 teaspoon ground cloves
2 teaspoons baking powder
1/4 teaspoon baking soda
1/2 teaspoon salt

1/3 cup shortening
1/3 cup sugar
1 egg
3/4 cup milk
3/4 cup molasses
2 medium-sized apples, peeled, cored and sliced
2 tablespoons butter

(Serves 8)

Sift and measure 2 cups flour. Combine with ginger, cinnamon, cloves, baking powder, baking soda and salt; sift again. Place the shortening in large bowl and beat it lightly; add the sugar and cream it with the shortening. Mix in the egg and beat the creamed mixture until light and fluffy. Combine the milk and molasses. Add the dry ingredients and the milk-molasses mixture alternately in small amounts to the creamed shortening. Stir well after each addition, but only until blended. Line a 9-inch heavy skillet neatly with 2 thicknesses of aluminum foil. Dot the foil with the butter. Arrange the apple slices attractively over the butter and spoon the batter over the fruit. Cover the skillet and place it over low coals* for 90 minutes or until a wooden toothpick comes out clean when inserted in the center of the cake. Do not lift the lid during the first 30 minutes of cooking.

* If you are simultaneously cooking a meat or fish recipe that requires that the coals be close to the grill, place 2 or 3 sheets of aluminum foil under the pan and push the coals to one side.

Apple Upside-Down Cake

Whip this delectable cake together about 1 1/2 hours before your guests arrive for dinner. Place it on the back of the grill and forget it while the rest of the meal cooks. A dessert that is baked outdoors is always appreciated by guests.

4 medium-sized apples, peeled and cored
1 tablespoon lemon juice
2 cups sugar
3 cups flour
1 tablespoon baking powder
1/4 teaspoon salt
1 cup vegetable oil

4 eggs, beaten
1 teaspoon vanilla
1/4 cup orange juice
1 1/2 tablespoons butter
1/2 cup chopped nuts
4 tablespoons sugar
1 teaspoon cinnamon
1 1/2 cups heavy cream

(Serves 8)

Thinly slice 2 of the apples. Sprinkle the slices with lemon juice and set aside. Chop the two remaining apples. Into a bowl, sift together the sugar, flour, baking powder and salt. Stir in the oil, beaten eggs, vanilla and orange juice. Beat until the batter is smooth and free of lumps.

Cover the bottom of a heavy skillet with 2 thicknesses of aluminum foil. Arrange the apple slices on the foil, dot with butter, and pour 1/2 the batter over the fruit in the pan. Mix together the chopped apples and chopped nuts; place them over the layer of batter. Combine the sugar and cinnamon and sprinkle half of this mixture over the nuts and apples. Pour in the remaining batter and top with the rest of the cinnamon-sugar mixture. Cover the skillet and place it on the back of the grill, near but not over the low coals. Cook for about 1 hour and 40 minutes, or until a toothpick comes out clean when inserted into the center of the cake. Place a large serving plate over the skillet and turn the cake onto it with the apple slices on top. Carefully peel off the aluminum foil. Serve with cold whipped cream in a separate bowl.*

* If the cake does not turn out of the pan neatly and in one piece, serve it topped with the whipped cream and no one will be the wiser.

Bing Cherry Omelet

8 egg whites	kirsch
8 egg yolks	confectioners' sugar
1/3 cup sugar	4 cups Bing cherries, cut
1 tablespoon water	in half and pitted
1/8 teaspoon salt	1 pint heavy cream
4 tablespoons butter	

(Serves 8)

Separate the egg yolks from the egg whites and place in separate bowls. Mix the sugar with the egg yolks and beat until thick and lemon-colored. Add the water and a few grains of salt to the egg whites and beat until they stand in peaks. Fold the egg whites carefully into the beaten egg yolks. Melt the butter in 2 medium-sized skillets. Pour the egg mixture into the skillets and cook until the omelets are brown on the bottom and the eggs are set on top. Fold the omelets in half and carefully slide them onto 2 serving dishes. Sprinkle generously with kirsch and confectioners' sugar and surround with the Bing cherries. Serve with a bowl of whipped cream flavored with sugar and vanilla.

Grilled Peaches

8 large ripe peaches	1 tablespoon rum
3 tablespoons currant jelly	

(Serves 8)

Dip the peaches in boiling water and pull off the skins. Cut the fruit in half and discard the pits. Arrange the peach halves on skewers. Mix together the jelly and rum. Brush the fruit with the jelly–rum mixture and broil until the peach halves begin to brown. Do *not* overcook.

Grilled Bananas

16 ripe bananas	1/8 teaspoon nutmeg
1/2 cup honey	1 1/2 cups heavy cream,
10 macaroons, crushed	whipped

(Serves 8)

Peel the bananas and brush them on all sides with the honey. Arrange them in a 1-inch deep oiled wire basket and grill over medium coals for 2 to 3 minutes on each side until nicely browned. Serve hot and pass a bowl of macaroon crumbs mixed with lightly sweetened nutmeg flavored whipped cream for guests to help themselves.

Jelly-Baked Apples

8 baking apples
1/4 cup raspberry jelly
3/4 cup almonds, finely
chopped
1/2 cup sugar

1 cup heavy cream,
whipped
Banana-flavored liqueur
to taste

(Serves 8)

Using a paring knife, carefully core the apples without cutting through the bottom. Peel the skin from the top 1/3 of each apple. Place the apples in a baking pan and fill with a mixture of jelly and chopped nuts. Sprinkle the top of the apples liberally with sugar. Bake slowly covered with foil until the apples are tender but not mushy. Serve warm, topped with whipped cream lightly sweetened with banana liqueur.

Recipes to Complement Your Barbecue

Hors d'Oeuvres

SERVE FIX-AHEAD cold hors d'oeuvres or a cold soup while the entrée and vegetables are cooking on the grill.

Antipasto

1 small cauliflower, separated into florets

15 small white onions (about 1-inch in diameter), quartered

1 small eggplant, cut into 3/4-inch cubes

1 cup string beans

1 cup button mushrooms

1 carrot, cut into 1/2-inch pieces

1 stalk celery, cut into 1/2-inch pieces

1 small green pepper

1 small red pepper

2 large cloves garlic, coarsely chopped

3/4 cup olive oil

2 small bay leaves

16 large ripe olives

10 large green pimiento-stuffed olives

4 canned pimientos, drained

1 cup tarragon vinegar

1 cup catsup

4 teaspoons mild yellow mustard

2 1/2 tablespoons brown sugar

Salt and freshly ground black pepper to taste

French bread or melba toast

(Serves 8)

99

Heat the olive oil in a large skillet, add the garlic and sauté until golden. Discard the garlic and add the raw fresh vegetables and the bay leaves. Cover and cook slowly until the vegetables are just barely tender when pierced with a fork.

Meanwhile, chop the ripe and the green olives coarsely and cut the pimientos into bite-size pieces. Add the olives and the pimiento to the vegetables in the skillet along with the wine vinegar, catsup, mustard and sugar. Continue to cook for about 8 minutes, stirring from time to time. Adjust the seasonings and turn the antipasto into a bowl; chill well. Drain off the excess oil* and serve with thin slices of French bread or melba toast.

* Excess liquid may be used to baste steak or kebabs.

Summer Vegetable Bowl

5 medium-sized carrots, cut into thin strips	16 cherry tomatoes
3 large green peppers, cut into thin strips	Garlic Mayonnaise (page 25), Hot Anchovy Dip (page 108), or Cheese and Nut Dip (page 108)
16 scallions	
1 bunch radishes	
3 medium-sized cucumbers	

(Serves 8)

Trim the scallions, leaving 3 inches of green top. Rinse and trim the radishes, leaving 1/2-inch of green leaves. Cut off a flat piece from the root end of each radish and make thin petal-shaped cuts around the radishes to create a rose effect. Soak all vegetables in the refrigerator in ice water for at least an hour. Drain well, and cut the unpeeled cucumbers into thin lengths before arranging all vegetables attractively over cracked ice. Service with Garlic Mayonnaise, Hot Anchovy Dip or Cheese and Nut Dip.

Honeydew Melon with Prosciutto Slices

1 large ripe honeydew
  melon
2 tablespoons lime juice

8 thin slices prosciutto
  (Italian ham)
8 lime slices
8 lemon slices

(Serves 8)

Cut the chilled melon in half and scoop out all the seeds and stringy fibers. Peel the halves, cut into thin slices, sprinkle with lime juice and chill well. At serving time, arrange the melon slices on 8 cold plates and top each serving with a slice of prosciutto and a slice each of lemon and lime. Serve immediately.

Bleu Cheese Celery

1 large bunch celery
1/4 cup cream cheese, at
  room temperature
1/2 cup butter, at room
  temperature

3/4 cup Bleu cheese, at
  room temperature
1/4 cup chives, minced
1/2 cup finely chopped
  walnuts

(Serves 8)

Scrub and trim the celery stalks, discarding the leaves. Combine the cream cheese, butter, bleu cheese, chives and walnuts to produce a well-blended mixture. Fill each celery stalk with the cheese mixture. Refrigerate for at least 2 hours and cut into 3-inch pieces. Serve cold.

Pickled Scallops

3 medium-sized white
  onions
5 large dill pickles
2 pounds scallops, washed
  and cut into 1/3-inch
  slices
4 cloves garlic, peeled
  and crushed

1 cup lime juice
1/2 cup lemon juice
3 tablespoons white wine
  (optional)
4 tablespoons sugar
Salt and pepper to taste
2 cups salad oil

(Serves 8)

Peel the white onions and cut them into very thin rings. Cut the pickles into 1/4-inch slices. Beginning with the scallops, make layers of the scallops, onion rings and pickle slices in a large wide-necked jar or bowl. Prepare a marinade by mixing the garlic, the lime juice, the lemon juice, the wine, the sugar, and the spices in a separate bowl. Slowly beat in the oil. Pour this marinade over the scallops, onion rings and pickle slices. Cover the jar and allow it to refrigerate overnight. Serve cold.

Lobster Chunks with French-Mustard Dip

3 cups cooked lobster meat chunks	1 cup sour cream
1/4 cup French-style mustard	1/2 cup finely chopped chives
	1 cup whipped cream

(Serves 8)

Cut the lobster in chunks and skewer each with an hors d'oeuvre pick. Refrigerate. Mix together the mustard and sour cream. Fold in the chives and the whipped cream. Refrigerate. Serve with the chilled lobster chunks.

Eggplant Appetizer

1 medium-sized eggplant	2 teaspoons lemon juice
2 large onions, chopped	1/4 teaspoon cinnamon
4 slices bacon, chopped	1/2 teaspoon salt
4 stalks celery, chopped	1/8 teaspoon each cloves and marjoram
4 tablespoons honey	
4 tablespoons catsup	

(Serves 8)

Peel the eggplant and cut it into 1/2-inch squares. Parboil eggplant for 3 minutes and drain well. Fry the onion, bacon and celery over a medium flame for 5 minutes. Add the eggplant and the remaining ingredients and cook, stirring constantly, for 4 minutes more. Serve cold or at room temperature on crackers.

Green Chili Meatballs

3/4 pound lean chuck, finely ground
3/4 cup corn flake crumbs
1 small onion, chopped
1 1/2 tablespoons hot green chili peppers, minced
1/2 teaspoon oregano

1 egg
1/2 cup light cream
Salt and freshly ground black pepper to taste
1/4 cup vegetable oil
1/4 cup butter

(Serves 8)

In a large bowl, mix together the meat, corn flake crumbs, onions, chili peppers and oregano. Beat the egg to a lemony froth; add it and the cream to the meat mixture. Sprinkle with salt and pepper to taste, and mix all ingredients thoroughly. Heat the oil and butter in a large skillet. Shape the meat mixture into tiny balls, and sauté them until they are brown on all sides. Serve piping hot with a sweet and sour sauce.

Crunchy Chicken Balls

Any combination plate of the following 6 recipes lends variety to a backyard barbecue. These particular recipes are not only delicious but are also high in nutrition.

4 small chicken breasts, skinned and boned
6 tablespoons red miso*
1/2 teaspoon salt
16 water chestnuts

2 tablespoons flour
6 tablespoons vegetable oil
Soy sauce

(Serves 8)

Grind the chicken breasts or chop them finely. Stir the miso and salt in with the chicken. Mince the water chestnuts and mix them, along with the flour, into the seasoned chicken meat. Form into small balls, allowing about 1 teaspoon of the mix-

* Soy bean paste available in health food stores and Oriental groceries.

ture for each. Fry in hot oil for 3 or 4 minutes or until brown on all sides. Serve hot, dipped in a little soy sauce if desired.

Cheddar and Walnut Balls

2 cups sharp Cheddar
cheese, grated

1/4 cup butter, at room
temperature

1 clove garlic, crushed

3/4 cup walnut halves,
finely chopped

2 teaspoons Worcester-
shire sauce

French-Mustard Dip
(page 102)

(Serves 8)

Blend the cheese with the softened butter. Work in the cheese mixture together with 1/2 cup of nuts. Season with the Worcestershire, mix thoroughly, and shape into bite-sized balls. Roll the balls in the remaining nuts. Chill for at least 1 hour. Spear each ball with a toothpick. Serve cold with mustard sauce.

Cold Shrimp Balls

1 pound boiled shrimp,
shelled and deveined

8 hard-cooked eggs,
shelled

1 teaspoon salt

1/2 teaspoon pepper

1 tablespoon fresh dill
weed, minced (or
1 teaspoon dried)

6 tablespoons sour cream

4 tablespoons wheat germ

(Serves 8)

Finely chop the shrimp and the hard-cooked eggs. Mix together the shrimp, eggs, spices and sour cream. Form into small balls and roll in the wheat germ. Refrigerate. Serve cold.

Avocado Balls

2 ripe avocados

4 tablespoons olive oil

1/2 cup lemon juice

2 cloves garlic, crushed

1 teaspoon chili powder

(Serves 8)

Peel and seed the avocados. Using a small melon-ball cutter, cut the pulp into balls. Mix the oil, lemon juice, garlic and chili powder. Place the avocado balls in a glass jar and pour the lemon juice marinade over them. Turn the jar once. Chill for several hours, turning the jar occasionally. Drain, insert a wooden pick in each ball, and serve cold.

Alfalfa Sprout Balls

If you're wondering what to serve your friends who are health food addicts—try these.

1 cup alfalfa sprouts	1 teaspoon sea salt
1 cup cream cheese	Generous pinch or two
3/4 cup unblanched almonds, chopped	of curry powder

(Serves 8)

Coarsely chop the alfalfa sprouts. Mix the sprouts, cream cheese, half of the chopped nuts, the sea salt and curry powder. Shape into balls and roll in the remaining chopped nuts. Chill and serve cold.

Hard-Cooked Eggs Stuffed with Salmon

16 hard-cooked eggs	1 tablespoon onion, minced
1/4 cup cooked salmon or shrimp, finely chopped	Mayonnaise
2 tablespoons sweet pickles, finely chopped	7 small pimiento-stuffed olives, sliced

(Serves 8–10)

Shell the hard-cooked eggs and split them lengthwise. Remove the yolks and press them through a fine sieve. Mix the yolks with the finely chopped fish, the chopped pickles and the minced onion. Add just enough mayonnaise to barely moisten the mixture and place a spoonful on each egg white. Decorate each egg with 1 slice of olive; chill and serve as an appetizer.

Eggplant with Miso

1 eggplant	2 tablespoons red miso*
3 tablespoons almond kernel oil	2 tablespoons sugar
	4 tablespoons water
8 scallions, chopped	1 tablespoon vinegar

(Serves 8)

Cut the eggplant into 3/4-inch cubes. Place the oil in a teflon skillet. Heat over high flame. Stir in the eggplant. Lower the heat to medium and cook for 5 minutes, stirring occasionally. Mix together the miso, sugar, water and vinegar. Pour this mixture over the eggplant. Stir over low heat for 3 or 4 minutes. Add the scallions and stir for 1 minute more. Serve hot as an hors d'oeuvre.

* Soy bean paste available at health food stores or Oriental groceries.

Deviled Dandelion Eggs

12 hard-cooked eggs	4 tablespoons mayonnaise
1/2 cup young dandelion leaves, finely chopped	1/2 teaspoon dry mustard
	1/4 teaspoon nutmeg

(Serves 8)

Cut the eggs in half lengthwise. Force the yolks through a fine sieve. Mix the sieved egg yolks, chopped dandelion leaves, mayonnaise and spices. Fill the hard-cooked egg whites with this mixture, using a pastry tube if available. Chill. Serve cold.

Oriental Almonds

Guests love these!

2 1/2 cups almonds	anise, cloves, ginger and nutmeg)
2 tablespoons butter	
1/8 teaspoon Chinese Five Spices (or a pinch each of powdered	1/4 teaspoon sea salt
	5 tablespoons soy sauce

(Serves 8)

Sauté the almonds in the butter over very low heat. Sprinkle with spices, add the soy sauce and stir until the nuts are dry.

Potato Medallions with Caviar

If your cook-out is one that is easy to prepare, you may have the time to serve these delectable little potato pancakes.

4 medium-sized potatoes	5 tablespoons heavy cream
3 tablespoons milk	4 tablespoons butter
1/2 teaspoon salt	Sour cream
4 tablespoons flour	Red and/or black caviar; or bits of flat anchovy fillets
4 eggs	
2 tablespoons sour cream	

(Serves 8)

Boil the potatoes until tender and purée them by forcing through a fine sieve. Mix the milk into the potato purée and set aside to cool. Stir in the salt and flour, then beat in the eggs, one at a time, beating thoroughly after each addition. Add 2 tablespoons of sour cream and the heavy cream and stir until the batter is smooth. Melt a bit of the butter on a griddle and drop tablespoons of the batter into the hot butter. Turn the medallions and cook until they are golden on both sides and brown around the edges.

Serve topped with a dollop of sour cream and a bit of caviar. These are rolled and eaten with the fingers.

These little potato pancakes can be cooked ahead of time and reheated over the fire on aluminum foil. Top with the sour cream and caviar, roll up and serve immediately.

Dips

Hot Anchovy Dip

*To be served with an attractively arranged platter of
hot or cold vegetables.*

3 cloves garlic, peeled
   and crushed
1/2 cup butter, melted

1/4 cup olive oil
1/4 cup anchovy paste

(Serves 8)

Place the crushed garlic in a saucepan with the butter, the oil
and the anchovy paste and heat over a very low flame. Do *not*
boil. Serve hot.

Cheese and Nut Dip

3 ounces Roquefort
   cheese
3 ounces cream cheese, at
   room temperature
1/2 cup sour cream
1/2 cup heavy cream

1 small onion, grated
2 tablespoons parsley,
   minced
1 tablespoon steak sauce
1/4 cup walnuts, finely
   chopped

(Serves 8)

Force the Roquefort cheese through a fine sieve with the back
of a spoon. Blend it into the softened cream cheese. Stir in the
sour cream, cream, onion, parsley, steak sauce and nuts. Chill.

Green Devil Dip

This unusual dip is hot enough to make you cry but tasty enough to keep you coming back for more. Serve this with tiny meat balls, vegetable cubes, shrimp or tortilla chips.

2 ripe avocados	1 tablespoon lime juice
1/2 4-ounce can hot green chili peppers	2 tablespoons mayonnaise
	1/4 cup heavy cream
2 tablespoons onion, chopped	1 teaspoon salt
1 clove garlic, peeled and crushed	

(Serves 8)

Peel the avocados, cut them in half, and remove the seeds. Coarsely chop the avocados and place them in a blender, along with the chili peppers, chopped onion, crushed garlic, lime juice, mayonnaise and salt. Blend for a few seconds until all ingredients are well puréed. Refrigerate at least 1 hour.

Refried Bean Dip with Corn Chips

3 1/2 cups Refried Beans (page 88)	3 1-inch cubes soft Jack cheese (or Longhorn Cheddar)
1/2 cup Italian Dressing (page 120)	Corn chips
1 small onion	

(Serves 8)

Mash the beans and dressing together with a fork, adding more dressing if necessary to bring the dip to the desired consistency. Peel and mince the onion. Cut the cheese into fine dice. Stir the onion and 1/2 of the cheese into the dip. Place in a serving bowl and top with the remaining cheese. Serve at room temperature with corn chips.

Oriental Egg Spread

8 scallions with 3 inches of
  green top
8 hard-cooked eggs, shelled
8 thin slices fresh ginger
  root, peeled

3 tablespoons white miso
8 teaspoons yoghurt

(Serves 8)

Finely chop the scallions, hard cooked eggs, and ginger root.
Mix the miso and yoghurt together. Stir in the egg mixture.
Chill. Serve as an hors d'oeuvre with crackers.

Cold Soups

Gazpacho

2 small onions, chopped
2 medium-sized cucum-
  bers, peeled and
  chopped
2 large cloves garlic,
  crushed
4 medium-sized tomatoes,
  peeled, seeded and
  chopped
1 medium-sized green
  pepper, chopped
4 cups French bread
  crumbs

1/4 cup red wine vinegar
6 cups clam juice
1/2 teaspoon salt
1 tablespoon tomato paste
3 tablespoons olive oil
Garnishes:
  Green peppers, chopped
  onions, chopped
  cucumbers, chopped
  croutons
  freshly ground pepper to
  taste

(Serves 8)

In a bowl, mix together the chopped vegetables, bread crumbs, wine vinegar, clam juice and salt. Whir a portion at a time in the blender until all is puréed. Return purée to the bowl and beat in the tomato paste and the olive oil. Cover tightly and chill in the refrigerator for 2 hours or more. Serve the cold soup in chilled soup bowls. Serve bowls of chopped green pepper, chopped onion, chopped cucumber and croutons as a garnish.

Iced Fish, Meat, and Cucumber Soup

This chilled cucumber soup laced with chicken,
shrimp and fennel is beautifully white and creamy.

2 1/2 cups plain yoghurt
2 1/2 cups milk
1 1/2 large cucumbers, peeled and chopped
3 small dill pickles, peeled and chopped
1 1/2 cups cooked shrimp, chopped
1 1/2 cups cooked chicken, chopped

6 tablespoons parsley, minced
2 1/2 tablespoons fresh fennel, minced
1 large leek, minced
3 tablespoons lemon juice
Salt and pepper to taste
6 hard-cooked eggs

(Serves 8)

Stir the yoghurt and milk together. Add the cucumbers, pickles, shrimp, chicken, parsley, fennel and leek. Stir in the lemon juice, salt and pepper, then chill the soup for at least 4 hours. Serve cold, garnished with sliced hard-cooked eggs.

111

Hlodnik

A gorgeous pink, chilled beet soup garnished with hard-cooked eggs and lemon slices. Its flavor is enhanced by the chopped shrimp, cucumbers and ham.

8 small beets, sliced
1/2 cup young beet tops, minced
1 1/2 cups water
5 tablespoons scallions, minced
1 tablespoon fresh dill, minced
1 1/4 cups sour cream
1/4 cup lemon juice
2 teaspoons vinegar

1 teaspoon salt
5 cups chicken broth
1 cup cooked shrimp
2 medium-sized cucumbers
1 1/2 cups cooked ham
Freshly ground black pepper
5 hard-cooked eggs
8 thin slices lemon

(Serves 8)

Place the beets and beet tops in a saucepan. Add the water and cook for 20 minutes, or until the beets are tender. Cool the beets, reserving the cooking water, and chop them very fine. Stir the chopped beets into the beet water, and add the scallions, dill, sour cream, lemon juice, vinegar, salt and chicken broth. Refrigerate for 3 hours or longer. Place soup bowls in the refrigerator. Chop the shrimp. Peel and chop the cucumbers. Dice the cooked ham. Chill well. Stir the shrimp, cucumbers and ham into the cold soup.

To serve, put 1 tablespoon of crushed ice in each chilled bowl and pour the soup over it. Sprinkle with the black pepper and garnish with the hard-cooked eggs, cut in lengths, and lemon slices.

Cold Guacamole Soup

*A penchant for using leftovers resulted in this
out-of-the-ordinary avocado soup. All the
ingredients contained in guacamole are here,
plus a generous supply of rich heavy cream.*

2 large ripe avocados,
 peeled and chopped
 (reserve the pits and
 add them to the
 chopped avocados to
 prevent discoloration)

2 tablespoons lemon
 juice

5 cups chicken broth

3/4 cup ripe tomatoes,
 peeled, seeded and
 coarsely chopped

1/4 cup Bermuda onion,
 peeled and finely
 chopped

2 cups heavy cream

1 1/2 tablespoons
 mayonnaise

1 teaspoon chili powder

10 drops Tabasco sauce

(Serves 8)

Reserve 3/4 cup chopped avocado pulp, add the pits and
lemon juice and refrigerate. Place remaining chopped avocado
in blender container with 1/4 cup chicken broth. Blend until
smooth, stopping occasionally to push the contents down
against the blades. Add the remaining chicken broth and
mix thoroughly. Place in a glass or enamel pot and slowly
bring to a boil. Lower the flame immediately and simmer
over very low flame for 5 minutes. Cool. Meanwhile, prepare the tomatoes and onion. Refrigerate. Put the mayonnaise in a small bowl, add the cream, a bit at a time,
stirring until smooth. Add the mayonnaise-cream mixture to
the cool avocado soup and chill well. Just before serving, stir
in remaining ingredients including the reserved chopped avocado with pit removed. Serve very cold, garnished with an ice
cube.

Cream of Almond Soup

The delicate flavor of almonds accents this creamy, smooth-textured soup. Serve in thin glass bowls or champagne glasses as a preface to an elegant outdoor meal such as grilled fowl.

3 cups blanched almonds
4 squares of lump sugar
5 cups chicken broth
1 1/4 cups milk

1 1/2 cups heavy cream
1/8 teaspoon ground cardamom
Salt and white pepper to taste

(Serves 8)

Using an electric blender, finely chop together 2 3/4 cups almonds and the lump sugar. Turn off the blender every few seconds and gradually add 3 tablespoons of cold water. Place the chicken broth in a saucepan. Add the almond-sugar mixture and simmer, covered, for 10 minutes. Heat the milk in a separate saucepan. Remove the soup from the heat, stir in the hot milk, add the cream, cardamom and salt and pepper to taste, and return to very low heat for a minute or two. Chill the soup and serve it very cold. This soup may also be served hot.

Chilled Avocado Soup

Few soups are as attractive and delectable as creamy avocado soup.

3 large ripe avocados, peeled and cut into 1/2-inch cubes
6 cups chicken broth
1 teaspoon lime juice
1 3/4 cups heavy cream

1/8 teaspoon nutmeg
Salt and white pepper to taste
Whipped cream
Lime Ice Cubes (page 128)

(Serves 8)

Place avocado cubes in blender container with 1/2 cup chicken broth. Blend until smooth, stopping once or twice to push the avocado cubes down against the blades. Mix in the remaining broth and lime juice and stir. Pour into a glass or enamel pot and bring to a boil. Lower the flame immediately and simmer over very low flame for 4 minutes. Stir in cream, nutmeg, salt and pepper; chill. Serve cold, topped with a dollop of whipped cream and a lime ice cube.

Salads

To prevent last minute panic, prepare your salad in advance and refrigerate it until the grilled meal is very nearly ready to serve. Toss the salad while your guests look on, and serve it before it has a chance to wilt.

Summer Salad

*Here's a lunch in a bowl or a salad to serve with
a plain meat meal.*

4 small cucumbers, finely chopped	5 tablespoons lime or lemon juice
10 scallions with 3 inches green top, finely chopped	5 tablespoons olive or safflower oil
4 medium-sized tomatoes, finely chopped	3 tablespoons fresh mint, finely chopped
4 small green peppers, finely chopped	2 tablespoons wheat germ

(Serves 8)

Toss the vegetables with lime juice, oil and mint. Chill well. Sprinkle with wheat germ just before serving.

Curried Summer Salad

4 medium-sized ripe
  tomatoes
4 hard-cooked eggs
2 cups cooked chicken
  breasts, cut in julienne
  strips
2 cups cooked whole
  green beans
1 1/2 cups cooked peas
1 cup cooked carrot
  slices
1 1/2 tablespoons tarragon
  vinegar

1 teaspoon curry
  powder
3/4 teaspoon salt
1/3 teaspoon freshly
  ground black pepper
1/2 cup vegetable oil
2 tablespoons finely
  chopped fresh chives
2 tablespoons minced
  fresh parsley

(Serves 8)

Peel the tomatoes, cut into quarters and remove the seeds, then chop coarsely. Peel the eggs and cut lengthwise in halves. Set the yolks aside and cut the whites into thin strips. Combine the tomatoes and egg whites with the chicken, green beans, peas and carrot slices. Place 3 egg yolks in a small bowl and mash thoroughly with a fork until smooth. Add the vinegar, curry powder, salt and pepper; blend until smooth. Add the oil, a tablespoon at a time. Beat the dressing vigorously, and pour it over the salad. Toss lightly several times. Just before serving, press the remaining egg yolk through a sieve held over the salad. Sprinkle with chives and parsley.

Salade Pierre

1 large head lettuce
3 scallions, minced
3 cups raisins, walnuts
  or pecans
1/2 cup apple, peeled and
  chopped

20 Greek olives
1/3 cup Cheddar cheese,
  diced
1/3 cup skinless Genoa
  salami, chopped

(Serves 8)

Remove the core and break the lettuce into bit-size pieces. Place in a large salad bowl and add the remaining ingredients, tossing to mix well with Zesty Dressing.

ZESTY DRESSING

1/2 cup tarragon vinegar
3/4 cup olive oil
2 teaspoons Worcester-
shire sauce

1 teaspoon dry mustard
1/2 teaspoon salt

Use a wire whisk to combine all ingredients thoroughly. Toss the salad with the mixture.

Greek Salad

1 medium-sized cucum-
ber, thinly sliced
1 bunch radishes
6 scallions
5 ripe tomatoes
1 head lettuce
24 Greek olives

1 1/2 teaspoons salt
1 1/2 teaspoons oregano
1/3 cup wine vinegar
1/2 cup olive oil
8 thin slices Feta cheese
16 flat anchovy fillets

(Serves 8)

Wash and thinly slice the radishes. Trim the scallions, but leave on 3 inches of green top. Cut the scallions into 1-inch pieces. Remove the stem ends from the tomatoes and cut into very narrow wedges. Shred the lettuce and place in a large bowl. Add the cucumbers, radishes, scallions, tomato wedges and Greek olives. Refrigerate until serving time. Just before serving, combine the salt, oregano and vinegar in a jar, cover and shake thoroughly. Add the oil and shake well again. Pour the mixture over the salad ingredients and toss quickly. Arrange portions in individual salad bowls. Top each bowl with a slice of Feta and 2 anchovies. Serve immediately.

Watercress and Grapefruit Salad

1 1/2 bunches watercress
2 fresh grapefruits

Orange Dressing
(below)

(Serves 8)

Wash the watercress thoroughly, drain well and pat dry with paper towels. Remove and discard the thick stems and arrange the leaves in a salad bowl. Cut the peel from the grapefruits, including the thick white inner skin. Gently separate the sections of each grapefruit, discarding the seeds and membranes. Place the grapefruit sections on the watercress leaves. Refrigerate. At serving time, toss the watercress and grapefruit sections lightly with the Orange Dressing listed under the recipe for Watercress Salad with Orange Dressing, below.

Watercress and Apple Salad

3 bunches watercress
5 scallions, finely chopped
2 medium-sized tart apples

Italian Dressing
(page 120)

(Serves 8)

Wash the watercress carefully, a few leaves at a time, making sure that both sides of the leaves are clean. Cut off the thick stems and pat the leaves dry. Wrap the watercress leaves in aluminum foil; chill. Peel and core the apples just before serving, slice them into very narrow wedges, and toss with the scallions and watercress before adding Italian dressing.

Watercress Salad with Orange Dressing

3 bunches watercress
8 scallions, each including
3 inches of green top
1/4 cup fresh or frozen
orange juice

2 tablespoons wine
vinegar
1/3 cup olive oil
1 teaspoon sugar

(Serves 8)

Rinse the watercress under running water to remove sand and any lurking snails, and pat dry with paper towels. Cut off and discard any thick stems. Arrange the watercress attractively in a large salad bowl. Trim the scallions, slice them thinly and scatter them over the watercress. Combine the orange juice, vinegar, oil and sugar and beat the mixture together thoroughly. Chill the Orange Dressing and the watercress separately for at least 30 minutes. To serve, toss the salad and dressing together lightly and serve immediately.

Cole Slaw

1 medium-sized cabbage	1/4 cup sugar
1 1/2 cups mayonnaise	1 1/2 teaspoons poppy seeds
2 tablespoons mild yellow mustard	3/4 teaspoon salt
1/2 cup cream	1/3 cup crushed pine- apple, drained
1/4 cup lemon juice	

(Serves 8)

Cut the cabbage into quarters and remove and discard the limp outer leaves and the hard core. Rinse the quarters under cold running water; drain thoroughly. Shred each quarter as finely as possible and place in a large bowl. Blend together the mayonnaise, mustard, cream, lemon juice, sugar, poppy seeds, salt and pineapple, and pour over the cabbage. Use two forks to toss the cabbage with the dressing. Chill thoroughly before serving.

Spinach and Tarragon Salad

3 cups fresh spinach
    leaves

1 cup parsley, finely
    chopped

5 tablespoons tarragon
    leaves, finely chopped

2 cups fresh zucchini,
    thinly sliced

1/3 cup olive or safflower
    oil

3 tablespoons lime juice

1 teaspoon salt

2 cloves garlic, crushed

(Serves 8)

Wash vegetables and drain on paper towels. Cut zucchini into thin slices. Toss the zucchini and remaining ingredients. Serve immediately.

SALAD DRESSINGS

Italian Dressing

1/2 cup tarragon vinegar

1/2 teaspoon dry mustard

1 teaspoon paprika

1 teaspoon salt

1/4 teaspoon pepper

1 cup olive oil

2 cloves garlic

3 tablespoons finely
    chopped pimientos

2 tablespoons minced
    green pepper

2 tablespoons minced
    onion

1/2 teaspoon oregano

(Makes 1 1/2 cups)

Measure the vinegar into a large jar that has a tight-fitting cover. Add the mustard, paprika, salt and pepper. Cover the jar and shake vigorously until the ingredients are well mixed. Add the oil; cover and shake again. Peel and halve the garlic cloves and add to the dressing together with the pimiento, green pepper, onion and oregano. Refrigerate overnight. Discard the garlic, shake the dressing thoroughly and pour over salad greens.

Avocado Salad Dressing

Quick, easy and super-delicious, this lovely dressing makes a tasty dip, too!

1 avocado
1/2 cup yoghurt

2 teaspoons lemon juice
2 teaspoons sugar

(Makes 1 cup)

Peel and mash the avocado. Add the yoghurt, lemon juice and sugar. Beat until smooth and rather fluffy.

Drinks

Martinis with Olives

Marinate overnight.

1 large jar green olives

Martinis to cover

(Serves 8)

Drain the olives, rinse them, and pat dry. Place the olives back in the jar. Make a pitcher of your favorite martinis and add enough to cover the olives. Marinate in the refrigerator overnight.

Banana Rum Cooler

1/2 cup milk
1 cup cream
1 banana

4 teaspoons honey
4 ounces rum
4 ice cubes

(Serves 2)

Blend all ingredients until the ice is fairly well cracked. Serve immediately.

Strawberry Cooler

*A grilled burger, an interesting vegetable kebab and a
strawberry cooler—a perfectly simple summer meal.*

1 1/2 cups fresh strawberries	4 ice cubes
3/4 cup cream	2 fresh mint sprigs
3/4 cup milk	

(Serves 2)

Rinse and hull the strawberries. Place in a blender with the
cream, milk and ice cubes. Blend until smooth. Serve immediately, topped with a mint sprig.

Crème de Menthe Cooler

5 ounces white crème de menthe	Club soda
	Mint leaves

(Serves 2)

Set out 2 well-chilled 12-ounce highball glasses. Place 4 ice
cubes in each glass. Pour 2 1/2 ounces of white crème de
menthe into each glass. Add enough club soda to fill. Stir once
or twice. Garnish each glass with 2 fresh mint leaves, and serve
immediately.

Green Velvet

1/2 cup green crème de menthe	1/3 cup crème de cacao
3 tablespoons cognac	1 cup vanilla ice cream

(Serves 2)

Place the crème de menthe, cognac, crème de cacao and
vanilla ice cream in the blender. Add 1/4 cup of cracked ice.
Blend at high speed until thoroughly mixed and foamy, about
1/2 minute. Fill 2 well-chilled large highball glasses with the
mixture, and serve each with a long sipping straw.

Comtesse

1/3 cup cognac
3/4 cup apricot liqueur
1/2 cup fresh orange juice,
   strained

1/4 cup pineapple juice
Champagne
2 1-inch strips orange
   peel

(Serves 2)

Place enough cracked ice in a cocktail shaker to fill it 1/3 full. Pour in the cognac, apricot liqueur, orange juice and pineapple juice; cover and shake well. Strain half of the mixture into each of 2 large chilled highball glasses. Add champagne to fill, stir briefly, and serve immediately, garnished with a twist of orange peel.

French "75"

4 ounces gin or vodka
1 tablespoon Bar Syrup
   (page 128)

2 1/2 tablespoons fresh
   lemon juice
Champagne

(Serves 2)

Fill 2 champagne glasses with crushed ice. Place enough cracked ice in a cocktail shaker to fill it at least 1/2 full. Add the gin, Bar Syrup and lemon juice. Cover and shake energetically until the ingredients are well mixed. Strain half of the mixture into each champagne glass, and add chilled champagne to fill.

Hawaiian Cocktail

2 ounces vodka
2 ounces orange juice
4 ounces pineapple
   juice

2 teaspoons coconut
   syrup
1 1/2 cups crushed ice
2 orange slices

(Serves 2)

Place the vodka, orange juice, pineapple juice, coconut syrup and the crushed ice in a blender. Cover and blend for 3 seconds. Pour into 2 tall glasses and top each with an orange slice and a fresh mint sprig.

Caribbean Julep

8 sprigs fresh mint	1/3 cup pineapple juice
Powdered sugar	1/4 cup lime juice
3/4 cup white rum	1 1/2 tablespoons grenadine

(Serves 2)

Rinse the mint sprigs and pat dry. Roll 2 of the sprigs in a little powdered sugar. Combine the rum, pineapple juice, lime juice and grenadine. Place 3 of the remaining mint sprigs in each of 2 highball glasses and bruise them with the back of a long-handled spoon. Fill the glasses with cracked ice and divide the mixture between the two. Stir lightly. Garnish each glass with a sugared mint sprig. Serve immediately.

Sangria

To my mind there is absolutely no drink so cooling and soothing on a steaming summer's day than a pitcherful of the Spanish-Mexican wine punch— Sangria. Every cook, it seems, has his or her own favorite recipe—try the following variations and choose yours.

1 bottle (4/5 quart) dry red wine	1 1/2 cups cold club soda
	16 ice cubes (optional)
1 1/2 cups cold pineapple or orange juice	1 small orange cut into thin slices
1/4 cup Bar Syrup (page 128)	

(Serves 8)

Mix wine, fruit juice and bar syrup in a pitcher. Refrigerate. To serve, place 2 ice cubes in each glass, pour in the wine punch, and add club soda and orange slices to suit your taste.

VARIATIONS

* Add 1 stick cinnamon to bar syrup during cooking.
* Slice 1 small peeled banana and/or ripe pear and add to the

pitcher of punch. This variation is the one served most often on Spain's Costa del Sol.

* Use a sharp knife or a vegetable peeler to cut the thin outer skin from the orange. Do not include any of the thick white inner skin. Press 1 tablespoon of sugar into the orange skin with the back of a spoon to release the orange oils. Add this skin to the wine punch during refrigeration. Remove the orange skin before serving the Sangria.
* Add 1/2 cup orange (or pineapple or banana) liqueur to the punch before refrigeration.

English Cobbler

Sip the cobbler, nibble the fruit—and have a cool and refreshing afternoon.

1 cup dark rum	4 teaspoons lime juice
1/2 cup strong tea	Strawberries
1 tablespoon sugar	Fresh pineapple wedges

(Serves 2)

Stir the rum, tea, sugar and lime juice into a pitcher half filled with cracked ice. Pack shaved ice into 2 large stemmed goblets until they are about halfway full, and then strain the cobbler into each goblet. Top with strawberries and pineapple wedges.

Fresh Orangeade

4 cups fresh orange juice	3 tablespoons fresh lemon juice
1/3 cup sugar (or more if you prefer)	Club soda or ginger ale
3 tablespoons fresh lime juice	4 orange slices

(Serves 4)

Combine the orange juice, sugar, lime juice and lemon juice. Pour the mixture over ice in 4 tall glasses. Fill the glass with club soda. Slit the orange slices halfway through and place one on the edge of each glass.

Orangeade with Mint

2 cups fresh orange juice
1/4 cup sugar
1/3 cup mint leaves

2 tablespoons lime juice
1 tablespoon lemon juice
Club soda or ginger ale

(Serves 2)

Bring 1 cup of orange juice to a boil, remove from the heat and stir in the sugar and mint leaves. Pour into a small pitcher and allow the mixture to cool. Stir in the remaining orange juice, the lime juice and the lemon juice. Fill 2 large highball glasses with ice. Strain the orangeade into the glasses, add club soda to the brim and garnish with additional mint leaves.

Lemonade with Sherbet

2 cups water
Juice of 3 lemons
2 tablespoons sugar
Lemon-flavored soda

Pineapple or orange sherbet
2 sprigs mint

(Serves 2)

Bring 1 cup of water to a boil. Add the lemon juice and the sugar; boil 3 minutes. Stir in the cold water. Chill the mixture. At serving time strain the lemon mixture into 2 tall glasses, fill with the cold lemon soda. Top each glass with a scoop of sherbet and a sprig of mint.

Cardinal Punch

5 cups cranberry juice
4 cups fresh orange juice
1/3 cup fresh lemon juice

3 quarts ginger ale
Sugar to taste

(Serves 10 to 12)

Pour the juices into a large enamel pot; mix by stirring. Place a large block of ice in a punch bowl. Pour the juice mixture over the ice; add 3 quarts of ginger ale and sugar to taste. Serve immediately.

Russian Punch

1 fifth vodka
Juice of 12 oranges
Juice of 6 lemons

1/2 cup grenadine
1 quart club soda

(Serves 8)

Pour the vodka into a large pitcher. Stir in the orange juice, lemon juice and grenadine. Place a solid block of ice in a punch bowl. Pour the vodka mixture over the ice, and add the club soda. Stir well and serve. If you desire, float thin orange, lemon or lime slices on top of the punch.

Minted Orange Tea

3 tea bags
15 mint leaves
2 1/2 cups boiling water

1/4 cup fresh orange juice
Sugar (if desired)
2 mint sprigs

(Serves 2)

Place the tea bags and the mint leaves in a pyrex graduate or pitcher. Cover with the boiling water. Allow to steep for 5 minutes. Then remove the tea bags and add the orange juice and sugar (if desired). Chill in the refrigerator. Fill 2 ice tea glasses with ice cubes and divide the chilled tea between the glasses. Garnish with mint sprigs and serve immediately.

Moroccan Brandied Coffee

3 ounces crème de
   cacao
2 ounces brandy
1 1/2 cups fresh hot coffee

1/4 cup heavy cream,
   whipped
1/2 teaspoon sugar
Bitter chocolate

(Serves 2)

Set out 2 stemmed 6- to 8-ounce glasses. Pour 1 1/2 ounces of crème de cacao and 1 ounce of brandy into each glass, divide the hot coffee between the glasses, and garnish each with whipped cream sweetened with the sugar. Top each drink with 1/2 teaspoon shaved chocolate.

Bar Syrup

4 1/2 cups sugar
1 1/3 cups water

Dissolve the sugar in the water and boil the mixture for 5 minutes. Allow to cool and pour into a jar. Seal tightly.

Strawberry, Lemon or Lime Ice Cubes

These ice cubes make a perfect garnish for cold soups or drinks.

**Strawberries, thin lemon   Water
slices, thin lime slices**

Place water in ice cube trays. Tuck a strawberry or a slice of fruit in each compartment. Freeze.

Desserts

Apricots in Orange Juice

*Prepare 2 days in advance of serving.
This Near Eastern dessert is a refreshing aftermath
to an outdoor meal.*

**1 1/2 cups tightly packed   1/2 cup honey
    dried apricots (about   4 teaspoons rosewater
    50)   (optional)
  6 cups fresh orange   1/3 cup whole blanched
    juice   almonds (about 50)**

(Serves 8)

Stir the apricots, orange juice, honey and rosewater together in a glass bowl. Refrigerate for 2 days, stirring occasionally. To serve, stir in the whole almonds. Serve cold.

Ginger-Melon

2 ripe honeydew melons, thinly sliced, chilled
Crystallized ginger, chopped

2 oranges, thinly sliced
2 lemons, thinly sliced
2 limes, thinly sliced

(Serves 8)

Arrange the chilled melon slices attractively on dessert plates and sprinkle with chopped ginger. Tuck slices of citrus fruit among the melon slices on each plate. Guests may squeeze citrus juice over the melon if they wish.

Melon Balls and Grapes with Cointreau

Marinate several hours.

1 1/2 pounds green seedless grapes
2 Honeydew melons
2 large cantaloupes
1 cup honey

3 teaspoons lemon juice
1/2 cup Cointreau or Grand Marnier
1 1/2 cups sour cream

(Serves 8)

Wash the grapes and remove the stems. Pat grapes dry with paper towels. Halve and seed the honeydew melons. With a melon-ball cutter, scoop balls of pulp from the honeydew. Reserve and refrigerate the honeydew shells. Cut both cantaloupes in half and discard seeds. Scoop out the pulp with the melon-ball cutter. Reserve and refrigerate the shells. Place the grapes, honeydew melon and cantaloupe balls in a large bowl. Combine the honey, lemon juice and all but 1 tablespoon of the Cointreau. Pour this marinade over the fruit and stir thoroughly. Chill the fruit for several hours and stir it from time to time. At serving time, smooth the sides of the honey-dew and cantaloupe shells and pile an equal amount of the fruit into each of them. Mix the sour cream with the remaining tablespoon of Cointreau and serve in a separate dish. Guests can help themselves.

Fresh Fruits with Whipped Cream

5 bananas, cut into
  1/2-inch cubes
5 pears, peeled, cored
  and chopped
5 peaches
6 purple plums, pitted
  and coarsely
  chopped
3 cups seedless white
  grapes

1/4 cup confectioners'
  sugar
1/2 cup kirsch
1/2 pint heavy cream
3 tablespoons granu-
  lated sugar
1/2 teaspoon almond
  extract

(Serves 8)

Prepare the bananas, pears and plums. Dip the peaches in scalding water for a few seconds and slip off the skins. Slice the peaches, discarding the pits. Place all of the fruit in a serving bowl and add the confectioners' sugar and kirsch. Toss the fruit lightly and refrigerate for 1 hour.

Immediately before serving, whip the cream with the granulated sugar and the almond extract. Serve the whipped cream in a separate bowl along with the bowl of fresh fruit.

Raspberries Chantilly

6 cups fresh raspberries
1 teaspoon vanilla
  extract

3/4 cup confectioners'
  sugar
3 cups heavy cream

(Serves 8)

Rinse the raspberries carefully and spread to dry on paper towels. Put the fruit in a serving bowl and sprinkle with vanilla and confectioners' sugar to taste. Whip the cream and stir it gently into the sweetened fruit. Refrigerate for at least 2 hours. Serve icy cold.

Jellied Melon with Strawberries

2 large ripe cantaloupes
1 package raspberry
   gelatine
2 cups sliced strawberries

1 cup heavy cream,
   whipped
2 tablespoons kirsch

(Serves 8)

With a sharp knife, cut a round plug from the stem end of each cantaloupe; the hole should be large enough to allow a spoon to be inserted. Set the plugs aside and scoop out the melon seeds. Prepare the gelatine as directed on package; allow to cool to room temperature.

Spoon 1 cup of strawberries into each melon cavity. Pour enough gelatine over the strawberries to fill the hollow melons. Replace the melon plugs and chill until the gelatine is firm. To serve, carefully cut each melon into 4 round slices, top each slice with the whipped cream flavored with the kirsch.

Peach-Stuffed Pineapple Halves

20 fresh peaches, peeled
   and sliced
1 cup kirsch
3 medium-sized fresh
   pineapples with leaves

2 boxes whole fresh
   strawberries, hulled
3/4 cup sugar

(Serves 8)

Cover peaches with kirsch; set aside to soak, stirring occasionally. Holding each pineapple upright, cut down through the leaves to the stem end. Use a sharp knife to hollow out the insides of each half. Allow at least 3/4 inch of the wall to remain intact. Coarsely chop the cutaway pineapple sections, discarding the hard cores. Drain the peach slices and arrange them inside each pineapple half. Cover with equal amounts of the drained, chopped pineapple. Roll the whole strawberries in the sugar and use them to top the pineapple halves. Refrigerate until serving time. Add more sugar, if desired; sprinkle with kirsch. Serve cold.

Cooked Fruits with Sauterne

2 pounds mixed dried
  fruits
1 cup sugar
3/4 cup sauterne or any
  other wine

1 lemon cut in slices
2 whole cloves
3 2-inch pieces
  cinnamon
1/3 cup raisins

(Serves 4)

Place the dried fruit in a saucepan, cover with water, and soak for 3 hours. Add the sugar, the wine, the lemon slices, the cloves, and the cinnamon pieces. Bring the fruits to a boil over medium high heat; then lower the heat and cook very gently until the fruit is tender when tested with a fork. Stir in the raisins. Serve hot or cool.

Strawberrries and Sugar

3 quarts fresh ripe strawberries

Coarse sugar
2 cups Cherry Heering

(Serves 8)

Hull the strawberries, rinse them, and pat them dry with paper towels. Heap the berries in a large serving bowl and serve with 2 smaller bowls of sugar and 2 bowls of Cherry Heering. Let your guests dip the strawberries first in the Cherry Heering and then in the sugar.

Melon Compote

2 cups strawberries, cut into quarters

2 cups honeydew melon balls

2 cups cantaloupe balls

2 cups watermelon balls

2 cups fresh blueberries

1/2 cup raisins

1/4 cup honey

1/2 cup orange- or banana-flavored liqueur

Mint leaves

(Serves 8)

Wash the strawberries and cut them in quarters. Put all of the fruit into a large bowl. Add the honey and liqueur and stir only long enough to coat all the fruit. Serve icy cold, garnished with mint leaves.

Bananas Deluxe

2 cups heavy cream

1/4 cup sugar

1 1/2 teaspoons almond extract

20 almond macaroons, finely crumbled

1/4 cup sherry

8 large bananas, thinly sliced

1 cup fresh sliced strawberries

1 cup fresh whole strawberries, with the leaves attached

(Serves 8)

Whip the cream until it is fairly thick. Continue beating as you sprinkle in the sugar a bit at a time. Stir in the almond extract. Spread 1/3 of the macaroon pieces over the bottom of a large shallow casserole or pie plate. Sprinkle with sherry. Arrange 1/2 of the banana slices over the macaroon pieces. Spoon 1/3 of the whipped cream over the bananas, and add 1/2 of the strawberry slices. Continue the layers ending with the macaroons and top with the remaining whipped cream. Garnish with the whole strawberries and chill thoroughly before serving.

Chocolate Soup with Whipped Cream

*Satisfy your sweet tooth with this rich
and creamy Chocolate soup.*

5 3/4 cups milk
  1/2 pound semisweet
      chocolate, grated
    2 teaspoons flour
  2/3 cup sugar

4 egg yolks
1 cup heavy cream
  Chocolate or mint
  cordial

(Serves 8)

Bring the milk and grated chocolate to a boil in large saucepan. Mix 1 or 2 tablespoons of the hot chocolate milk with the flour, and add to the soup as it boils. Stir in the sugar and remove from the stove. Add the egg yolks, stirring constantly, and return to low heat only long enough to warm the soup.

Serve hot or cold in small bowls as a special dessert, with a dollop of whipped cream and a few sprinkles of chocolate or mint cordial.

Chocolate Ice Box Cake

  3/4 cup coffee
  1/2 cup light rum
   20 petit beurre biscuits
    5 eggs
  3/4 cup confectioners'
      sugar
   10 ounces German
      sweet chocolate

3 tablespoons sweet
  butter
1 1/2 cups chopped
      pecans, optional
   10 petit beurres,
      crushed
      Maraschino cherries

(Serves 8)

Mix together the coffee and rum. Very quickly dip each biscuit into the coffee-rum mixture and line a buttered bread pan with the moistened biscuits. Separate the eggs into two bowls. Add the confectioners' sugar to the egg yolks and beat to a creamy broth. Melt the chocolate with the butter in the top of a double boiler over hot water. Beat the chocolate-butter mixture into the egg yolks and sugar. Beat the egg whites until they are stiff but not dry; fold them into the egg yolk mixture along with the crushed petit beurres and the chopped nuts. Gently spoon this filling into the biscuit-lined pan and chill the cake in the refrigerator overnight. Loosen the edges and carefully unmold the dessert from the pan onto a serving dish. Decorate the edges of the cake with whipped cream rosettes and maraschino cherries. Additional whipped cream may be served in a separate bowl.

Chocolate Ice Cream Cups with Crème de Menthe

8 ready-made semi-sweet chocolate cups; or 9 ounces semi-sweet chocolate

Boiling water

8 paper baking cups (used for cupcakes)

8 marrons glacé

1 pint vanilla ice cream

Crème de menthe

8 maraschino cherries

(Serves 8)

If ready-made chocolate cups are not available prepare your own. Place the chocolate in bowl, cover with boiling water and allow to stand until the chocolate softens slightly. Pour off all but 1/4 cup of the water. Mix the chocolate and the remaining water until the mixture is smooth. Set out 8 paper baking cups. Swirl the chocolate mixture with a spoon to cover the inside of each cup. Put the chocolate-coated cups in muffin tins and place them in the freezer. If the chocolate seems thin in any areas swirl with chocolate once more and refreeze. Remove the chocolate cups from the freezer one at a time and peel the paper from each very quickly so the cup does not melt. Place a well-drained marron and a scoop of ice cream in each cup and refreeze until serving time.

To serve top the ice cream with crème de menthe and a maraschino cherry and pass immediately.

Balkan Fruit and Nut Fritters

Zest of 2 lemons
(grated outer rind)
Zest of 3 oranges
4 medium-sized
apples, peeled and
grated
2 1/2 cups self-rising
flour
4 teaspoons baking
powder
1 teaspoon cinnamon
1/2 teaspoon nutmeg
1/2 teaspoon allspice

1 1/4 teaspoons almond
extract
1 teaspoon vanilla
extract
1 1/2 cups milk
1 cup walnuts, finely
chopped
1 cup pecans, finely
chopped
Vegetable oil
Coarse granulated
sugar

(Makes about 50)

Combine the flour, baking powder, cinnamon, nutmeg and allspice and sift together into a large bowl. Add the almond and vanilla extracts to the milk, stir this liquid thoroughly into the dry ingredients. Mix the lemon and orange zest, the grated apples, the walnuts and pecans into the batter.

To fry the fritters, fill a deep kettle at least halfway full of oil (to ensure that the fritters will not stick). Heat to 365° F. Drop the batter by rounded teaspoons into the hot oil. When the fritters turn puffy and golden brown, remove with a slotted spoon and drain on paper towels. Roll each fritter in the sugar while still warm. Serve with fruit.

Raspberry Sauce

*Spoon this delectable sauce over fresh fruit or
ice cream.*

1 1/2 pints raspberries,
mashed
2 cups sugar

2 cups water
1/4 cup framboise or
cassis

(Serves 8)

Place the raspberries in a saucepan. Add the sugar and water, bring the mixture to a boil and allow to simmer over very low heat, for about 15 minutes. Stir the mixture frequently until it reduces to a thick sauce. Cool slightly. Purée the sauce by pressing through a fine sieve with the back of a spoon. Stir in the framboise or cassis and return the sauce to low heat for about 5 minutes. Serve hot or cold as an accompaniment to fruits, mousses, puddings, or ice cream.

Cantaloupe Halves with Fresh Fruit Salad

1/2 cup fresh blueberries
1/2 cup peaches, peeled, pitted and sliced
1/2 cup strawberries cut into quarters
2 bananas, peeled and sliced

1/4 tablespoon confectioners' sugar
1 tablespoon lime juice
1/3 cup kirsch
4 ripe cantaloupes
8 whole, ripe strawberries with leaves

(Serves 8)

Toss the fruit gently in a bowl with the sugar. Sprinkle with the lime juice and kirsch. Cut the cantaloupes in halves and discard the seeds. Mound sweetened berries in the center of each melon half and top each with a whole strawberry. Refrigerate at least 1 hour before serving.

CAMPING

A
Successful
Camping
Trip

CAMPING IS a word that means many things to many people. One camper may hop into his $30,000 motor home, drive to an ocean-side trailer camp, plug into the electrical outlet there, turn on his air conditioner, settle into his easy chair, seldom emerge from his expensive cocoon, and then regale his friends back home with tales of his rugged camping trip.

Another camper may never venture far from public camping grounds. He may pile his car high with stoves and ovens, hammocks and camping chairs, refrigerators and even a small portable bar. He finds his home away from home not so much in communing with nature as in being bumper to bumper with other campers. His camping horizons reach only as far as his wheels will comfortably carry him.

There are the "let's-make-it-hard-for-ourselves" campers. They strenuously avoid the public sites, the "short-drive-to-the-grocery-store" camping conveniences, and strike out for themselves wherever their ingenuity may take them. They often motorboat to some out-of-the-way place that is not necessarily back to nature but is, at least, solitary.

Others are "live-off-the-land" campers. They bike and hike and motorcycle to the most remote of wilderness settings, where they pick wild berries, chew wild herbs and build their fires from real, honest-to-goodness fallen trees.

Each one of the above-mentioned campers I have been.

I've loaded the car at 3 A.M., driven through the dark and the glimmering dawn to claim the choice campsite at Lake George, only to discover that this best of all sites, an island of our very own, would not be vacated until noon. I've circled that island for four sweltering hours in a motorboat with one whimpering infant and one pesky 5-year-old (not to mention one grouchy husband). The wait was worthwhile! That island was totally delightful and my 5-year-old learned to steer the motorboat in which we zapped to the grocery store located on another island.

I've camped on a farmers' island (Grindstone Island, to be exact), in the Saint Lawrence river. The campsite was located on a steep hill amid the stubbles of an unshaded field. The farmer's family watched in total amazement while we erected our tent in the middle of a storm. We had never dealt with a suspension tent before and we had forgotten the instructions. It was a rain-drenched hour and a half and several temper tantrums later that the last bar of our tent slipped into the last aluminum tube, the elastic ropes sprung into place and our tent popped into shape. Was the isolation worth the trouble and inconvenience? Not really. The field mice scurried whenever we took a step, the grasshoppers sang all day, the crickets screeched all night and the fishing was terrible, but if I had it to do over again . . . I would.

There are obvious differences between "backyard cooking" and "camping out." Whether you prefer luxurious or primitive camping, you will have a more enjoyable time if equipment and food lists are well thought out. Most camp sites now have grocery stores nearby, but camping trips are for enjoyment, not grocery shopping, and it is wise to plan menus carefully and bring along all supplies except milk, eggs, meats, fruits and vegetables.

- Read the following pages carefully before you begin making up your equipment lists.
- If possible, discuss the terrain of your planned campsite with campers who have had experience in the area.

- Consult your camping equipment salesman if you are puzzled about what equipment you should buy. Most of these salesmen are camping "bugs" and can be of great help.
- Determine whether your site will be near a lake or ocean, a grocery store, or in the wilderness.
- Make up menus for every camping day based on the above and prepare grocery lists. If you are camping where the fishing is good (or is supposed to be), be sure to plan some meals around fish. However, it's best not to *count* on fish dinners until you actually see the fish. Bring along "back-up" dinners in case the fish aren't biting. (As a bride, I brought along slivered almonds, vegetables and pasta for all the fish we were bound to catch. The fish were uncooperative and we ate dried beef with slivered almonds for nearly a week.)
- If possible, prepare the first night's meal, either wholly or in part, before you leave home. Refrigerate it in an ice box while you are traveling to your site. This makes setting up camp less of a strain and gets your trip off to a good start.

Just as there are "different strokes for different folks," there are different tips for different trips. The technical skills the public-site camper needs to know are minimal—how to work a gasoline stove, reflector oven, Dutch oven, etc.—and suggestions and recipes for correct cooking with each one. These skills are discussed in some detail in the remainder of this chapter.

The wilderness camper must know a bit more, for often his comfort and/or safety depend upon his ability to make proper use of what nature so generously supplies. We have begun, then, with a description of the available equipment and, for the more serious camper, have included detailed instructions on making fires and finding water.

Equipment

PORTABLE CAMP STOVES

A seemingly endless display of models and prices for all cooking purposes often confronts the first-time purchaser of portable camp stoves. There are 1, 2 and 3 burner stoves, any of which may use gasoline, butane, propane, naptha, alcohol or kerosene. Some fold into compact suitcase-like units for easy transportation; others can be conveniently fitted into a hiker's pocket.

Your best buying guide through this maze of stoves is the knowledgeable salesman in a reputable store, who will help you choose the stove most suited to your needs and purse.

Although when I camp I carry as little equipment as possible, I always take along my Coleman 2-burner gasoline stove for main meals and my butane 1-burner for picnic lunches or impromptu cooking. I like to live off the land, supplementing my camp-stove cooking with a wood fire only when absolutely necessary. Camp stoves should be used whenever possible or convenient in order to preserve the ecology. They also serve to heat the tent on camping trips if bad weather drives you indoors, although *adequate ventilation must be provided*.

A word about 1-burner stoves that travel easily in pocket or pack. Low in cost, these small stoves usually adapt to gasoline, outdoor motor oil or even lighter fluid in a pinch.

Whether you travel by boat or car and where you will camp really dictates what to take along. The main idea is not to duplicate your own backyard. Roughing it has its own many challenges and satisfactions.

GASOLINE CAMP STOVES

Efficient, inexpensive gasoline-burning stoves are highly regarded by most experienced campers. Most are compact units, either mounted on legs that fold or fitted like a suitcase for tabletop use, which make them ideal for packing, with adjoining cover and side pieces which perform as a windshield.

Gasoline burners consume little fuel and have a simple operating mechanism. Use a funnel to fill the gas tank, close the filler cap tightly (and remove the tightly-closed gasoline supply can to a safe distance), pump up the air pressure in the tank, turn on the valve, wait a few moments to allow the air to escape, and light the burner with a match. The unleaded gasoline available in most camping or resort areas is best, since

it keeps the generator from clogging and heats more quickly than leaded gasoline. Carrying a spare generator, easily installed with a small wrench or pliers, is always an excellent idea. Also important is a working knowledge of the inner parts of your stove, since no two stoves behave identically.

PROPANE CAMP STOVES

Propane camp stoves are efficient, very safe and easy to operate, although they cost more than gasoline stoves. Propane is a nonpoisonous and nonlethal pressurized gas, avail-

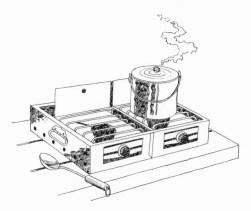

able in small, easily attached, disposable containers or the more economical 5-, 10- or 20-pound tanks. Unlike gasoline models, propane stoves require no pumping or generator change; you need only attach the container or tank, turn on the valve, and light. The flame will be clean and very hot, since propane seldom clogs the stove, and changing the fuel tanks is simple.

Disposable propane containers are not always interchangeable, however, and if you run out of your brand, you may not be able to purchase others until you return home. Sometimes these propane units are susceptible to temperature variations, and do not function well if the weather is too cold. Never throw propane containers into a campfire when empty. Drop them in trash baskets or bury them under the ground instead.

BUTANE CAMP STOVES

A petroleum derivative similar to propane, butane or "bottle gas" is likewise packaged in disposable cans for attaching to camp stoves. However, the container cost is higher and butane's heating ability is lower. Butane camp stoves, nonetheless, prove handy as supplementary units because the packaged containers are so compact and convenient to use.

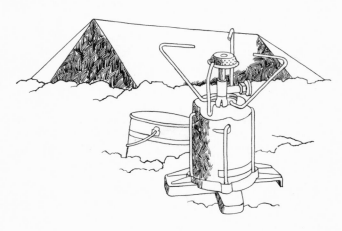

A SUCCESSFUL CAMPING TRIP

ALCOHOL CAMP STOVES

Alcohol stoves come in various models and use the methyl or denatured alcohol sold in hardware and paint stores as shellac or paint solvent. Alcohol is a safe fuel that burns with little soot or odor, but food will take longer to cook because alcohol heats slowly. These are best used as a 1-burner or supplementary unit.

TIN CAN STOVES

Fun to make and use, but hardly adequate for serious cooking, are stoves fashioned from the larger-sized cans whose contents have already been eaten. Twigs, bark and even charcoal serve as fuel for these improvised stoves.

CAMPING

WOOD STOVES

Rugged portable wood-burning stoves will, in addition to wood, burn solid fuel of any kind: brush, charcoal or waste. They are excellent for cooking, since most models have a built-in oven, draft controls and a telescoping stovepipe. If a spark arrester is attached, a woodstove may be used where there might be danger from an open fire. Propane and gasoline stoves are more efficient and do not require foraging for wood. Never cut down living trees for use in wood stoves. Freshly cut wood burns poorly and killing trees is bad for the ecology.

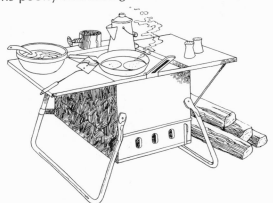

REFLECTOR OVENS

Freshly made pies, cakes, muffins and quick breads, baked beneath the cool quiet greenery of your campsite, add to the enjoyment of outdoor eating. A "must" for serious camp cooking is a good-sized reflector oven, which will enable you to turn out any quantity of baked goods or even a small roast over any open hardwood fire.

A reflector oven may be made of aluminum, tinned iron or sheet steel. Either folding or rigid models are available, but each should have a horizontal middle shelf for baking and side panels to keep the heat in. Heat bounces off the sloping roof and back panel of the oven as its open side faces the fire, and is reflected back on both the top and bottom of the food baking on the middle shelf.

Reflector ovens are exceedingly efficient and ensure even baking, but a steady blaze is a most important ingredient. Since temperature controls are absent you should experiment carefully with various recipes until you learn to use your oven. Square or rectangular baking pans are better than round ones which may overhang the shelf. Turning your pans from time to time will help prevent scorching.

Grease and crusted foods should be scoured from the oven after each use because heat reflects best from a shiny surface. In a pinch, however, you may line yours with gleaming aluminum foil.

DUTCH OVEN

The skillet is the traditional pan for campfire cooking but less known and just as versatile and useful is the Dutch oven. It is one of the most serviceable items you can buy for camping, or even for a backyard barbecue. It will bake very efficiently over a campstove or charcoal and also will double for casserole cookery. A Dutch oven is any good-sized heavy pot with a tight-fitting cover, with or without a set of 3 legs and sometimes equipped with a bail handle. It will satisfactorily bake your biscuits or quick breads, turn out long-cooking pot roasts and stews, fry your foods in a pinch, and work wonders with hole-in-the-ground cooking.

Cast iron Dutch ovens are preferable to aluminum ones; cast iron heats slowly and evenly and retains the heat long after the pot leaves the fire. Conventionally, these should have a tight-fitting cover to seal in the moisture and flavor. The cover may be indented so that coals can be placed on top when baking, or it may have a flat surface and a raised rim so that it can be reversed to hold the coals.

Frequent use will improve the quality of the foods cooked and baked in your Dutch oven, but it must be seasoned first. Grease the entire inner surface lightly with vegetable oil. Set the Dutch oven in a slow 225° F. oven for a couple of hours, then use a paper towel to remove the surplus oil.

Preheating your Dutch oven is essential, especially when baking. Grease the bottom lightly before baking to prevent scorching, or set the greased baking pan containing the dough on a wire rack or trivet. Use round baking pans for maximum efficiency, and a wire lifter or tongs to remove the food when finished. Place the Dutch oven on your camp stove or over hardwood coals. Dutch ovens with legs are best when cooking with coals; coals may also be set on the oven's cover. A little practice will teach you techniques for timing your baked goods and casseroles. Don't forget the value of maintaining a steady heat when cooking with coals.

The Dutch oven is ideal for hole-in-the-ground cookery. Beans, stews or other casseroles can cook for hours without special attention from the cook. This method of camp cookery calls for digging a large hole, which is then lined with stones. Build a fire with dead hardwood (or use charcoal) and let it burn until reduced to glowing embers. Rake all but a 2-inch layer of coals out of the bottom of the pit and scatter them over the hot stones. Place your 3-legged Dutch oven over the bottom coals, or rig up your legless oven so that it doesn't touch the coals; set some of the coals on the cover, push the hot stones around the sides and top, cover with a tin sheet or aluminum foil to keep out the dirt, and fill in the hole. When you return from your day's hike or fishing expedition, you'll have a special treat in store.

THE COOK'S CAMPING EQUIPMENT

I travel with enamel pots and plates because I feel that food tastes better and retains more of its nutritional value when cooked and served in or on enamel or glass. Most camping equipment is aluminum, however, so if you find aluminum more convenient, by all means use it.
- Plates and cups for each person
- Stainless steel spoons, knives and forks for each person
- 2 or 3 sharp knives of different sizes for paring and slicing
- Set of measuring spoons
- Set of measuring cups
- Grater
- Bread board or cutting board
- Small set of mixing bowls
- Sturdy salt shaker and pepper mill
- Roll of heavy-duty aluminum foil
- Long-handled fork
- Large serving spoon
- Spatula

- Wheel-type can opener
- Bottle opener
- Keys for opening cans
- 2 1-gallon pots
- 2 8- or 10-inch frying pans
- Coffee pot
- Kettles
- Dutch oven or large heavy pot with a cover, made of cast-iron and designed to set directly on the grill. One of the handiest items for baking over campfires.
- Hinged wire basket
- Portable grill
- Ax
- Shovel
- Pot grip or pump pliers
- Asbestos mitt
- Grease can for saving bacon or meat drippings. Should have a tight-fitting cover.
- Waterproof meat and bread bags
- Small container of detergent
- Scouring soap pads or metal sponges
- Dish cloths
- Paper towels
- Paper plates
- Collapsible candle lanterns or tin-can lamp
- Portable refrigerator of some sort
- Kitchen tarp
- Dining tarp (optional)
- 2 small containers of wooden matches dipped in wax
- I folding cookstove

TIPS FOR CAMPERS

Getting ready:
- Buy dehydrated foods to keep weight to a minimum.
- Use chunk bacon rather than strip bacon. This makes it easier to scrape off any mold that might form.

- Remove plastic wrapping from bacon and wrap in cheese-cloth. When you are ready to cook, dip the bacon in cold water and it will curl less.
- To save space, insert waxed paper between bread slices, place them in a plastic bag, and press them together to one-third of their original size. When you unpack, the slices will spring back to their original shape.
- Make a mixture of instant coffee and dry milk, as you like it, to eliminate extra containers.
- Wrap butter in waxed paper and then in strips of wet cotton to prevent melting. Place this in a metal or wooden box and cover with newspaper. Keep the cotton moist.
- Make your own ice blocks to keep perishables fresh by filling milk containers with water and freezing. Leave the ice in the container; the melted water can be used as drinking water at the site.
- Use rice in the salt shaker to absorb any moisture and prevent the salt from sticking or clogging.
    At the site:
- Use white wood ashes mixed with flour for baking soda.
- When baking bread, place the dough in a greased skillet and prop against a rock or log facing the fire.
- Or wrap a long strip of the dough around a green hardwood stick, place it over the fire and turn the stick until the dough is brown.
- An egg variation: Cut a large onion in half, remove the center, leaving several of the outer layers. Break an egg into the onion shell and place it on the coals. Remove when the egg is done as you like it. Serve on toast.
- To make a double boiler, place one pot on 3 stones inside a larger pot.
- Use a green sweet gum or maple stick for the skewer to make your kebab tastier.
- If maple syrup ferments or molds, heat the syrup to the boiling point and skim off the scum. (This will restore its natural flavor.)
- Keep perishables fresh or liquids cool by anchoring them in watertight containers in a shaded stream.

Fire Building

A fire glowing in the darkness, turning to red embers—a fire to cook over and to be warmed by. This is the image most of us eagerly bring to mind when we plan our camping trips. What would camping be without a campfire?

However, because the back country camping areas and the national parks are so densely used, there has been an increasing concern on the part of ecology groups and conservationists about how and where campfires should be built. The National Parks of the Future has prepared a report commissioned by the Conservation Foundation of the U.S. Government National Parks Service setting forth certain policies on wilderness management so that the parks can be kept free of man's impact. Their aim is to enable each individual to enjoy the experience of nature without the feeling that someone has been there just five minutes before. The remains of a campfire—blackened logs, fire-scorched rocks—are really another form of litter on the landscape.

The report does not recommend giving up your campfires but does strongly suggest that you consider your site carefully. Build your fire well away from the trail so its remains will not be seen by people using the trail. Scout around for the remains of a campfire and build yours in the same place.

Also, be careful about burning only the trash which will burn. Aluminum foil in particular is virtually indestructible. The most practical way to dispose of foil is to use it over again as often as possible and then bury it well under the forest floor. A succession of outdoor campers will thank you for this as well as for your care in selecting your site. These simple precautions will do much to keep the wilderness unspoiled.

Picking a Site

In picking a suitable site for building your campfire, the first step is to determine whether a fire may be built. Permission must be obtained for fires on private or posted property.

Signs or fire wardens will direct you to the designated areas in public camping grounds.

General rules of common sense and fire safety will help you select the best locations in the wilderness. A good wood supply is important, and standing or leaning dead hardwood trees and branches are the best source. Water should be close at hand so that the fire may be completely extinguished when your cooking is finished.

Take care that the site you choose is protected from the wind. Wind is usually strongest between 2 and 4 or 5 P.M., although wind currents may be very different on high peaks, in deep valleys and near the seacoast. Breezes usually blow off a lake and up toward higher ground during the day; at night they reverse and move toward the water. Knowing wind direction will help you in planning your fire and cooking arrangements, and will prevent smoke from getting in your eyes during those peaceful moments when you're sitting around the campfire. In any case, keep the prevailing winds in mind so that smoke or sparks from the fire will not damage your camping gear or set a forest fire.

Never camp in tall dry grass where fire hazards abound, and avoid swamps, which all harbor mosquitoes. Heavy brush and water sites may attract black flies and no-see-ums as well as you. Hollows may be plagued with insects; hilltops or mountain crests may be far away from water or exposed to winds or lightning; and flash floods may occur in dry gullies. If you camp at the seaside, remember to build your fire well above high tide level.

Ideally, your campfire site should be flat and fairly well sheltered. Rocks, dirt or sand make the best surfaces. Never build your fire too close to the base of a tree—it may injure the roots. And stay away from tree stumps or peaty ground where your fire might smolder undetected for days before bursting into active flames. Scrape the forest floor clear of leaves and debris right down to an area of bare dirt or rock at least 6 feet in diameter before beginning your fire building. Replace the leaves when you are breaking camp and you are sure your fire is dead.

SELECTION OF WOODS
TINDER

Bark from the white birch, which on mature trees flaps loosely in a breeze, makes the best tinder because it burns readily even after a thorough soaking, but its removal leaves an ugly permanent scar. Always use birch bark from dead trees or fallen branches. Cylinders made from dead birch branches make fine tinder where the wood inside has rotted. Squeeze the bark cylinder, shake out any of the cadmium layer that may be clinging to the inside, stuff thin birch twigs, small pieces of birch bark, or split kindling into the hollow and light your tinder. The inner kindling will dry out the cylinder and it will soon be blazing.

There are many evergreens which will serve for tinder when sufficiently dry and brittle if there are no birches near your campsite.

Dead cedars can be easily stripped of their bark. Dry bark from living red and northern white cedar trees will make good tinder, but take care to shave off only the *outside* bark with a knife or ax so no irreparable damage is done. "Fat" pine, fir and spruce make exceptionally fine tinder. Jack pine, red pine and red spruce all drip their sap in death, and the pockets of pitch thus created in the knots, bends and butts of these dead limbs can be shaved off or chopped up for an instant blaze.

Dried stumps from any softwood tree readily yield their bark for tinder, and wood from *abandoned* beaver dams makes excellent fire-building material. The tidy beavers gather and/or fell small aspen and poplar trees (among others) to build their dams. Both aspen and poplar burn cleanly and with practically no smoke. Snap off any protruding dry pieces of wood from the dam and use them for tinder. *Warning!* Do not disturb beaver dams or houses that are still being used by the beavers! The beaver dam is necessary to the ecology and is protected by law in some states!

Do not burn hemlock at all since this fine tree is becoming quite scarce. Avoid tamarack bark—it will not burn.

If any of the sources of tinder mentioned above are not

available, don't despair. Dead or even green sage brush is easy to light and burn. Long lengths of dried hay or weeds, tied together in bunches of 5 or 6 and knotted in several places, may smoke a bit but should start a fire in favorable weather. Pine needles are practically worthless as tinder, unless they are very dry, wrapped in newspaper, placed under a teepee of prayer sticks and ignited. Omit the pine needles from the package of newspapers and nothing will be lost.

A prayer stick, sometimes called a frizz or fuzz stick, is a fairly standard method of starting a fire. Prepare the prayer stick with your knife or ax from dry, seasoned softwood sticks. Shave very thin strips from all sides of the stick along as much of its length as possible, curling them under as you go without cutting the shavings off. Tie 6 or 7 of these together, teepee-fashion, or stack them crisscross fashion under slightly larger kindling; ignite and your fire is started.

Some woodsmen scorn the use of prayer sticks as tedious and unnecessary, but they are most practical when conditions are wet because there's dry wood under the wet bark. During rainy weather you will need to assemble, and keep sheltered, a good supply of wood for tinder and firewood. Wood split from inside the rain-shielded sides of dead hardwood or evergreen stumps will be dry enough to burn in a rainstorm. Your fire-building efforts, too, will need protection in wet weather. A rain poncho, canvas tarp, or even a sheet of plastic will serve if propped up where there is no natural overhang. A dry place for your fire may be found by turning over a flat rock and using the drier ground underneath. A pile of rocks may also supply a foundation for your fire.

HEAVIER FIREWOODS

Once your tinder is in place, you will need to lay on heavier and longer-burning kindling and firewood to produce suitable coals for a good cooking fire. Standing dead hardwoods are excellent because they burn slowly while giving off strong heat, and reduce to hot, long-lasting coals. Following is a list of some of the more common trees most suitable for firewood.

CAMPING

Never use living trees! They do not burn well and their death will be mourned by many generations of campers.

Apple
Ash
Birch (White or Yellow)
Hickory
Holly
Hornbeam
Ironwood
Locust
Oak
Osage Orange
Rock Elm
Rock Maple

All wood, of course, has both good and bad qualities—some are difficult to get started—hickory, often rated the top hardwood, is sometimes difficult to split into usable size. In general, the woods to avoid for their unpleasant qualities of excessive smoke, strong odor or danger from sparks are:

Balsam Fir
Basswood
Black Ash
Box Elder
Cottonwood
Elm
Hemlock
Pin Oak
Pines
Spruces
Tamarack
Tulip
Willow

Firewood should come from dead branches or small dead logs cut to fit the size of your fireplace. Don't forget to split your firewood in half lengthwise, because split wood burns faster and hotter than whole logs.

BUILDING YOUR FIRE

Start your fire building by first assembling tinder, kindling of very thinly split hardwood or hardwood sticks, and your heavier fuel—split hardwood logs. Lay two 1-inch-thick kindling sticks in your fireplace in the shape of a V; the point of the V should be toward the wind. Pile the tinder lightly between the sticks, and stack other kindling sticks teepee-fashion over the tinder. A teepee fire without heavier logs serves as a quick, hot fire for boiling water or heating soup. Another method of stacking kindling is to lay it crisscross or log cabin fashion in several layers over 2 very small logs on either side of the tinder. In either case the air circulation essential to fires will be provided: fires need oxygen to burn. Light the tinder close to the ground while kneeling with your back to the wind. As the tinder and kindling burn briskly and settle, add more kindling in crisscross fashion as necessary until the fire is well established. Then you may lay on the heavier split hardwood logs, also in crisscross fashion, which allows room for the important upward draft. The result will be a solid and long-burning fire.

Make sure that your fire is no larger than your needs. A great roaring blaze is a heartwarming sight, but it also means a larger supply of firewood must be cut, is often too hot to get close enough for cooking, has a remarkable tendency to scorch food, and is more likely to start forest fires. Aim instead for a goodly amount of cooking coals in a reasonably short time. The fire must die down to glowing gray coals before you start to cook.

FIRE STARTERS

An absolutely foolproof means of lighting a fire is a must for every camper who expects to eat hot meals in the wilderness. Always carry wooden kitchen matches which have been dipped in paraffin and stored in a waterproof container. Commercial fire starters are handy, but they may be burdensome on hiking trips and sometimes flare up when ignited. One commercial product that's compact and safe is a box of tiny cubes or disks of urea-formaldehyde, but they are fairly expensive. Canned Heat and Sterno are popular fire starters, especially in inclement weather. Candle stubs light easily and burn long enough to dry out and catch even wet tinder. Rolled newspapers soaked in paraffin and then dried and cut into short lengths make an effective homemade fire starter.

FIREPLACES

Many camping areas provide ready-made fireplaces, but if you're hiking or backpacking you'll probably have to construct one of your own. Size and layout depend on the number of people you'll be cooking for and how long you'll be using the fireplace.

Quick fireplaces can be made on a rock base, or lacking that, on dirt or sand. Scoop out the dirt or sand to form a shallow trench, find 4 large rocks to set at each corner, and lay your grill in place with the rocks to hold it down. That's all there is to it. When you no longer need a fire, don't forget to erase all signs that you passed that way. The wilderness should be left as wild as you found it.

A more permanent fireplace may be constructed if you're

planning to camp on one site for several days. The most convenient construction is a horseshoe shape, made by stacking flat rocks in a 2-foot semicircle. A good height for the rocks is 8 inches. The grill is anchored on all corners, but one side of the fireplace is left open to allow convenient feeding of the fire. The opening should face the prevailing wind to provide for upward draft. A special consideration in leaving one side open, although many campers may prefer to build a completely circular fireplace for safety reasons, is that it enables you to make good use of your reflector oven.

A keyhole fireplace is a modification of the circular type. The side of the circle facing the wind is extended by continuing the line of stacked rocks into a narrow extension of the fireplace to form a keyhole shape. Cooking is done in the narrow alley leading to the circle, where a constant fire is maintained to produce additional hardwood coals.

FIRE SAFETY

Safety should be the first *and* last consideration when building a fire. Use fireplaces to enclose fires, clearing the ground of sticks and leaves first. If you're making a fire in an exposed area, dig a trench for your fireplace and replace the dirt afterward. Build a fire no larger than your needs and never leave a fire unattended for *any* reason.

Take time to put out your fire completely. Begin to bank it as soon as the cooking is done. Knock apart whatever is left of the big logs and scatter the coals to the sides of the fireplace. Douse the coals with water and mix them about in the resulting mud, repeating the process as many times as it takes to ensure that no live sparks remain. If no water is available, cover the embers with sand or dirt and stir thoroughly to make sure they are suffocated. Test the spot where the fire was built—if you can press your hand down into it and feel no heat you can be sure it is out. Cover the fireplace area again with additional dirt or rocks and make a final check before leaving.

Finding and Purifying Water

Finding water in wilderness areas is seldom a problem. There is usually a tumbling, bubbling mountain stream, a spring or a lake close at hand that you may discover without too much difficulty. Determining whether the water is fit to drink is a difficult and important question. Don't assume that wilderness water is automatically pure: within the clearest cup may lurk the most virulent organisms gathered as the stream coursed past cabins and fishing camps. The application of a few basic rules concerning water purification will assure your continued good health during your camping or hiking trip.

BOILED WATER

A tried and true method for killing germs is to boil your water before drinking it. Boiling is well worth the extra time and trouble it takes—getting sick is far worse. Any questionable water should be boiled for at least 5 minutes. Boiled water's flat taste is somewhat improved by aerating it with a vigorous shake before drinking, or by the addition of a little salt. It can be made more pleasant to the taste by stirring bits of charred hardwood from the campfire into the pan of boiled water. Simmer for 20 minutes longer, and skim off the sediment or allow it to settle. Water that has been muddied or discolored by animal or mineral pollution can be filtered through sand or several layers of clean cloth to clean it. Then, of course, it must be boiled.

Halazone tablets, which may be purchased inexpensively in a drugstore, will purify water chemically with a minimum of effort. Several tablets dropped into a quart of water will generally purify it in half an hour, although I tend to be a bit over-cautious and prefer to wait an hour before using the water for drinking. Be sure to disinfect the mouth of your container with the water and halazone mixture immediately after the tablets dissolve.

Iodine tablets, or 2 or 3 drops of tincture of iodine, serve the same purpose as halazone tablets when you put 2–4 tablets into a quart of water and wait for one hour. Disinfect the mouth of your container after shaking up the mixture. Once again, I use the maximum quantity.

Collected rainwater and falling or clean snow when melted are safe to drink, as is fresh running spring water at its source. The higher you go up in the mountains, the greater the chances are that the water will be pure. A good rule to remember is that as water runs down the mountainside it has more chance to come in contact with pollution, whether animal, mineral or man-made. Drinking water melted from ice should be boiled.

To locate fresh water near the seashore, dig a shallow hole in the sand below the high water mark while the tide is out. As the lightweight fresh water makes its way down to the sea it will collect and float in the hole.

Finding water in desert areas presents more of a problem. Wherever there is green vegetation there is almost sure to be water, even if you have to dig down into the ground to find the hidden source. Since water always runs downhill, the lowest point of a dry stream bed may possibly provide you with a bit of water after a long hike and very hard digging. Your walking efforts will probably be better rewarded by following a trail well traversed by wild game, since animals instinctively know where the water supply is. The desert cacti also store moisture in their spiny segments, which may be extracted by mashing the ends with judicious care. The large barrel cactus considerately provides its own bowl. Do not, however, kill the slow-growing cactus unless your life depends on it.

Campfire
Cookery

Filling Soups

Bread and Cheese Soup Pot

*Soups are warm, filling, nourishing and delicious.
They may be cooked in one pot and served in the
high-sided camp plates with a sandwich, frank or
burger for a well-rounded meal.*

2 tablespoons butter	1 teaspoon whole
3 large onions, sliced	peppercorns
6 stalks celery with	1/2 teaspoon salt
tops	5 cups chicken stock
1 bay leaf	1 French bread
	1/2 pound Swiss cheese

(Serves 4)

Melt the butter in a large saucepan or skillet. Cut the celery
and celery tops into 1-inch pieces. Sauté the onions, celery
and spices for 5 minutes. Add the chicken stock; cover and
simmer for 1 hour.

Meanwhile, cut the bread into thin slices and grate the
cheese. Arrange the bread slices and grated cheese in alternate
layers in a casserole. Strain the broth, reheating if necessary,
and pour slowly over the bread and cheese. Serve at once.

Japanese Shrimp Soup

4 or 5 cups chicken broth or packaged dried chicken soup, prepared according to directions	1/2 cup white or red miso*
	1/2 cup minced scallions; or minced wild onions
1 8-ounce can shrimp, coarsely chopped	1/8 teaspoon powdered ginger
	Tabasco sauce

(Serves 4)

Bring soup to a boil and add chopped shrimp. Combine the miso and 1 cup of hot soup and gradually stir the mixture back into the remaining soup. Add the scallions and ginger and continue to cook for 3 minutes. Stir in a few drops of Tabasco sauce and serve hot.

* Miso, a soy bean paste, can be purchased in health food or Oriental grocery stores. It needs no refrigeration and is therefore ideal for camping trips.

Lima Bean, Barley and Mushroom Soup

1/2 cup large dried lima beans	1 medium-sized onion, chopped
2 tablespoons coarse pearl barley	2 tablespoons dried parsley
8 bouillon cubes	1/2 cup celery, finely diced
1 quart water	1 cup carrots, finely diced
1 jar dried chipped beef	1/4 teaspoon dill weed
2 tablespoons dehydrated sliced mushrooms	1/2 teaspoon celery salt

(Serves 4)

Wash the lima beans and barley in cold water, and drain well. Place the beans and barley in a soup kettle. Add the water and all remaining ingredients to the kettle; cover and bring to a boil. Cook gently for about 2 hours, or until the lima beans are soft. Serve the soup steaming hot.

166

Warm and Filling Kidney Bean Soup

Soak overnight. Prepare garlic croutons at home and store them in a plastic bag. For convenient campsite cooking pre-measure spices and wrap them in plastic or foil.

1/2 cup dried kidney beans
3 cups water
2 ounces salt pork, diced
1 medium-sized onion, chopped
1 carrot, chopped
2 stalks celery, including leaves, chopped
3 1/2 cups water
3 peppercorns

1 small bay leaf
1 teaspoon saffron
Salt and freshly ground pepper to taste
1 avocado (if available)
Lemon juice
3 scallions with 3 inches of green top
1 hard-cooked egg, chopped
garlic croutons

(Serves 4)

Place the beans in a large saucepan with water to cover; soak overnight. Drain the beans and set aside.

Place the salt pork in a heavy soup kettle and fry over medium heat until crisp. Add onions, carrots and celery to the soup kettle and sauté until the onions are transparent, about 5 minutes.

Bring the water to a boil and add to the soup kettle together with the drained beans, peppercorns, bay leaf and saffron. Cover the pot and simmer for 3 hours or prepare in a Dutch oven and pit-cook until the beans are tender. Adjust the seasonings. Dice the avocado and sprinkle with lemon juice. Chop the scallions. Serve the soup hot, garnished with avocado, scallions, chopped egg and garlic croutons.

Guatemalan Bread Soup

1 1/2 tablespoons butter
1 medium-size
  onion, chopped
1 tomato, peeled,
  seeded and
  chopped
1/8 teaspoon sugar
1/2 teaspoon flour
1/2 cup water
1 package dried
  onion soup mix

4 cups water
1 clove garlic, minced
1 1/2 tablespoons cook-
  ing oil
4 slices whole-wheat
  bread, fresh or stale
2 hard-cooked eggs,
  sliced
Parmesan cheese,
  grated

(Serves 4)

Melt the butter in a large heavy skillet. Sauté the onion and tomato until the onion is transparent. Sprinkle with sugar. Mix together the flour and water and stir into the vegetables. Bring to a boil, stirring constantly. Add the onion soup mix and water and simmer for 15 minutes. Sauté the garlic in the oil. Remove the crusts from the bread. Fry bread slices in the oil until golden brown on both sides. Serve the hot soup in individual bowls topped with sautéed bread slices, hard-cooked egg and grated Parmesan cheese.

Onion Soup

This soup provides a filling camp lunch. The delicious little Pennsylvania Dutch dumplings or "rivvels" are easy to prepare.

2 tablespoons butter
1 1/2 cups chopped
  onions
5 cups beef con-
  sommé or 2 pack-
  ages dried onion
  soup plus 5 cups
  water

2 1/2 tablespoons flour
2 eggs
Salt and freshly
  ground black
  pepper to taste
1/2 cup grated cheese

(Serves 4)

Melt the butter and sauté the onions until golden and transparent. Pour the consommé into a large kettle and bring it to a boil. Add the sautéed onions, lower the heat, and simmer for 10 minutes.

Meanwhile, prepare the rivvels as follows: Measure the flour into a small bowl, stir in the eggs and cut the dough into narrow pieces. Allow it to dry for 10 minutes. Rub pieces of the dough between the sides of your palms until bits break off and fall into the simmering soup. Let simmer 15 minutes. Adjust the seasonings. Serve hot, with a bowl of grated cheese on the side.

Pistou

A tablespoonful of this distinctive paste will enliven almost any soup. Prepare a small jarful to take with you on your next camping trip.

5 slices bacon	6 tablespoons Parmesan
2 egg yolks	cheese, grated
3 cloves garlic	1 teaspoon olive oil
1 teaspoon dried basil	

Boil the bacon for 3 minutes in one cup of water, drain and chop. Place the yolks in the blender with the bacon, garlic and basil, and blend until all ingredients are puréed. Pour the purée into a bowl. Stir in the grated Parmesan cheese and olive oil. This will keep on ice for 2 days.

Swiss Cheese-Wild Onion Dumplings

These tiny golden dumplings make any plain soup a fancy one in minutes.

3 tablespoons butter	1 tablespoon minced
1/2 cup grated Swiss cheese	wild onion (1 teaspoon dried dill,
2 tablespoons flour	onion flakes or other
1 egg yolk	spice may be substituted)

(Serves 4)

Cream all ingredients together. Dust hands with flour and form the cheese mixture into dumplings the size of filberts. Drop into boiling soup. When the dumplings rise to the surface, boil for a few seconds more. Serve immediately.

Corn Dodger Dumplings

2 cups white corn-
meal
1 teaspoon salt

1 1/2 cups boiling water
1 tablespoon bacon
fat

(Makes 16)

Combine the cornmeal and salt in a large bowl. Add enough of the boiling water to make a batter that can be shaped with the hands. Stir in the bacon fat and refrigerate for at least 20 minutes. Bring 3 quarts of lightly salted water to a boil in a deep kettle. Form the batter into dumplings and drop into the boiling water. Cook for 20 or 30 minutes, or until the dumplings are light. Add to soup just before serving.

Wild Blackberry or Dewberry Soup

1 pint blackberries
1 1/4 cups light sweet
wine
1 2-inch stick of
cinnamon

2/3 cup granulated
sugar
Pinch of cloves
1 1/2 cups sour cream,
kept on ice

(Serves 4)

Pick over the berries, discard any bad ones and set aside 1/2 cup of the largest to use as a garnish. Place the remainder in a strainer and run cold water over them. Pour the washed berries into a soup kettle and add the wine, cinnamon, sugar and cloves. Place on medium-high heat and bring slowly to a boil. Lower heat and cook gently for about 5 to 8 minutes. Strain soup into a bowl, pressing as much of the berries through the strainer as possible. Place on ice overnight or for at least 4 hours.

When ready to serve, fold in the cold sour cream. Serve at once with cinnamon toast as a breakfast treat or as a dessert soup. Garnish with the reserved berries.

Dried Fruit Soup

Semi-prepare this sweet and tart dessert soup at home and continue the cooking in camp.

1/4 cup dried apples
1/2 cup dried apricots
1/4 cup dried pears
1/2 cup dried pitted
    prunes
1/4 cup dried peaches
1/2 cup golden raisins
  3 whole cloves

1/2 cup plus 1 table-
    spoon sugar
1/4 cup tapioca
  2 cups water
1/2 stick cinnamon
1/4 cup lemon juice
1/2 cup grape jelly

(Serves 4)

At home, soak the dried fruit in the water for 2 hours. Drain the fruit, placing the liquid in a large soup kettle. Dice the fruit and add it to the liquid in the kettle, along with the whole cloves. Cook over low heat until the fruit is tender. Pour the liquid through a strainer into a saucepan or jar. Place the fruit in another jar.

At the campsite, add the sugar, tapioca, water and cinnamon stick to the strained soup. Return this to the stove and boil for 30 minutes, stirring occasionally until the soup is clear. Lower heat and stir in the lemon juice and jelly until the jelly melts. Add the fruit and a little more lemon juice if the soup is too sweet for your taste. Reheat and serve hot.

Eggs and Potatoes

Salami Eggs

3 tablespoons butter
2 medium-sized
onions, sliced
1/2 pound salami, thinly
sliced

4 eggs
Salt and freshly
ground black pepper
to taste

(Serves 4)

Heat the butter in a skillet over medium coals. Sauté onions until lightly browned. Place the cooked onions in a bowl and keep them warm.

Sauté the salami slices on both sides and arrange neatly in the bottom of the skillet. Top with the onions and cook briefly. Make shallow wells by pressing the onion rings in 4 places with the back of a spoon. Break an egg into each well, season with salt and pepper, cover and cook until the eggs are set. Serve immediately for a quick lunch or supper.

Pumpernickel Eggs

Absolutely delicious.

2 tablespoons butter
2 tablespoons
vegetable oil
4 thick slices pumper-
nickel bread
8 eggs

1 2-inch square
Cheddar (or other)
cheese
1/8 teaspoon each salt
and pepper
1/4 teaspoon oregano

(Serves 4)

Heat the butter and oil in a large frying pan. Cut the pumpernickel slices into 1/2-inch cubes and sauté in the butter and oil, stirring to brown on all sides. Break the eggs into the pan over the bread. Cut the cheese into 1/2-inch cubes and distribute over the eggs. Add salt, pepper and oregano, cover, and cook over low heat until the eggs are set.

Bull's-Eye Eggs

8 slices bread
4 tablespoons butter or
bacon fat
8 eggs

Oregano
Salt and freshly ground
black pepper to taste

(Serves 4)

Trim the crusts from the bread slices. Cut circles about 1 1/2 inches in diameter from the center of each slice. Melt the butter in 2 skillets. Place the bread slices in the skillets and break an egg into each hole. Fry several minutes, then turn and continue cooking until the egg yolks reach the desired consistency. Sprinkle with spices and serve immediately.

One-Dish Bulghour and Eggs

Bulghour is ideal for camping trips. This Middle-Eastern cracked wheat product is light in weight, high in nutrition and a tasty substitute for potatoes, rice or pasta.

4 onions, chopped
3 tablespoons butter
1 cup bulghour
2 cups water

1 package onion soup
mix
4 eggs

(Serves 4)

Melt the butter in a heavy skillet and sauté the onions for 8 minutes. Add the bulghour and continue to cook, stirring constantly, for 5 minutes more. Stir the onion soup mix and water together and add to the bulghour. Place over low heat, cover the skillet and cook, stirring occasionally until the bulghour is almost tender. Make 4 depressions in the bulghour with the back of a spoon, drop an egg into each depression. Cover and cook until the eggs are the desired firmness. Serve immediately.

Sliced Potato Omelet

2 large onions, finely
  chopped
4 medium-sized potatoes,
  thinly sliced
3 tablespoons olive oil

4 eggs
Salt and freshly ground
  black pepper to taste
8 large pimiento-stuffed
  olives

(Serves 4)

Heat the olive oil in a large skillet and add the onions and potatoes. Cover and cook slowly, stirring from time to time until potato slices are tender but not brown. Remove onions and potatoes from the pan, chop finely and set them aside. Beat the eggs well and add the onions, potatoes and salt and pepper to taste. Scrape the skillet well and, if necessary, remove any excess oil, leaving just enough to coat the bottom of the pan.

Cut the olives into 1/4-inch slices and arrange in the skillet. Spoon the potato-egg mixture over the olives and cook until the omelet is brown on one side and the eggs are set.

Loosen the sides of the omelet with a spatula, hold a plate firmly over the skillet, then turn the pan upside down and transfer the omelet onto the plate. Heat a little oil in the skillet and slide the omelet back into the pan. Brown and serve at once, olive side up.

Cointreau Omelet

1 1/2 tablespoons butter
4 eggs
2 tablespoons con-
  fectioners' sugar
Pinch of salt
3 tablespoons Coin-

treau or any
orange-flavored
liqueur
4 tablespoons apricot
jam

(Serves 4)

Heat a 10-inch skillet or omelet pan over medium coals until it is very hot; melt the butter and when it is sizzling, quickly add the well-beaten eggs to which a 1/4 teaspoon of sugar and a pinch of salt have been added. Shake the pan as you stir the eggs briskly with a fork until the top of the eggs begins to set. Remove the pan from the fire and tip it slightly as you roll the omelet up into an oval shape with the fork. Slide the omelet off the pan into a large heat-proof dish. Sprinkle it with the remaining sugar and cover with aluminum foil to keep it warm. Mix 2 tablespoons of the liqueur with the apricot jam in a small saucepan and heat briefly. Pour 2 additional tablespoons of the liqueur over the sauce. When the liqueur is warm, ignite it. Pour the flaming sauce around the omelet, then cut it into four slices and serve immediately.

Dessert Omelet

4 **egg yolks**	2 **tablespoons butter**
4 **egg whites**	**Kirsch**
3 **tablespoons sugar**	**Confectioners' sugar**
1/2 **tablespoon water**	2 **cups wild berries**
Salt	1/2 **pint whipped cream**

(Serves 4)

Mix the sugar with the egg yolks and beat until thick and lemon-colored. Add the water and a few grains of salt to the egg whites and beat until they stand in peaks. Fold the beaten egg whites carefully into the egg yolks. Melt the butter in a medium-sized skillet. Pour the egg mixture into the skillet and cook until the omelet is brown on the bottom and the eggs are set on the top. Fold the omelet in half and carefully slide it onto a serving dish. Sprinkle generously with kirsch and confectioners' sugar and surround with the berries and cream.

Hash Browned Potatoes

A camping classic. Be sure you pack a grater with your camping equipment.

6 **medium-sized potatoes**	1/2 **teaspoon salt**
6 **tablespoons vegetable oil**	1/8 **teaspoon sage**
2 **medium-sized onions**	1/8 **teaspoon thyme**
	1/8 **teaspoon pepper**

(Serves 4)

Peel the potatoes and grate them on a medium-sized grater. Allow the potatoes to drop on several thicknesses of paper toweling set beneath the grater to absorb any liquid. Blot excess moisture from the top of the grated potatoes with additional paper towels. Heat 3 tablespoons of the oil in a large skillet and arrange the potatoes in pancake form over the bottom.

While the potatoes brown on one side, peel and grate the onions, taking care to catch any juices. Flatten the potatoes slightly with your spatula and scatter the onions, onion juice and spices over the top.

When the potatoes are crispy brown on one side, cut the pancake into quarters. Lift each quarter carefully from the pan and set on a plate. Add the 3 remaining tablespoons of oil to the skillet, turn the quarters carefully and return them to the skillet to get brown and crispy on the other side. Serve immediately.

Steamed Potatoes

No need to carry extra skillets on camping trips when foil-wrapped potatoes are so easy to prepare. Fold a 2-foot piece of aluminum foil in half, and crimp the 2 side edges to form a 12-inch square pocket. Place 4 peeled and thickly sliced potatoes inside and top with one of the following combinations. Crimp to seal the open edge of the pocket and wrap the whole pouch in heavy-duty quilted foil.

(Serves 4)

Herbed Potatoes

1 1/2 tablespoons butter

1 small onion, peeled and chopped

1 teaspoon fresh sage (or 1/4 teaspoon dried)

1 teaspoon fresh thyme (or 1/4 teaspoon dried)

1/8 teaspoon salt

Pepper to taste

Sesame Potatoes

1 1/2 tablespoons butter

1 large onion, peeled and chopped

2 tablespoons sesame seeds

1 tablespoon minced parsley

1/4 teaspoon salt

Pepper to taste

Main Courses

Fried Brook Trout with Lemon Mustard Butter

4 medium-sized brook trout

1/2 teaspoon salt

1/3 cup milk

1/2 cup flour

3 tablespoons oil

5 tablespoons butter

2 1/2 teaspoons French-style mustard

1 teaspoon dried parsley flakes

2 tablespoons lemon juice

(Serves 4)

Clean, wash and dry the trout. Mix together the salt and milk. Dip each trout in the milk mixture, then roll in flour. Heat the oil and 3 tablespoons of the butter in a large skillet. Fry the trout until they are tender and crispy. Quickly stir the mustard, the remaining butter, and the parsley flakes into the butter in the pan. Add the lemon juice, bring to a boil, and pour the hot lemon-mustard butter over the fish.

Trout with Egg-Cheese Sauce

4 small trout
2 tablespoons butter
Salt and pepper to taste
1/4 cup dry white wine
2 egg yolks
1/2 cup sour cream

2 tablespoons minced wild onions or 1 1/2 tablespoons minced, dried onions*
1/2 cup grated or slivered Swiss cheese

(Serves 4)

Split and clean the trout, leaving the heads intact. Place the butter in a skillet and sauté the trout 5 minutes on each side. Pour in the wine, then cover and simmer over a slow fire for 5 minutes, or until the fish are almost done. In a small bowl, beat the egg yolks lightly and blend in the sour cream and the juices from the pan. Pour this mixture over the fish, top with onions and cheese. Cover and cook over low heat 8–10 minutes longer, or until the fish is done.

Oatmeal-Crusted Trout

4 trout (or more if you have them)
3/4 cup butter
Salt and pepper to taste

1 1/2 cups oatmeal
2 whole lemons

(Serves 4)

Wash and clean the trout and dry them well. Heat the butter in a large skillet over medium coals. Season trout with salt and pepper. Place the oatmeal on a sheet of aluminum foil, dip the fish in the butter and roll them in the oatmeal, making sure that the oatmeal adheres to each side. Arrange the fish in the hot butter in the pan. Sauté until golden brown on both sides, turning once. Cut the lemons into 8 wedges to garnish each serving.

* If dried onions are used, add with the wine.

Pike with Anchovy Butter

1 3- to 4-pound pike
Salt
1 medium-sized onion
1 tablespoon lemon juice

1/3 cup butter
7 anchovy fillets
1 lemon

(Serves 4)

Clean the pike and rub salt over all surfaces. Peel the onion and slice it into thin rings. Place the pike in a large heavy skillet, arrange the onion rings over the top and sprinkle with 1 tablespoon lemon juice, then set the fish aside for 15 minutes. Melt the butter, mash the anchovy fillets in it and heat for 3 minutes. Pour this anchovy butter over the fish and seal the top of the skillet with a double thickness of aluminum foil. Set the skillet over medium coals and cook the fish until it flakes easily when pierced with a fork, about 30 minutes. Serve hot with plenty of sauce and lemon wedges.

Baked Muskellunge Steaks

A game-fish found in Canada and very difficult to land, muskellunge is a rare treat. If the muskies aren't biting, this recipe may be prepared with any other variety of pike.

4 medium-sized muskel-
lunge steaks
Salt and pepper to
taste
4 tablespoons butter, at
room temperature
3 tablespoons minced
onions
1/4 teaspoon dried thyme
1 tablespoon flour

1 can or package of
dried mushroom
soup*
1 1/2 cups milk
1 tablespoon bottled
horseradish, drained
1/2 teaspoon sugar
1/3 cup grated or slivered
cheese

(Serves 4)

* If dried soup is used, add 1/2 cup water along with the milk.

179

Sprinkle the fish steaks with salt and pepper. Melt the butter in a heavy skillet. Sauté the fish steaks for 8 minutes, adding the minced onions and the thyme after the steaks are turned. Sauté the fish until nearly done. Mix together the flour, mushroom soup, milk, horseradish and sugar. Stir until smooth. Bring the sauce to a boil over medium heat, stirring constantly. Pour the sauce over the fish and sprinkle with the cheese. Cover the pan and cook 10 minutes longer. Serve immediately.

Fish Stew with Eggs

2 medium-sized onions, minced

3 tablespoons butter, oil or bacon fat

2 medium-sized tomatoes, peeled

4 large potatoes, peeled
Minced wild onions and herbs (if available)

Large pinch each saffron and fennel seeds

2 1-inch pieces of orange rind (if available)

4 small fillets of fish, cut into 2-inch pieces

4 eggs

4 slices stale bread, buttered

(Serves 4)

Heat the butter or oil in a deep skillet and sauté the onions. Cut the tomatoes into quarters and remove seeds. Coarsely chop tomatoes before adding to the skillet. Cut potatoes into 1/4-inch slices and place them in the skillet. Add onions and herbs, saffron, fennel seeds, and orange rind. Cover with water to a depth of at least 1/2-inch above the ingredients. Bring to a boil. Immediately lower the heat, cover, then simmer the stew until the potatoes are nearly tender. Add the fish pieces and cook for 10 minutes more. Remove the stew from the flame and carefully break 4 eggs, one at a time, into the broth. Cover and poach gently over very low flame until egg white is firm but yolks are still soft. Place the stale bread slices in 4 soup plates, ladle potatoes and 1 egg over each slice and pour in the hot stew.

White Beans and Sausage in a Skillet

Begin this recipe at least 3 hours before serving.

1 1/2 cups dried white
beans

1/2 pound sausage or slab
bacon

2 medium-sized
tomatoes

3 medium-sized onions

1 large clove garlic

3/4 cup olive oil

1/2 teaspoon salt

1/4 teaspoon thyme

Freshly ground black
pepper to taste

(Serves 4)

Wash the beans and remove any dark or otherwise imperfect beans. Place the beans in a saucepan with water to cover. Bring to a boil over high heat. Remove the pan from the fire and soak beans for 1 hour. Drain beans thoroughly, cover with fresh water and simmer for 1 1/2 hours, or until tender. Drain beans and set aside.

Meanwhile, cut 1/2 pound of sausage or bacon into 2-inch lengths. Fry until crisp and drain well on paper toweling. Reserve. Peel the tomatoes, cut into quarters and shake out the seeds. Peel and slice the onions. Peel and mince the garlic. Place the olive oil in a skillet and sauté the tomatoes, onions and garlic until the onions are lightly browned and transparent. Add the beans, salt and thyme to the skillet and cook over low heat for 10 minutes. Adjust the seasonings. Gently stir in the sausage or bacon pieces and continue cooking 10 minutes longer. Serve hot.

Steak Diane

If you feel festive, try the following recipe.

Sirloin steak to feed 4

3 tablespoons butter

3 tablespoons finely
chopped scallions or wild
onions

2 tablespoons cognac

2 tablespoons sherry

(Serves 4)

Trim most of the fat from the steak. Heat 2 tablespoons of the butter in a large skillet over a medium fire and gently sauté the scallions until they are golden. Add the steak and cook it to the desired degree of doneness, turning often. Just before serving, pour in the cognac, heat it slightly and set it aflame. Remove the steak to a serving platter, add the sherry and the remaining tablespoon of butter to the pan juices, swirl briefly to blend and pour over the hot steak.

Drunken Hunter's Stew

1 1/2 pounds Spanish
    sausage or garlic
    sausage
1/2 pound cooked lamb
3 large onions, thinly
    sliced
3 tablespoons vegetable
    oil
3 tablespoons flour

1/2 cup vodka
2 cups red wine
3 tablespoons tomato
    paste
2 cups tomato juice
2 1/2 pounds sauerkraut,
    drained
2 large potatoes

(Serves 4)

Cut the sausage into 1/2-inch slices and the lamb into 1 inch cubes. Set aside. Heat the oil in a skillet and sauté the onions until they are golden and transparent. Blend the flour in with the onions. Gradually stir in the vodka, wine, tomato paste and tomato juice. Cook gently, stirring constantly, until the sauce thickens. Remove the sauce from the flame.

    Rinse the sauerkraut in water and drain well. Peel and slice the potatoes. In a large pot, alternate layers of sauerkraut, sausage, meat, potatoes and sauce to form 4 layers. Cover and simmer for 2 1/2 hours over low heat or place in a Dutch oven and cook in a pit. Serve hot.

Veal Steak with Green Pepper and Orange Sauce

1 veal cutlet, 1 1/2
   inches thick
1/8 teaspoon salt
1/8 teaspoon pepper
2 tablespoons butter
2 medium-sized green
   peppers

2 medium-sized
   tomatoes, peeled
2 medium-sized onions
1/2 teaspoon orange zest
   (grated outer rind)
1 3/4 cups orange juice
1 1/2 teaspoons cornstarch
1 tablespoon water

(Serves 4)

Sprinkle the veal with salt and pepper. Melt the butter in a Dutch oven and brown the cutlet on both sides. Remove the seeds and white pith from the green pepper. Cut the tomato into quarters and remove the seeds. Coarsely chop the green pepper, tomato and onion. Mix together and add, along with the orange zest, to the meat in the Dutch oven and cook over low coals for a few minutes. Pour the orange juice over the meat and vegetables and simmer, covered, until the veal is tender, about 1 hour. Place the meat on a serving platter and keep it warm. Mix the cornstarch and water together thoroughly, and add to the liquid in the skillet. Cook for a few minutes over hot fire, stirring constanly until the sauce thickens, adding a bit more orange juice if the sauce is too thick. Pour the sauce over the veal and serve hot.

Veal Chops and Sausage with Tomatoes

8 veal chops
1/8 teaspoon rosemary
1/8 teaspoon salt
1/8 teaspoon freshly
ground black pepper
1/4 cup flour
1/4 cup vegetable oil
4 cloves garlic, chopped
4 small onions, chopped
2 medium-sized green
peppers, chopped
2 cups sliced mushrooms

10 canned plum tomatoes,
mashed
6 tablespoons tomato
paste
4 teaspoons sugar
6 cups canned chicken
broth
1 teaspoon curry powder
2 whole bay leaves
Salt and freshly ground
black pepper to taste
1 pound kielbasa (Polish
sausage)

(Serves 8)

Sprinkle the chops with the rosemary, salt and pepper, then roll them in the flour. Heat the oil in one large skillet or two smaller ones, and brown the chops on both sides. Arrange the garlic, onions, peppers, mushrooms and tomatoes on top of the veal chops. Mix together the tomato paste, sugar, chicken stock and spices, then pour mixture over the vegetables. Skin the kielbasa, cut into 1/2-inch thick slices and tuck these around the chops, making sure they are covered by the sauce. Cover the pan and place over medium heat for 2 hours, or until the veal is tender. Serve hot over rice or cous-cous. This recipe is particularly good when the ingredients are placed in a Dutch oven and pit-cooked.

Chicken Breasts with Rosemary

4 large chicken breasts,
boned and skinned
4 teaspoons rosemary leaves

Salt and white pepper to
taste
4 teaspoons butter

(Serves 4)

Keep chicken breasts thoroughly chilled. One hour before serving time, press the rosemary into the chicken breasts with the heel of your hand. Refrigerate 1 hour longer. Place in a hinged wire basket and grill over medium coals (or sauté in oil and butter), until the chicken is no longer pink. Do not overcook. Serve sprinkled with salt and pepper and dotted with butter.

Spicy South American Skillet Beef

2 medium-sized onions, thinly sliced

3 medium-sized tomatoes; or 1 cup canned tomatoes, drained and chopped

2 tablespoons vegetable oil

1 pound ground lean chuck

1/2 teaspoon sugar

1/4 teaspoon thyme

1/2 teaspoon oregano

1/8 teaspoon freshly ground black pepper

Salt to taste

2 teaspoons powdered cloves

1 package dried onion soup mix

1 cup water

3 hard-cooked eggs, chopped

10 stuffed green olives, sliced

(Serves 4)

Peel the tomatoes, cut into quarters, remove seeds, then chop coarsely. Put the vegetable oil in a skillet, add the chopped meat, onion, tomatoes, sugar, thyme, oregano, pepper, salt and cloves. Place over medium high flame and stir until the meat is brown. Stir together the onion soup mix and water; add to the meat. Cook until all of the liquid evaporates. Pour off any excess fat. Garnish with the chopped eggs and the sliced olives. Serve immediately.

Rice with Bacon and Smoked Sausage

1/2 cup diced bacon
1/2 cup thinly sliced kielbasa (Polish sausage), or other smoked sausage
2 medium-sized onions, finely chopped
2 cloves garlic, finely chopped

2 medium-sized green peppers, thinly sliced
1 1/2 cups rice
1 3/4 cups boiling water
1 cup tomato juice
1 teaspoon salt
1/2 teaspoon sugar

(Serves 4)

Sauté the bacon and kielbasa in a skillet until the bacon is slightly browned. Add the rice, garlic and onion, and sauté, stirring occasionally, until the onion is golden and transparent, and the rice is lightly browned. Remove the skillet from the heat and stir in the green peppers, boiling water, tomato juice, salt and sugar. Place the skillet over medium coals and bring the mixture to a boil. Move skillet further from the coals and simmer, covered, for about 30 minutes, or until the rice is tender when a grain is rubbed between the thumb and forefinger.

Campfire Sausage and Beans

1 medium-sized onion, thinly sliced
1 medium-sized green pepper, cut into 1/2-inch squares
1 or 2 tablespoons vegetable oil
1 15-ounce can baked pork and beans
1 15-ounce can butter beans, drained

1 small can sliced mushrooms, drained
5 ounces ready-to-eat smoked sausage
1/2 cup catsup
1/4 cup mustard
2/3 cup maple syrup
1 teaspoon oregano
5 whole cloves
2 small bay leaves

(Serves 4)

Heat the oil in a large saucepan over a low fire and gently sauté the onion slices and pepper squares until the onion is slightly transparent, about 3 or 4 minutes. Add the baked beans, butter beans and sliced mushrooms and stir well. Cut the sausage into bite-size pieces and add to the beans, together with the catsup, mustard, maple syrup, oregano, cloves and bay leaves. Cook the beans, stirring occasionally, until all the ingredients are piping hot. Serve immediately.

Sausage in a Pot

2 1/2 pounds potatoes
1 1/3 pound kielbasa
   sausage
2 tablespoons butter
3 medium-sized onions,
   coarsely chopped

1 tablespoon paprika
1 teaspoon marjoram
1 teaspoon sugar
1 teaspoon salt
1 1/2 cups tomato juice,
   beef broth or water

(Serves 4)

Peel the potatoes and cut into 1/2-inch slices. Cut the sausage into 1-inch slices. In a skillet, brown the sausage in butter. Add the onions and sauté until golden and transparent. Stir in the paprika, and add the potatoes, marjoram, sugar, salt and tomato juice, beef broth or water. Cover and cook over low heat until the potatoes are tender. Serve hot.

Chili Con Carne

Save time and effort—measure and place the needed spices in a small plastic bag when you pack groceries for your camping trip.

1 1/2 pounds lean beef
1 tablespoon oil
1 28-ounce can
   tomatoes
1 large onion, finely
   chopped
2 large cloves garlic,
   finely chopped
2 1/2 tablespoons chili
   powder

1 teaspoon salt
1/2 teaspoon ground
   cumin seed
1 teaspoon oregano
2 20-ounce cans red
   kidney beans
3 cups cooked macaroni
   (optional)

(Serves 4)

Cut the lean beef into small cubes. Heat the oil in a deep heavy pot and brown the meat well on all sides. Drain the canned tomatoes, reserving the juice, and chop the tomatoes coarsely. Add the tomatoes, reserved juice, onions and garlic to the meat, along with the chili powder, salt, cumin and oregano. Stir in the kidney beans with their juice. Reduce the heat, cover and simmer the chili for 2 1/2 to 3 hours, stirring occasionally. Add a little hot water during the cooking if the chili seems too thick. If desired, this may be placed in a Dutch oven and cooked in a pit. To serve, place 1/2 cup of cooked macaroni in each serving bowl, and spoon the piping hot chili over it.

Puddings, Bread and Fruit

Cheesey Corn Pudding

3 tablespoons butter	3 egg yolks
1 small onion, chopped	3 egg whites
3 tablespoons all-purpose flour	1/2 teaspoon salt
	White pepper to taste
2 cups milk	1/8 teaspoon garlic powder
1 cup Cheddar cheese, grated	1 package frozen corn; or 1 can corn, drained

(Serves 4)

Melt the butter in a skillet. Add the chopped onion and sauté until transparent. Remove from the heat and stir in the flour, pressing out any lumps with the back of a spoon. Return the pan to the heat and gradually add the milk, stirring constantly until the mixture thickens. Add the cheese and stir until the cheese melts and the sauce is smooth. Cool slightly. Beat the egg yolks, salt, pepper, garlic powder and corn into the cheese mixture. Set aside to cool.

Meanwhile, beat the egg whites until they are stiff but not

dry. Gently but thoroughly fold them into the pudding. Pour the corn pudding into a well-buttered, large heavy skillet. Fold a 3-foot piece of aluminum foil into a 5-inch square pad. Cover the skillet with a lid and place it on the aluminum foil pad. Bake over medium coals for 1 hour. Serve immediately.

Skillet Bread Pudding

1 1/2 cups milk
10 slices white bread
2 tablespoons butter
1/4 teaspoon salt
1/2 teaspoon cinnamon
1/4 teaspoon cloves

1/4 teaspoon nutmeg
2 egg yolks
1/3 cup sugar
1/4 cup sherry
1/4 cup white raisins or chopped dates

(Serves 4)

Heat the milk in a saucepan but do not let it boil. Trim the crusts from the bread and cut the slices into 1/2-inch cubes. Stir the butter into the hot milk and add all at once to the bread. Allow the bread to soak in this mixture for 10 minutes. Stir in the seasonings, egg yolks, sugar, sherry and raisins. Mix thoroughly and pour into a heavy buttered or oiled skillet. Cook, covered, over medium coals for 30 minutes. Turn the pudding and cook, covered, for 30 more minutes. Serve warm, topped with a bit of jam mixed with lemon juice or Lemon Curd (see page 239).

Squaw Bread

Squaw bread is a large, round, fried bread that is delicious with butter and jam.

5 cups all-purpose or unbleached white flour
2 tablespoons baking powder

1 1/4 teaspoons salt
1 1/2 tablespoons melted butter
2 cups milk
Oil for frying

CAMPING

At home, measure 4 cups of flour, baking powder and salt. Sift together and place in a container to take with you. At the campsite, place the pre-sifted ingredients in a large bowl. Melt the butter and add to the milk. Add the milk and butter mixture, a little at a time, to the dry ingredients, beating until the dough becomes stiff. Sprinkle the remaining cup of flour on a pastry board or other flat surface and knead lightly until all of the flour has been worked in. Roll the dough into three circles about 1/8 inch thick and 10 inches in diameter.

Heat 3 or 4 tablespoons of oil in a 10-inch skillet. When the oil is hot, fry each bread until crisp and light brown on both sides. Serve hot.

Cream Scones

1/2 cup butter
4 cups all-purpose or unbleached white flour, sifted
2 3/4 teaspoons cream of tartar

1 1/2 teaspoons baking soda
1 egg
6 tablespoons sugar
1 cup sour milk

(Makes 5 dozen)

Melt the butter over hot water. Combine the sifted flour, cream of tartar and baking soda, and sift together. Beat the egg in a large bowl and stir in the sugar and sour milk. Blend in the dry ingredients and mix together thoroughly. Add the melted butter, a little at a time, beating the dough after each addition. Dust a pastry board or other flat surface lightly with flour and roll the dough out to 1/4-inch thickness. Using the edge of a drinking glass, cut the dough into 3-inch circles. Slice each circle into quarters and dust with a light sprinkling of flour. Cook on a hot griddle for 10 minutes, or until golden brown on each side.

Toast from the Grill

Toast to go with your morning eggs and coffee is quickly prepared by spearing your bread on the tines of a long-handled fork or clipping it into a hinged wire basket. Simply grill on both sides over charcoal or your campstove. If you've made bacon for breakfast, fry the bread slices in the bacon fat left in the skillet for delicious skillet toast.

Australian Busters

These soft thin cheese biscuits are superb.

8 tablespoons butter
2 cups flour, unsifted
3 1/2 cups grated Cheddar, loosely packed

6-7 tablespoons water
A pinch or two of cayenne pepper

(Makes 12)

With your fingers, rub the butter into the flour until the particles are very small. Once again, using your fingers, lightly mix in the grated cheese. Stir in the water and cayenne pepper with a fork. Roll the dough out to 1/4-inch thickness, cut into 3-inch rounds, prick each biscuit ten times with a fork, and place on a greased pie pan or aluminum camp plate. Bake for 15 minutes in a preheated Dutch oven.

Baked Apple with Raisins and Prunes

4 large McIntosh apples
4 heaping tablespoons golden raisins
12 prunes, pitted

4 tablespoons honey
1/8 teaspoon cinnamon
1/8 teaspoon nutmeg
4 teaspoons butter

(Serves 4)

Remove the seeds and cores from the apples without cutting through the blossom ends. Scoop some of the pulp from the apples and chop together with the raisins and the prunes. Mix this filling with the honey, cinnamon and nutmeg and blend well. Fill the hollow of each apple with this mixture and top each with a teaspoon of butter.

Wrap each apple loosely in a 2-foot piece of foil folded

in half. Twist the ends of the foil together to seal. Place over low coals until the apples are tender. Serve hot with cream or Lemon Curd (see page 239) if desired.

Stewed Apricots and Honey

24 dried apricots
1/4 cup honey
1 cup fresh orange juice
1 cup water

1 stick cinnamon
3 cloves
1/8 teaspoon powdered anise

(Serves 4)

Rinse the apricots and place all ingredients in a skillet. Simmer until the fruit is fairly soft and the syrup is thick. Serve warm or cold. Save the cinnamon stick to nibble on.

COOKING
BY THE
SEA

COOKING BY THE SEA

CAMPING AND/OR COOKING on or near a beach is probably the most fascinating outdoor activity there is. Here is a lesson in sensuous living. One is warmed by the sun and caressed by the ever-present breezes. The grasses answer in response to the whispering of the winds and the crack and boom of the surf stirs the soul. Our coasts are long and amply stocked with creatures so exquisitely beautiful, so fascinatingly structured and so incredibly delicious as to totally confound the eye, the intellect and the palate. My seaside camping adventures have ranged geographically from Rhode Island to the Virgin Islands, from Washington State to southern California, and each place provided an abundance of edible sea creatures inspiring indeed to any cook. If you live or vacation near the ocean, by all means try the exhilarating pastime of foraging for your own food.

Here follows a list and description of favorite seashore tidbits with suggestions for preparing them.

Fish

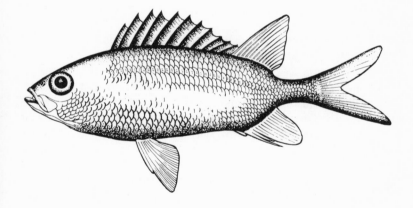

I PERSONALLY AM content to cook the fish others catch but there are those who find it especially soul-satisfying to catch, prepare and cook the fish. If you can't catch the fish yourself, take advantage of the fish markets and ask for fish that have been brought in that very morning. Following is a listing of salt-water and fresh-water fish, to help you in your selection.

195

Salt-Water Fish

BARRACUDA Principally known to anglers as a voracious game fish, some varieties of barracuda, or sea pike, are edible, especially if smoked beforehand.

BLOWFISH Spiny-finned blowfish puff themselves into a globe-like shape when disturbed. Only the flesh near the spine is edible. Other names for this fish are sea squab, globefish or puffer.

BLUEFISH Found along the Atlantic and Gulf coasts, blue-tinted bluefish are tireless game fish with a surprisingly subtle taste when broiled or baked.

BUTTERFISH Broiled or sautéed in lots of butter or oil, these very small silvery fish from Atlantic coastal waters have a rich and delicate flavor.

CALIFORNIA BLACK SEA BASS Sometimes weighing up to 700 pounds, the flavorful meat of this very large fish from the Pacific coast is sold mainly as steaks or fillets. Also called jewfish.

CALIFORNIA KINGFISH The tasty flesh of this Pacific coast fish is delicious broiled, baked or fried. Size ranges from 3/4 to 1 1/4 pounds.

COD or *CODFISH* is found mainly in North Atlantic waters, although a close relative makes its home in the Pacific. A well-known food fish which can weigh up to 50 pounds, cod can be served in many different ways: fresh or salted, pickled, smoked, flaked or as fillets or steaks.

CROAKER There are a number of varieties of this game fish which emits a croaking or grunting sound through an air bladder. Croakers are tasty either broiled or fried.

CUSK is a game fish from northern waters, similar in taste and texture to cod.

EELS are found in both fresh and marine waters, although they always return to the sea to spawn. The fatty layer which covers eel flesh can be removed along with the skin before cooking this fish, which is considered a real delicacy.

FLUKE, also known as summer flounder, is a member of the flatfish or flounder family. Fluke can be found on the Mid-

Atlantic coast during the summer months and makes delicious eating.

GROUPERS   There are many varieties of groupers, all of which belong to the sea bass family. Found in Atlantic waters and the Gulf of Mexico, groupers range in weight from 5 to 15 pounds, and may be prepared whole, in steaks or fillets.

GRUNION are small, flavorful fish and are considered excellent for eating. They can be caught on shore without fishing lines, since they lay their eggs directly on the beach at certain times of the year.

HADDOCK is a smaller relative of and closely resembles the cod. This popular edible fish from Atlantic waters may be cooked in many ways. Lightly smoked haddock is called "finnan haddie."

HAKE also resembles and is related to the cod, with tender and flaky white flesh. Hake can be found in the Atlantic and Northern Pacific oceans and is sometimes marketed as cod.

HALIBUT   This flatfish may sometimes weigh up to 700 pounds, although 50 to 100 pounds is the average. Found in northern waters, it is usually sold as steaks or fillets. Young halibut from 2 to 10 pounds are marketed as chicken halibut.

HERRING are small food fish found in both Atlantic and Pacific waters. Most of the herring caught end up smoked, pickled or salted, although some are sold fresh. Sardines are really young herring.

LING COD is found on the Pacific coast. Although not a species of cod, this relatively small fish can be prepared in most of the same ways.

MACKEREL is a familiar and important food fish, related to the tuna, with a delightfully rich flavor. Averaging about 16 inches long, it can be prepared in many different ways.

The SPANISH MACKEREL is a choice game fish which usually is found in southern Atlantic waters during most of the year, although it migrates north during the summer.

MULLET   The many varieties of this fish, which is found in both salt and fresh water, are prized world-wide. Gray mullet is a favorite from the waters of the Carolinas and Florida and is generally broiled or baked whole.

OCEAN PERCH is the usual label under which a group of salt-water fishes—rosefish, redfish or sea perch—are marketed as frozen fillets. All these members of the perch family are delightfully mild in flavor and suitable for any method of preparation.

POLLOCK comes from North Atlantic waters. A relative of the cod, it is a flavorful fish and is usually marketed as frozen fillets.

POMPANO The silvery blue pompano which is caught in the waters of the South Atlantic and the Gulf of Mexico is a highly prized favorite with fish fanciers. There is also a California pompano which is actually a kinsman of the butterfish.

PORGY Sometimes known as scups, porgies in their many varieties are found in Atlantic and Gulf waters. They may weigh up to 2 pounds.

REDFISH comes from the family of ocean perches and is usually sold under that name. This game fish weighs anywhere from 2 to 25 pounds.

RED SNAPPER is a large and colorful inhabitant of the warm southern waters of Florida and the Gulf of Mexico. Red snappers grow as large as 2 to 3 feet and may weigh up to 30 pounds. They are equally delicious whether broiled, baked, fried or served in soups.

SABLEFISH This Pacific coast fish, sometimes wrongly called Alaska black cod, can be prepared in any number of ways, although it is extra delicious when smoked or kippered.

SALMON, that most highly prized of fishes, is exceedingly popular everywhere, whether fresh, smoked, salted, dried or canned. Most of the salmon consumed in the U.S. comes from the Pacific coast, principally the Columbia River, Puget Sound and Alaska. The Chinook salmon and the King salmon are the most popular west coast varieties, varying in color from red to pink, and in size from 5 to 50 pounds. Canada's Atlantic waters supply most of the salmon for the east coast. They are slightly smaller and paler than their western counterparts.

SEA TROUT is the name given to such small food fish as the spotted weakfish (or spotted sea trout), the white sea trout, and the weakfish. The latter is a tender-tasting game fish, blue-tinged in color, which makes Mid-Atlantic waters its home. Sea trout are usually prepared whole.

SHAD is a delicate and tender-tasting fish highly prized by gourmets, native to Atlantic waters, but introduced during the last century to the Pacific coast where it now flourishes. Shad's exceedingly bony structure dictates that it be boned or cut into fillets before being eaten.

SHEEPSHEAD Dwelling in the Gulf of Mexico and Florida and California waters, the sheepshead is related to the porgy, and is cooked whole or in fillets.

SMELT are to be found off both the east and west coasts of the U.S. The small silvery smelt is related to the salmon, and like the salmon, swims up rivers and streams to spawn. It has mild flavor, is tender and rich in oil, and is usually served crisply fried.

SOLE Although fillets of sole are a popular item in American markets and restaurants, the *true* sole you buy must be European: Dover or Channel sole, which is purchased frozen. True American sole varieties are usually too small and bony for eating. The fresh fillets marketed as sole in this country are really varieties of flounder: the gray sole, the lemon sole, the winter flounder, the yellowtail and the dab. Sole is closely related to the flounder; both are small-mouthed flat fishes, and may be prepared in identical manners.

SQUID is a marine mollusk related to the octopus whose popularity used to be confined to Spain and Italy. Now it is available in the U.S. on a wider basis, and is delicious batter-fried, baked or sautéed.

STRIPED BASS makes its home in both Atlantic and Pacific waters. Averaging 15 to 18 inches long, this game fish is growing in popularity as a commercial food fish. Another name for it is rockfish.

STURGEON The popularity of this exceedingly fine fish has contributed to its scarcity. Its meat is somewhat on the dry side, like tuna, and it is considered a great delicacy when smoked, although smoked sturgeon, like the caviar that is the sturgeon's roe, is quite expensive.

SURF PERCH, which inhabits the shallow waters of the Pacific coast, is a small, striped food fish, sometimes known as blue perch.

SWORDFISH, a fine game fish popular with anglers, may be found in the warmer waters of both the Atlantic and Pacific coasts. Easily identified by the swordlike point of its upper jaw, the firm and well-flavored meat is mainly sold as steaks.

The TAUTOG, or BLACKFISH as it is sometimes called, is found in Atlantic waters, where it is known to anglers as a fine game fish. Its weight averages from 2 to 3 pounds and its length runs from 12 to 18 inches.

TUNA   This very familiar and much-liked fish is related to the mackerel. Many varieties are found on both coasts; bonito is a favorite on the west coast. The white albacore is the finest part of the flesh with a taste similar to chicken; other parts of the tuna meat range from white to purple red. Tuna may be eaten fresh, smoked or salted, although most people know and prefer it canned.

WHITEBAIT are very small fish from the waters of northern Europe and are thought to be the young of various fishes like the sprat and herring. Usually eaten whole because of their size, they are delicious fried.

WHITING is a small delicately flavored fish found in Atlantic waters from New England to New Jersey. Gray-skinned with silver undersides, its white flesh makes it excellent for fish fries. Another name for this fish is silver hake.

YELLOWTAIL of the Pacific coast is a fine game and food fish with a juicy, pleasant taste, although the texture of its flesh is somewhat coarse.

Fresh-Water Fish

BASS   Members of this large family of fresh-water fishes are often described by their characteristics—striped, spotted, small-mouthed, large-mouthed, rock, black, white, yellow and so on —or by their regional names. Some smaller species of bass are called perch. Most bass are excellent game fish, and many species can be found in the northern, central and southern areas of the U.S. They are tasty whether broiled, baked, fried or poached.

BLUEGILL SUNFISH, also known as bluegill bream or just bream, is a small popular game fish usually found stocked in ponds. It can be broiled or pan-fried, using lots of butter or oil.

BUFFALO FISH are found in the Midwest. Varieties include the common buffalo, also known as the redmouth or bigmouth; the small-mouth buffalo; and the round or prairie buffalo, sometimes called the rooter. It is similar to carp and when smoked is especially tasty.

BURBOT At home in the northern U.S. and Canada, this fresh-water fish is a member of the cod family. Its liver and liver oil are especially nutritious, while the meat itself can be prepared like cod.

CARP is a large fresh-water fish introduced into American waters from China, and may weigh up to 60 pounds. Sometimes it has a muddy flavor which can be removed by keeping the live fish in clear water for a few days, or by bleeding it before cleaning, and seasoning it well.

CATFISH are a numerous family, all of which have a transverse mouth surrounded by barbels which resemble cats' whiskers. Catfish must be skinned before eating, and are served fried, poached or in soups. They are especially popular in the South.

CHUB are related to the carp and their soft flesh is similar in texture to the whitefish. They are excellent when smoked.

CRAPPIES are found in New England, southern Canada, and throughout the Mississippi Valley. About 12 inches long and weighing about 1 pound, both black and white crappies are tasty broiled or pan-fried.

LAKE HERRING are related to the whitefish and abound in the Great Lakes region. They can be smoked, salted, or prepared fresh for broiling, baking or sautéeing.

PIKE are a family of game fishes noted for their ferocity. Varieties of pike include the common pike, the pickerel and the muskellunge or muskie. They inhabit the waters of cooler areas in the U.S. and Canada. Pike usually weigh from 2 to 10 pounds, although the pickerel is larger and the muskellunge sometimes reaches a length of 4 feet.

PIKE PERCH are large perch that have assumed many of the habits and superficial characteristics of pike, although they are of a different family. Some of the varieties are the sauger or sand pike, the blue perch pike, and the walleyed pike, which is an important food fish. Perch may be found in the fresh waters of the Middle Atlantic states and the Mississippi and Missouri valleys, and in the Great Lakes.

TROUT are a popular variety of fresh-water fish highly esteemed for their delicate flavor. There are many members of this fish family, which is kin to the salmon and whitefish. Whether the large or salmon variety, or small like the speckled or brook trout, this game fish is delicious served in any number of ways.

WHITEFISH are found primarily in America's northern lakes and are an important food fish, especially when smoked. They range in weight from 2 to 6 pounds and may be cooked whole or in fillets. A caviar is sometimes made from the whitefish roe.

Preparing Fish

If you have caught the fish yourself, here are a few tips on preparing them for the pan.

Cleaning and dressing your fish begins with a sharp knife, although a few minutes of pre-soaking in cold water will make scaling easier. First, scale the fish by holding it firmly down by the head on a flat surface. Begin at the tail and scrape toward the head, taking care to clean well around the gills and base of the head. Slit the entire underbelly and discard the entrails. Carefully remove the pelvic fins located underneath the head, and, if desired, cut off the head just above the collarbone. A large fish may need to have its backbone snapped in half before the head can be completely severed from the body. Next cut away the pectoral fins (which are situated behind the gills) and the tail. Removing the large back dorsal fin and ventral fins on the back underside requires some finesse: make cuts on either side of each of these fins and then pull them forward with a quick movement to make sure that the small base bones come out along with the fins. Last, wash the fish thoroughly in cold water to remove any clinging bits of innards or dark matter. Now you are ready to cook your fish whole or to cut it into steaks or slice it into fillets.

FILLETING

Use the same sharp knife to bone the fish if you are making fillets. First, split the fish along the length of its back. Lay the fish flat, and cut through to the backbone at the head end. Then angle your knife flat and slice the fillet away from the bones on this one side. The fillet can then be lifted intact from the bones. Reverse the fish, and follow the same procedure on the other side.

SKINNING YOUR FILLETS

Lay the fillet on a flat surface, skin side down. Grip it by the tail and, beginning at the tail end, cut through just to the skin; then with your knife at a flat angle, slice the fillet completely away from the skin.

Recipes

Fish is at is best when grilled, sautéed or fried whole. Preheat and oil a hinged wire basket, place the fish in it and broil over medium coals, basting with melted butter (mixed with herbs if you wish). When the fish loses its transparent look and flakes when pricked with the tines of a fork, it is done. A 5-pound fish takes about 1/2 hour. DO NOT OVERCOOK.

To foil-cook, wrap the whole fish in a double thickness of oiled foil and place the package directly in the coals. Test for doneness as above.

Sauté the whole fish in butter and herbs in a fairly heavy skillet until it tests done or dip the fish in melted butter and breadcrumbs, or rolled oats or cornmeal, and fry in 1/2-inch oil and butter, mixed. Any fresh fish will taste delicious prepared as described above if you do not overcook it. Remove the fish from the wire basket or skillet *the moment* it tests done.

Flounder Fillets Meunière

1/2 **cup butter or oil**
8 **flounder fillets**
1/2 **cup flour**
    Salt and pepper to taste
2 **tablespoons butter**
4 **tablespoons finely chopped onion**

2 **cloves garlic, finely chopped**
2 **teaspoons each fresh chervil, parsley, thyme, tarragon**
1/2 **cup dry white wine**

(Serves 8)

Heat the butter in a large frying pan. Dip the fillets in lemon juice, pat dry with paper towels and dust them lightly with flour. Sprinkle with salt and pepper and sauté them in the butter. Remove the fillets from the pan when they are brown on both sides and put them aside where they will keep warm. Add 1 tablespoon of butter to the pan, and when it sizzles, blend in the chopped onion and garlic and cook for about 1 minute. Add the fresh herbs and wine, salt and pepper to taste, and simmer for 5 minutes. Pour the wine sauce over the fillets. Sprinkle with fresh chopped parsley, dill or wild fresh herbs. Serve with lime wedges, if desired.

Spicy Sea Bass Steaks

3 medium-sized onions
4 medium-sized tomatoes
2 tablespoons hot red peppers, chopped
3 cloves garlic, crushed
1 1/2 tablespoons olive oil
1 teaspoon oregano
1/4 teaspoon thyme
Salt and freshly ground black pepper to taste

8 sea bass steaks
1 teaspoon thin outer yellow skin of a lemon, grated
10 pimiento-stuffed olives, sliced
3 tablespoons lemon juice
3 tablespoons sesame oil

(Serves 8)

Peel the onions and slice into thin rings. Peel the tomatoes and seed them by cutting them in quarters and shaking out the seeds; slice the quarters. Remove and discard the seeds and stems from the peppers and chop the peppers finely. Rub the garlic over the fish. Oil the bottom of a very large skillet and arrange a mixture of 1/2 the vegetables to cover. Sprinkle oregano, thyme, salt and pepper over the vegetables. Place the sea bass steaks on top, sprinkle with grated lemon rind and arrange the remaining vegetables and the olives over the steaks. Sprinkle the lemon juice and oil over all the ingredients and cover the pan tightly. Cook over slow coals for 20 to 30 minutes or until the vegetables are tender.

Barbecued Halibut Steaks with Bleu Cheese Marinade

8 halibut steaks, 1-inch thick
1/2 cup vegetable oil
1/2 cup lemon juice
4 tablespoons bleu cheese

1/2 teaspoon oregano
1/4 teaspoon freshly ground black pepper
Parsley sprigs

(Serves 8)

Arrange the halibut steaks over the bottom of a shallow glass casserole. Prepare a marinade by mixing the oil, lemon juice, bleu cheese, oregano and pepper. Pour this marinade over the fish and refrigerate overnight if you have a refrigerator available. Before cooking the steaks, drain them and reserve the marinade. Place the fish in a well-oiled hinged wire basket and broil for 5 to 7 minutes on each side, brushing frequently with the marinade. Serve immediately, garnished with parsley.

Striped Bass with Potatoes in a Skillet

3 1/2 pounds striped bass (4 large fillets)	2 1/2 cups tomato purée
Salt, pepper, thyme, paprika	2 teaspoons sugar
1/4 cup butter	3 tablespoons lemon juice
1/4 cup vegetable oil	Salt and freshly ground black pepper to taste
4 onions	2 tablespoons minced fresh parsley
6 medium-sized potatoes	3 tablespoons minced chives
2 tablespoons vegetable oil	
3 tablespoons butter	

(Serves 8)

Sprinkle the fillets with salt, pepper, thyme and paprika. Heat 1/4 cup butter and 1/4 cup vegetable oil in a very large skillet and brown the fillets on both sides. Remove the fish from the skillet to a large plate and set them aside. Peel and thinly slice the onions and the potatoes. Add the 2 additional tablespoons of oil and 3 of butter to the skillet and fry the potatoes and onions until the potatoes are very nearly tender. Arrange the reserved fish fillets over the potatoes and onions. Stir together the tomato purée, sugar, lemon juice, salt and pepper and pour the mixture over the fish. Cover and cook for 15 minutes. Sprinkle the fish with the minced parsley and the chives and serve hot from the pan.

Seaside Stew

3 medium-sized onions	3 pounds fresh fish,
3 tablespoons butter	cleaned and split
2 pounds fresh spinach	2 cloves garlic, minced
Salt and freshly ground	1/4 cup vegetable oil
black pepper to taste	8 slices stale bread

(Serves 8)

Peel the onions and slice them into thin rings. Heat the butter in a large deep skillet and sauté the onion rings until transparent. Rinse the spinach thoroughly to remove all sand and shake out the excess water. Add spinach to the onion rings. As the spinach wilts, sprinkle it with salt and pepper to taste. Cut the fish into 1-inch pieces, add water to cover, and bring to a boil. Add the vegetables to the fish, and simmer the bouillabaisse, covered, for 15 minutes, or until the fish is tender. Meanwhile, fry the garlic in the oil and add the bread slices one at a time, browning each slice on both sides. Add additional oil if needed. Place the sautéed bread slices in individual soup plates, ladle vegetables and fish over the bread and cover all with broth. Serve immediately.

Greek Seafood Stew

2 1/2 cups lobster meat in	3 cups white wine
1-inch chunks	3 cups clam juice
1/4 cup good quality	24 small clams
olive oil	36 shrimp, shelled, with
6 cloves garlic, finely	tails intact
chopped	2 bay leaves
4 1/2 large tomatoes	1/2 cup finely chopped
3 cups tomato juice	parsley

(Serves 8)

Heat the olive oil in a heavy skillet. Sauté the lobster pieces and garlic for 3 or 4 minutes, turning the lobster meat once or twice. Peel, seed, and chop the tomatoes, and add them to the skillet, together with the tomato juice, wine, and clam juice. Bring the mixture to a boil. Carefully wash and scrub the clams and add them to the boiling soup. Cover and cook for about 10 minutes, or until the shells begin to open. Stir in the shrimp, bay leaves, and parsley, and cook for several minutes more, covered, until the shrimp turn pink. Serve with French bread.

Balkan Fish Chowder

A cool night on the beach is an excellent time to try this warming fish chowder.

2 pounds haddock fillets
2 1/2 cups water
6 thin slices smoked salmon
2 tablespoons tomato paste
4 tablespoons butter
5 tablespoons all-purpose flour
12 cups bottled clam juice

3 small sour gherkins, minced
2 tablespoons capers
1 1/2 cups cooked shrimp, chopped
2 1/2 cups heavy cream
Salt and pepper to taste
2 tablespoons chives, minced

(Serves 8)

Place haddock fillets in a kettle. Cover with 2 1/2 cups of water and simmer gently for 5 minutes, or just enough to poach the fillets. Remove the fish from the water and set it aside. Poach the smoked salmon in the kettle for a minute, then remove and reserve with the fish fillets. Cut the salmon and fillets into bite-sized pieces. Stir the tomato paste into the water simmering in the kettle, add the butter and blend in the flour. When the mixture is slightly thickened, add the clam broth, minced gherkins, capers, and the reserved fillet and salmon pieces. Heat thoroughly, then add the chopped shrimp and stir in the heavy cream. Season to taste with salt and pepper. Serve hot, sprinkled with chives.

Oyster Stew

4 cups oysters, shucked,
  with their liquor
4 tablespoons butter
5 cups milk
2 1/2 cups heavy cream

3/4 teaspoon whole thyme
1 teaspoon salt
Freshly ground black
  pepper to taste

(Serves 8)

Simmer the oysters with their liquor in the butter until the edges of the oysters begin to curl. Scald the milk and cream and add to the oysters along with the thyme and the salt. Simmer over very low heat for 10 minutes but *do not allow to boil.* Serve hot, sprinkled with pepper.

Fish and Shellfish Stew

2 pounds striped bass
16 mussels
16 clams
3 tomatoes
2 small hot red peppers;
  or 1 large sweet red
  pepper
1 large sweet green
  pepper
3 cloves garlic, minced
1 large onion
4 medium-sized potatoes

1/2 cup vegetable oil
3 cups clam juice
3 cups dry white wine
32 shrimp, shelled and
  deveined
1/2 eel, cleaned and cut
  into 1 1/2-inch lengths
1/2 pound fillet of sole
1/2 teaspoon whole saffron
  Salt and freshly ground
  pepper to taste

(Serves 8)

Clean and rinse the bass and wipe it dry. Thoroughly scrub the mussels and the clams with a small stiff brush and set them aside. Peel the tomatoes, cut them into quarters and shake out the seeds. Chop the red pepper. If you do not care for spicy dishes, substitute a sweet red pepper for the hot red peppers. Remove the stem, seeds and the white pith from the green pepper and chop together coarsely. Peel the onion, cut it into slices and separate into rings. Peel the potatoes, cut them into thin slices and set them aside. Heat the oil in a soup kettle and sauté the potatoes until they are lightly browned and nearly tender. Add the onion and continue cooking until the rings are golden and transparent. Stir in the prepared vegetables, the clam juice, wine, bass, mussels, clams, shrimp, eel, sole and the saffron. Return the stew to the heat and cook gently for 10 minutes, or until the fish is done. Adjust seasonings and serve piping hot.

Grilled Salmon

8 salmon steaks, cut 3/4-inch thick	Salt and freshly ground black pepper to taste
Vegetable oil	Lemon wedges
Lemon juice	

(Serves 8)

Brush both sides of the fish with the oil, sprinkle both sides with lemon juice and arrange the steaks in a well-oiled hinged wire basket. Grill over medium coals for 5 to 6 minutes; brush the top surface with oil again, turn over and grill for 5 to 6 minutes more or until the steaks flake easily when pierced by a fork. Sprinkle with salt and pepper and serve hot, garnished with lemon wedges and Dill Cream Sauce.

DILL CREAM SAUCE

1 1/2 cups sour cream	2 scallions with 3 inches green top
3 tablespoons fresh dill, minced	1/4 teaspoon salt

Mix the sour cream and the dill, trim and mince the scallion and add it along with salt to the sour cream. Stir well. This sauce may be served hot or cold.

Salmon Steaks in Sour Cream Sauce

8 small salmon steaks
Salt and freshly ground
black pepper
Flour
1/3 cup butter
16 large mushrooms
1/4 cup sherry

1/4 cup white wine
1 cup sour cream
1 cup heavy cream
2 hard-cooked egg yolks,
pressed through a sieve
2 tablespoons minced
parsley

(Serves 8)

Sprinkle the salmon steaks with salt and pepper and roll them in flour. Melt the butter in 2 large skillets and sauté the steaks over medium coals until they are golden on both sides and flake when pricked with the tines of a fork. Transfer all the steaks to one of the skillets and keep them warm. Wash and slice the mushrooms and sauté them for several minutes in the butter in the empty skillet. Stir in the sherry and the white wine and cook for 2 minutes over hot coals. Remove the pan from the heat and stir in the sour cream. Add the heavy cream a little bit at a time, and cook for a few minutes longer. Add more salt and pepper if desired. Arrange the salmon steaks on a platter, pour the hot sauce over them, sprinkle with the sieved egg yolks and the minced parsley and serve immediately.

Shad Roe on Toast

4 pairs of shad roe
Flour
1 1/2 cups butter
8 slices bacon
Parsley, finely
chopped

8 slices white bread
Lemon juice
Salt and freshly
ground black pepper
to taste

(Serves 8)

Divide the shad roe into 8 serving pieces and dip in flour. Melt the butter in a skillet. Remove the skillet from the fire and dip the roe in the butter to coat both sides. Wrap each piece of roe in bacon and place in a well-greased hinged wire basket; broil over low coals until the bacon is fairly crisp, turning frequently. Add the parsley to the melted butter and place the skillet on the back of the grill to keep warm. Toast the bread slices and butter them lightly. Place the roe on the buttered toast, sprinkle each piece with the lemon juice and the salt and pepper. Pour some of the parsley butter over each serving.

Shellfish

Blue Mussels

MUSSELS MAY NOT yet be the favorite seafood delicacy of the Eastern coast but their popularity is certainly on the rise. The mussel has been looked down upon if not blatantly ignored by residents of the U.S.—a strange prejudice since mussels abound from Canada to North Carolina. The French have long considered the mussel a delicacy and, as for myself, I prefer its tenderness and delicate flavor to that of the clam.

You will recognize the blue mussel by its elongated, blue-black shell with its lovely violet inner shell, and by the black silky beard that it spins to attach itself to pilings and rocks. To gather blue mussels in New England, look for old mussel shells along the shore and wade into the water where you see them. Unattached mussels are usually dead and should not be gathered; instead pull up 3-inch-long mature attached mussels from the rocks that line the shore at low tide, pull off their beards, scrub them well and prepare them as you desire. Since the shameful pollution of our coastal waters is so prevalent, it is wise not to eat mussels, or any other shell-fish, without cooking them first.

Mussels with Peppery Broth

3 dozen mussels
1/2 cup dry white wine
1/3 cup wine vinegar
3/4 teaspoon thyme

1/3 teaspoon dried red pepper
2 1/2 tablespoons lime juice

(Serves 8)

Scrub the mussels thoroughly under running water, and arrange them in the bottom of a large kettle. Add the wine, vinegar, lime juice and spices and bring to a boil over medium to hot coals. Continue to boil for about 2 minutes, then remove the mussels from the kettle and shell them. Mussels are done when the shells open. Do not cook them beyond this point or they will toughen. Discard any that do not open. Serve the mussels hot with the liquid in which they were cooked, or chill and serve them in the half shell on a bed of crisp lettuce with Mussel Sauce.

Mussel Sauce

1/3 cup chopped sweet pickles
1 1/2 teaspoons English mustard

1/4 teaspoon Worcestershire sauce
1 1/2 cups mayonnaise

(Makes 1 3/4 cups)

Stir the pickles, mustard and Worcestershire sauce into the mayonnaise and mix thoroughly. Serve cold.

Mussels in White Wine

2 1/4 cups white wine or
    vermouth
3/4 cup water
2 scallions with 3 inches
    green top, finely
    chopped
3 tablespoons minced
    fresh parsley
1 1/2 tablespoons sugar

3 tablespoons prepared
    mustard
3/4 teaspoon powdered
    thyme
1 1/2 tablespoons minced
    fresh dill
5 dozen mussels
1/4 cup butter

(Serves 6)

Combine the wine, water, scallions, parsley, sugar, mustard, thyme and dill in a large jar with a tight-fitting cover. Take this mixture along to the beach with you. Scrub the mussels and remove all beards. To ensure that the mussels will be free of grit, rinse them thoroughly in at least 3 changes of water. Arrange the mussels in a large heavy kettle and pour in the wine mixture. Stir in the butter and place the kettle over a high fire. Simmer the mussels, tightly covered, for 5 minutes. Uncover, stir the mussels again, cover, and continue to steam only until the mussels open. Do not overcook or the mussels will become tough. Be sure to discard any that remain closed. Serve the mussels in bowls with thick slices of French bread to sop up the steaming broth.

Periwinkles

Who ever heard of eating a periwinkle? I have, for one, and so have countless Englishmen. My first culinary experience with periwinkles was inspired by a young Englishwoman who was working for us at the time. A cockney lass, she entertained me with stories of the foods available in England that were not available here. Among these were "winkles" which were, according to her, an "andsome" dish. After several weeks I realized that "winkles" were, in fact, periwinkles, and that "andsome" meant handsome or delicious and not "and then some," as I had supposed. Our camping trip that year was along the New England coast and one of my finds was a section of coastline literally teeming with periwinkles. I picked a gallon of the black-shelled beauties in about 20 minutes and began preparing them immediately, following my favorite recipe for escargots. I had no previous experience with periwinkles and when they resisted all of my efforts to dislodge them from their shells with a safety pin and a crochet hook, I decided to simmer them for a few minutes to see what, if anything, would happen. I cooked these periwinkles in sea water, lined the pot with a bit of seaweed, and inadvertently made a very important discovery: salt in the cooking water causes periwinkles to firm up or toughen slightly so they may be pulled more easily from their shells with a safety pin.

Periwinkles can be found on the Atlantic shore from Canada to New Jersey. If on your next trip to the beach, you decide to search for periwinkles, here's what to look for. Periwinkles in the more northern waters have small, spiral-shaped, brown, black or olive colored shells, and live where rocks are washed by the surf. Further south, look for marshy areas only lightly surf-washed. The best tasting periwinkles are around 3/4 of an inch across or slightly larger. Smaller periwinkles tend to be a bit more bother than they are worth, and the larger ones are no tougher than slightly smaller ones. Serve the "winkles" swimming in garlic butter, in seafood stews or dipped in fritter batter and fried.

Clams

There are clams and there are clams . . . and almost all of them are delicious.

Quahogs are known by several other names—Littlenecks, Cherrystones, Hard Clams, Round Clams—and by any name they taste as sweet. The Quahog seems to be the easiest to find and therefore the most rewarding to look for.

The Quahog prefers tidal streams and inlets where there is a mixture of fresh and salt water, mud and sand. I have found the best clamming tool for seaside clamming to be the human foot, although a clam rake may be used if you prefer. Walk along a muddy sand beach at low tide and dig your toes in about 1-inch deep. When you find one clam your meal is usually nearby, for clams seem to like to congregate in beds. If your luck is poor on the beach, take a plastic bucket that will float fairly well, wade out a bit deeper into the water and use your feet to "feel" the muddy bottom. You will soon learn to "feel out" the smooth, round, chalky-white or grey shells of the quahog. Reach down with your hand, a strainer or a pair of oyster tongs, and snatch the clam from its muddy home and place it in the bucket. Place the clams in fresh water to which you have added a handful of cornmeal. The clams will void their sand and be ready to cook in several hours.

When the clams are small, they are delicious raw, but since so much of our coastal waters (as well as our lakes, rivers and streams) are polluted, I do not advise eating them without cooking. Gather about 15 per person and serve them well-heated, but not boiled, in a stew. If the clams are medium-sized (about 3 inches across) gather about 10 to 12 per person and steam them or fry them in fritter batter. Any clams that are over 3 1/2-inches should be ground or finely chopped and used in chowder. In this case, gather 6 to 8 per person.

Clams on the Half Shell

Never eat raw shellfish unless you are absolutely sure they come from unpolluted waters.

4 dozen clams

(Serves 8)

Scrub the clams thoroughly and rinse them well to remove all particles of sand. Shuck them carefully in order not to spill the juice, and arrange the shucked halves on a bed of ice. Serve with Tomato-Scallion Sauce.

Tomato-Scallion Sauce

1/2 cup tomato, peeled,
seeded and finely
chopped
1/2 cup finely chopped
scallions with 3 inches
green tops

3/4 cup wine vinegar
1/2 teaspoon salt
Coarsely ground black
pepper to taste

Mix all ingredients thoroughly. Chill. Serve on the side with clams on the half shell.

STEAMER CLAMS OR NANNYNOSES

Steamer Clams, also known as Nannynoses or Long Clams dwell in abundance all along the Atlantic coast from Labrador to Cape Hatteras. They are as equally abundant in New England and so easy to find and harvest that no one need go hungry who spends any time along the shore. Simply walk any tidal flatlands where the tide recedes twice daily and you will probably notice a series of little spurts of water jumping up around your bare toes. These are the frightened steamers, withdrawing their siphons as you approach. Use a spading fork to dig a hole wherever you see a good-sized spurt and you will most likely find a 3- or 4-inch Steamer Clam, with a brittle, oval, chalky-white shell, yours for the taking. There may be limits on the amounts of clams you are allowed to take at any one time so, once again, check with the local authorities before you begin to dig. When you have gathered the clams, soak them in fresh water with a handful of cornmeal to cause the clams to void the grit and sand.

EASTERN RAZOR CLAMS AND STOUT RAZOR CLAMS

The Eastern Razor Clam is easily recognized by its thin, elongated shell and is found in wet sandy shores and tidal flats from Greenland to Florida. Its usual size is around 6 inches, although it often grows to be much longer, and it is only about 1 inch in width. There is absolutely no way you can mistake a Razor for any other clam because it so closely resembles the old-fashioned straight-edged razor from which it got its name.

The difficulty with these clams lies not in recognizing them but in catching a glimpse of them at all. These energetic bivalves are ferocious diggers and when they are disturbed, in seconds they can disappear straight down into the sand. The best way to capture these delicious but elusive creatures is to look for a series of squarish holes in the sand near the water's edge. Use a pair of kitchen tongs, quickly reach down into the hole and secure the clam. Hold on tightly while you dig away the sand around the lower portion of the clam, place the clam in your bucket and sit quietly until the rest of the holes begin to fill with water. This generally means the other clams are rising to the surface once more. Simply repeat the process until your bucket is filled with Razors. Wash the clams and allow them to stand in clear, clean sea water to which a handful of cornmeal has been added for 3 hours while they void the sand in their shells. Prepare these Razor Clams as you would any other and eat them the same day as they do not keep well.

Quahog Chowder

1 1/2 dozen large quahogs in their shells	Salt and freshly ground black pepper to taste
Cornmeal	
1/4 pound piece salt pork	4 cups milk
2 medium-sized onions	2 cups heavy cream
6 large potatoes	2 tablespoons butter
2 tablespoons flour	Dash each of paprika and thyme

(Serves 8)

Soak the quahogs for 3 to 4 hours in fresh water mixed with a handful of cornmeal. Shell the clams and reserve their juice. Chop and render the pork in a large soup kettle over medium heat. Grind or mince the quahogs and drain them, reserving all the juices. Peel the onions and chop them coarsely.

Remove the salt pork from the kettle. Sauté the onions in the fat until they are golden and transparent. Peel and dice the potatoes and add them to the onions in the kettle. Blend in the flour, salt and pepper. Add the quahog juices and additional boiling water to just cover the potatoes, cover the kettle and cook until the potatoes are soft. Place the milk and cream and the ground clams in a saucepan and heat to just under a boil. Remove the quahog chowder from direct heat and quickly stir in the hot milk and cream. Adjust the seasonings. Garnish with bits of butter and a dash of paprika and thyme.

Old New England Clam Chowder

36 clams, shucked, and
    their juice
2 ounces salt pork
6 medium-sized
    potatoes
2 large onions
4 cups water
2 small bay leaves,
    crumbled

2 tablespoons butter,
    softened
2 1/2 tablespoons flour
5 cups milk
3 cups light cream
Salt and freshly
    ground pepper to
    taste

(Serves 10)

Strain the clams and remove any small bits of shell. Reserve the clam juice. Mince the hard parts of the clams but keep the soft parts intact. Dice the salt pork and sauté it until it is golden brown. Peel and dice the potatoes and onion and add them, together with the water and bay leaves, to the salt pork. Boil gently until the potatoes are tender but not mushy.

Meanwhile blend the butter and flour. Add this, the milk, cream, clams and their juice to the potato mixture. Stir over low heat until the soup comes to a low boil and thickens slightly. Serve hot.

220

SHELLFISH

Cioppino

*Discovering a few fresh mussels whose shells have
opened after you gather them needn't be a cause
of alarm. Squeeze both sides of the shell together
firmly. Any mussels that do not stay closed
should be discarded.*

1 pint raw clams	7 medium tomatoes
1 pint raw mussels	3/4 cup olive oil
10 cups water	3/4 cup tomato purée
5 tablespoons dried mushrooms	3 1/2 cups red wine
3 medium-sized onions	Salt and pepper to taste
2 green peppers	1 medium sea bass
1/3 cup parsley	3 small live lobsters
5 cloves garlic	1 pound large raw shrimp
1 teaspoon salt	

(Serves 8)

Arrange the raw clams and mussels in their shells in a large
bowl. Cover with the water. Allow to soak for 3 hours, changing the water several times. Chop the dried mushrooms, cover
with water, and soak for 1 hour.

Meanwhile, peel the onions and chop them very fine.
Rinse the peppers, discard the stems and seeds, and chop very
fine. Wash and chop the parsley. Peel and chop the garlic
cloves. In a small cup, mix the chopped garlic with the salt,
pressing the salt in with the back of a spoon. Peel the tomatoes,
seed them by cutting into eighths and shaking out the seeds,
and chop them coarsely. Drain the clams and mussels. Scrub
the shells thoroughly. Place them in a saucepan with 1 1/2 cups
of water, and steam them until they open. Strain and reserve
the liquid.

Heat the olive oil in a deep soup kettle. Drain the dried
mushrooms and add them, together with the onions, peppers,
parsley and the garlic-salt mixture, to the hot oil. Sauté for 5
minutes over low heat, stirring occasionally. Add the chopped
tomatoes, the reserved liquid from the clams and mussels, the

tomato purée and the wine. Sprinkle with salt and pepper to taste, bring to a boil, reduce the heat, and allow the soup to simmer, covered, for 30 minutes.

While the soup is simmering, slice the sea bass into 2-inch pieces. Cut up the live lobsters. Shell the shrimp and devein them. Add the bass, lobster pieces and whole shrimp to the soup. Cook for 10 minutes, or until the lobster turns a bright red. Add the clams and mussels in their shells and cook just long enough to heat through. Serve immediately with hot, buttered, crusty Italian bread.

Crabs

The Rock Crab, Jonah Crab, Lady Crab, Green Crab, Blue Crab and the Stone Crab all dwell in eastern coastal waters, while the Dungeness Crab, the Swimming Crab, the Gulf Blue Crab and the Red Crab abide along our West coast. These crabs each have their distinctive markings, but one thing they have in common is an incorrigible fighting spirit and a willingness to take on anyone or anything, even the looming monster you must appear to be to these small creatures. Chase a crab for a short distance and he will stop, brace himself and raise his claws, ready for battle. Discount neither his courage nor his pinching claws—both make him a genuine menace of the shallows. One pinch and you will respect him for life.

ROCK CRABS AND JONAH CRABS

These crabs are very similar in appearance and in habitat. They generally measure 4 inches across and prefer rocky shores along the tide lines of New England. Rock crabs may be identified by their oval shape and brown-spotted yellowish shells, which may reach a size of 4 or 5 inches across from side to side. The Jonah crab has a rough reddish-brown shell, its legs are thicker and shorter, and its undershell is tinged with yellow. Both the Rock and Jonah crabs may be sought out in pools of water left among the rocks by the receding low tide, or even among the rocks themselves. However, few people go out with the express purpose of catching these crabs, but inadvertently catch them on a hook while fishing. Be advised that crab meat in the natural state comes packaged in the shell, not in a tin or jar; it's exactly the same meat you pay so handsomely for in fancy fish stores. If you should happen upon a spot where Rock Crabs or Jonahs are plentiful, by all means scoop them up in a net and cook them following any of your favorite recipes, for this is the finest treat, bar none, that nature has to offer.

BLUE CRABS

The Blue Crab is a familiar and colorful crab common along the Atlantic coastline from southern New England to Florida, usually making its home in shallow mud-bottomed bays, inlets, and streams. Its large claws, its 6-inch shell along with the 2 sharp spiny projections which point sideways from the carapace, make this crab distinctive and easy to spot. Multi-colored, its shell is dark green on top with a white underbelly and blue feet. The tips of the spine are marked with red. When blue crabs shed or molt their old shells, and the new ones have not yet hardened around them, they are called soft-shelled crabs.

The Blue Crab prefers mud to sand and rocks and may be hunted in the same areas clams are often found. This large (6-inch) crab is notorious for his pugnaciousness and also for his delicate and delicious meat. Crabs may be caught in almost any kind of primitive trap, but I must admit that my only experience has been in fishing for them with hook and line. The most rewarding "crab fishing" is performed from a dock or pier, where you've accidentally caught crabs while angling for fish. Set up as many lines as you have on hand or can handle comfortably (6 or 7 are not too many), bait the hook with a piece of fish or meat, tie a sinker to it and hope for the best. Test the lines occasionally and if you feel a crab on the end, pull him toward you ever so slowly and scoop him up in a net. You won't *always* catch crabs, but it's a relaxing way to spend a lazy hour or two and when they *do* start biting, you may easily pull in 15 or so in a short period. Simply place them in a large burlap bag and look forward to an ambrosial meal.

SOFT SHELL CRABS

This soft, white crab is merely a Blue Crab who has shed his too-tight old shell and is waiting for another, larger shell to form around him. In this state of undress the crab is not only easy prey and excellent eating but marvelously nutritious as well. Dip the crab in a beaten egg, roll him in crumbs, fry him in butter and consume every bit of him. What could be better than this delicious morsel without the nuisance of picking the meat out of the shell?

Unfortunately, your chance of catching more than one Soft Shell at one time is quite remote unless you help nature along a little. If you intend to stay at the shore a while, and if you have found a particularly good crabbing area with one or two Soft Shells among your harder shelled captives, begin to look among your catch for Blue Crabs with a slightly separated top and bottom shell and a streak of white showing through. These are crabs that are about to molt and these you may imprison in a wire pen beneath the surface of the water until they shed their shells and . . . *voila!* Soft Shelled Crabs!

Scallops

Few of us are unfamiliar with the beautiful scallop shell that is seen in sculpture and paintings and even on billboard signs. The perfection of the scallop shell can only be matched by the delectability of its contents. Contrary to most beliefs, the entire scallop and not just its tender white abductor muscle is edible and absolutely delicious. Scallops are not the easiest of seafoods to find; they swim rapidly, rest on one side, and never crawl or burrow, but they are very much worth the effort.

The most common variety of scallop dwelling on eastern

shores is the Bay Scallop, which can usually be found in bays and inlets all the way south from Massachusetts Bay to the Carolina coast. Shell color varies widely, running from white to black, and covers nearly every color in between.

If you intend to go scalloping, be sure to check with natives or local authorities to find out if you need a license to gather these jet-propelled little creatures, and if there is a limit to how many you may take from the water. The most telling sign of the presence of live scallops is the abundance of dead scallop shells along the shore. Wherever you see these (very often along tide pools, sheltered shores or around eel grass), wade out or use your snorkle and fins to search under-water for these active bivalves. When you find them, simply scoop them up with a net, put them in a bag and hurry them back to camp or kitchen. Scallops do not "clam-up" as clams do, and it is an easy matter to slip a sharp knife between their shells, cut their abductor muscles, dip the whole scallop—muscle and all—in egg and crumbs and fry them until they are golden and succulent. Scallops may be prepared following any clam or scallop recipe.

PICNICS
HOT
AND
COLD

THERE ARE TWO varieties of picnics . . . the cold "let's-pack-a-sandwich" type, and the planned picnic, which may or may not include a hot dish or two cooked at the picnic site. My suggestion is to pick several recipes from the following section and mix and match to suit yourself.

Probably the most enjoyable picnic is the "late-breakfast" picnic. Here is a formula for a memorable one.

Fill large baskets and/or refrigerator boxes with ingredients for 1 hot egg dish and 1 hot meat dish, a salad, dough for biscuits and many homecooked jams, butters and relishes to go with all. Drive to a scenic picnic site where there are fireplaces and wooden tables. Serve cold fruit juices or Bloody Marys while the egg dish is cooking. Enjoy the egg dish while the meat dish is cooking. Rest awhile or take a short, leisurely walk, then reassemble at the picnic table and serve the salad, the relishes and the meat dish, now done to perfection. Bake the biscuits and serve them with the homecooked jams and butters and strong coffee or tea. Relax on the pine needles or in the shade of a tree and spend several hours doing absolutely nothing.

Cooking
at the
Site

Shrimp Omelette Deluxe

2 cloves garlic
1/2 cup lemon juice
3/4 teaspoon salt
2 pounds shrimp, cooked, shelled and deveined
2 small onions, sliced
4 medium-sized tomatoes
2 green peppers

2 tablespoons butter
1/2 cup scallions, coarsely chopped
8 eggs
4 tablespoons heavy cream
1/2 teaspoon salt
1/4 teaspoon thyme

(Serves 8)

At home, peel and crush the garlic and place it in a large jar. Add the lemon juice, the salt, and the shrimp and marinate in the refrigerator overnight. Peel and seed the tomatoes by cutting them into quarters and shaking out the seeds. Remove the stem, seeds and white pith from the green pepper. Cut the tomatoes and the green pepper into 1/4-inch slices and place them in a jar.

At the site, drain the shrimp and reserve the marinade.

Melt the butter in a skillet and sauté the onion and green pepper over low heat for 5 minutes. Pour in the reserved marinade and cook again until the liquid is absorbed. Arrange the sliced tomatoes, the chopped scallions and the shrimp on top of the cooked vegetables. Beat together the eggs, cream, salt and thyme and pour the mixture over the shrimp. Cover the skillet and cook over low heat until the eggs are set. Loosen carefully around the edges and across the bottom of the pan and turn the omelette onto a warm plate. Cut into wedges and serve hot.

Chipped Beef and Eggs on Toast

4 3-ounce jars chipped beef

3 cups water

8 hard-cooked eggs

8 tablespoons butter

1/2 cup flour

1 tablespoon French-style mustard

5 cups cold half and half cream or evaporated milk

8 slices bread

8 large pimiento-stuffed olives, sliced

(Serves 8)

At home soak the beef for 10 minutes in the water. Drain well. Tear the chipped beef into bite-sized pieces and place in a jar. Peel the eggs and chop the whites. Force the yolks through a sieve. Place the whites and the yolks in separate jars. Keep the three jars on ice until you reach the picnic site.

At the site melt the butter in a skillet, add the flour, and stir together over medium heat for 2 minutes, pressing out any lumps with the back of a spoon. Stir in the mustard. Add the half and half all at one time and cook over low heat, stirring constantly, until the sauce has the consistency of heavy cream. Stir in the chipped beef and the chopped egg whites and cook over medium low heat until the sauce thickens slightly. Toast the bread over the fire and cut into 1-inch strips. Pile the toast strips on individual plates, top with the chipped beef mixture, and garnish with the sieved egg yolks and olive slices.

Beer-y Eggs

2 cans beer
3 1/2 teaspoons Wor-
    cestershire sauce
    Juice of 1 lemon

2 cups catsup
Salt
16 eggs

(Serves 8)

Pour the beer into a very large skillet and set aside for 45 minutes. When the beer has settled, stir in the Worcestershire sauce, lemon juice, catsup and salt. Place on medium heat and bring the mixture to a boil. Carefully slide the eggs into the sauce and cook gently until they are the desired firmness. Remove the eggs with a slotted spoon. Serve on buttered toast and ladle some of the hot broth over each serving.

Red-Eye Ham Sandwiches

8 small slices ham, 1/2-inch
    thick
2 cups black coffee

1 cup heavy cream
8 slices bread

(Serves 8)

Sauté the ham in a skillet over medium heat, turning once, until the slices are golden brown. Set the ham aside, drain off most of the fat in the skillet, and return the skillet to the fire. Add the coffee and cream to the skillet, stir briefly to blend them, and arrange ham slices in the mixture. Simmer for 15 minutes. Place 8 slices of bread on serving plates, top the bread with the ham slices, and pour the sauce over the sandwiches. Serve hot.

Tarragon Chicken

3 3-pound frying
chickens, cut into
pieces
1/2 cup butter
Salt and freshly
ground black pepper
1 large onion, finely
chopped
1 1/2 cups canned chicken
consommé

1 1/2 cups dry white wine
2 cups Easy White Sauce
(page 35)
1/2 cup finely chopped
fresh tarragon; or
2 1/2 teaspoons dried
tarragon leaves

(Serves 8)

Rinse the chicken pieces and pat dry. Melt the butter in a large skillet and brown the chicken, a few pieces at a time. Sprinkle the browned chicken liberally with salt and pepper and set aside. Pour most of the fat from the skillet, add the chopped onions and sauté until golden. Gradually stir in the consommé, wine, white sauce and tarragon leaves. Cook gently for 20 minutes. Place the reserved chicken pieces in the sauce, cover and simmer for 25 minutes. Serve hot.

Chicken Hash

5 chicken breasts, boned
and skinned
6 large potatoes
2 large onions
1/2 teaspoon thyme

1/4 teaspoon salt
1/8 teaspoon pepper
3 tablespoons oil or butter
1/4 cup heavy cream

(Serves 8)

Cut the chicken into fine dice with a very sharp knife. Peel and mince the potatoes and onions. Combine the chicken, potatoes, onions and spices. Place mixture in a jar and refrigerate until ready to cook. Melt half the butter in a heavy skillet, add the chicken, potato and onion mixture and fry over medium heat until the bottom is crusty and brown. Pour the cream over the hash and continue to cook until the cream disappears. Turn the hash out onto a large plate. Melt the remaining butter in the skillet and slide the hash, brown-side up back into the pan. Cook until the bottom is brown and the potatoes are tender. Serve with catsup and fried eggs.

Sausages and Apple Rings

1/4 cup water
2 pounds small sausages
8 McIntosh apples

1 cup sugar
4 tablespoons flour
1/2 cup sausage drippings

(Serves 8)

Place the water in a skillet, add the sausages and cook until the water evaporates and the sausages are brown on all sides. Remove the sausages from the skillet to a serving dish; keep warm. Cut the apples into thick slices and remove the cores. Roll the apples in a mixture of the sugar and flour. In another skillet, heat the sausage drippings until hot. Add the apple slices and cook over medium coals until they are tender and golden.

Arrange the apples attractively around the sausages and serve hot.

Nine-Day Beef

This unique beef dish takes 9 days to make but requires very little time each day. Take it on a camping trip, a picnic, or serve it in your own backyard with hot hors d'oeuvres, vegetables and dessert. When wrapped in aluminum foil and refrigerated, this beef will keep for several weeks.

6-8 pound rump of beef
1 cup dark brown sugar
3/4 cup coarse salt
1 cup juniper berries
2 tablespoons pepper-
corns

2 tablespoons whole
allspice
1/8 teaspoon powdered
cloves
1 1/2 cups water
Onions

(Serves 8)

233

Rub all sides of the meat with the brown sugar, using the fingertips to work it in. Place the meat in a large covered dish and store it in the refrigerator for 2 days. Put the salt, juniper berries, peppercorns, allspice and cloves into a mortar and, using the pestle, pound the ingredients until the peppercorns and the allspice are finely crushed.

For the next 9 days, work 2 1/2 tablespoons of this spice mixture into all sides of the meat each day. On the tenth day, rinse the beef under cool, running water.

Place the spiced beef in a covered casserole, add the water, and bake at 275° F. for 5 hours, or until the meat is tender. Remove the meat from the oven, cool it, and wrap it well in aluminum foil. Place a weight on top of the foil-wrapped meat and refrigerate for 12 hours. When ready to serve, cut the spicy beef into thin slices and serve with very thinly sliced onions.

Take
Along
Recipes

Potato and Carrot Ball Salad

5 cups potato balls
2 cups carrot balls
2/3 cup vegetable oil
1/4 cup tarragon vinegar
1 1/4 teaspoons salt
Freshly ground black
pepper to taste

1/4 cup fresh parsley,
minced
1/4 cup minced chives
2 tablespoons fresh
tarragon, minced
French dressing

(Serves 8)

Peel several potatoes and use the large end of your melon ball
scoop to cut enough balls to measure 5 cups. Use the small
end of your melon ball scoop to cut carrots into balls. Place
the potato and carrot balls in boiling salted water, reduce the
heat, cover, and simmer until they are tender but not mushy.
Lift the potato and carrot balls from the water a few at a time
so that they do not break, drain them and place in a large
bowl. Combine the oil, vinegar, salt and pepper and pour over
the hot balls. Allow to cool to room temperature. Gently mix

in the parsley, chives and tarragon. Toss all ingredients with a light coating of French dressing. Serve at room temperature.

Mother's Own Potato Salad

3 pounds potatoes	1 teaspoon sugar
6 hard-cooked eggs	3/4 teaspoon salt
1/3 cup finely chopped onion	3/4 teaspoon poppy seeds
1/2 cup finely chopped celery	5 pimiento-stuffed green olives, cut in half crosswise
1/3 cup finely chopped sweet pickles	10 black olives
1 1/3 cups mayonnaise	Pimiento, cut in thin strips
3 tablespoons mild yellow mustard	Paprika
3 tablespoons cider vinegar	

(Serves 8)

Leave the potatoes in their jackets and boil until they are tender but still firm. Cool slightly, peel, and cut into 1/2-inch chunks. Peel the hard-cooked eggs and dice 5 1/2 of them, reserving 1/2 of the sixth. Place the potatoes and eggs in a large bowl. Add the chopped onion, celery, and sweet pickles. Blend the mayonnaise with the mustard, vinegar, sugar, salt and poppy seeds and pour the dressing over the potato mixture. Stir carefully until the salad is well coated with dressing. Cover and refrigerate for at least 4 hours or even overnight—potato salad improves with standing. Just before serving, place the reserved egg half in the center of the salad. Decorate by arranging the olive halves, pimiento-side up, around the egg. Cut 4 petals from each of the black olives and place them around the olive halves to form "flowers." Arrange pimiento strips radiating out from the egg. Sprinkle the edges of the salad with paprika.

Pepper Slaw

1 large green cabbage
2 medium-sized carrots
1/2 large Spanish onion
1 small sweet red pepper, finely diced
1 small green pepper, finely diced

3/4 cup sugar
1 cup vegetable oil
1 1/2 cups white vinegar
3/4 teaspoon salt
3/4 teaspoon pepper

(Serves 8)

Cut the cabbage into eighths and remove the tough outer leaves. Cut away and discard the hard core. Wash the wedges and thoroughly drain them. Use a large chopping knife to shred the cabbage as finely as possible. Peel and shred the carrots. Peel the onion, cut it into quarters and slice it thinly. Place the shredded cabbage and carrots in a large bowl together with the onion slices and the diced red and green peppers. Mix the sugar, oil, vinegar, salt and pepper. Toss the cabbage, carrots and onion slices, pour the oil and vinegar mixture over them, and toss again. Refrigerate at least 6 hours or overnight, stirring occasionally. Drain if desired. Serve cold.

Whole Cauliflower Salad

1 large cauliflower
1 1/2 cups sugar
2 cloves garlic, minced
1 tablespoon mustard seed; or 1/2 teaspoon dry mustard
1 1/2 teaspoons celery seed; or 1/2 teaspoon celery salt
1 1/2 teaspoons whole allspice; or 1/2 teaspoon powdered allspice
1 1/2 teaspoons whole

cloves; or 1/2 teaspoon powdered cloves
1 1/2 teaspoons turmeric
Equal portions of vinegar and water to cover
1 small head Boston lettuce
2 hard-cooked eggs, finely chopped
4 tablespoons minced scallions

(Serves 8)

Rinse the cauliflower and trim the stem so that the whole vegetable will stand upright on a plate. Cut out a slim triangular notch 2 inches deep from the core of the cauliflower. Place the sugar, garlic and spices in a deep kettle slightly larger than the cauliflower. Mix with enough vinegar and water to completely immerse the head of cauliflower. Bring this marinade to a boil, add the cauliflower, cover, and simmer until the cauliflower is tender, about 20 minutes. Cool the cauliflower and refrigerate it in the mixture until cold. To serve, arrange Boston lettuce leaves on a plate. Drain the cauliflower thoroughly and stand it stem down in the center of the plate. Sprinkle with the hard-cooked eggs and top with the scallions. Divide into 8 wedges and serve cold with lettuce leaves and Piquant Mayonnaise.

Piquant Mayonnaise

1 cup cauliflower marinade
1 cup mayonnaise

2 scallions with 3 inches green top, minced

Boil down 1 cup marinade until it measures 1/4 cup. Cool this syrupy liquid and stir it into the mayonnaise. Place the mayonnaise on a sauceboat, garnish with the scallions and chill until time to serve.

Honeydew Melon Balls with Benedictine

2 small ripe honeydew melons
6 medium-sized ripe peaches
1/4 cup Benedictine

1/4 cup confectioners' sugar
3 tablespoons orange juice

(Serves 8)

Cut the melons in half, scoop out and discard the seeds and fibers, and cut the pulp into small balls. Peel the peaches by slipping them into boiling water for an instant and pulling off the skins. Cut them into very thin slices. Combine the melon balls and peach slices; sprinkle with Benedictine, sugar and orange juice. Stir the fruit carefully to avoid breaking. Refrigerate until well chilled. Serve cold.

Oatcakes

2 cups oatmeal, uncooked	3 tablespoons butter, melted
1/2 teaspoon baking soda	1/2 cup hot water
3/4 teaspoon salt	

(Makes about 35)

Measure the oatmeal, soda and salt into a bowl. Melt the butter and work it into the oatmeal along with the hot water, using a wooden spoon; then, when the mixture is cool, use the hands until the mixture is well blended and forms a firm ball. Flour a board or tabletop and your hands and press the dough out, dipping your hands frequently in flour. When the top of the dough is no longer sticky, roll it out until it is about 1/3-inch thick. Cut the dough in 2-inch circles with a glass or cookie cutter dipped in flour.

Liberally grease a griddle or skillet and cook the oatcakes over medium-low heat until lightly brown. Turn and brown on the other side. Reheat at picnic site.

Lemon Curd

Cook this ahead and take a jar along on your picnic or camping trip. Spread on oatcakes or toast for a super breakfast or snack.

2 lemons	1 cup sugar
2 tablespoons butter	2 eggs

Grate the thin yellow outer rind from the lemons. Do not include any of the bitter white underskin. Place the lemon rind in the top of a double boiler with the juice from the lemons, the butter and the sugar. Stir over low heat until the sugar is completely dissolved. Beat the eggs and add them to the pan. Cook over hot water stirring constantly until the lemon curd thickens. *Do not allow it to boil.* Spoon into a sterilized jar and refrigerate.

Vegetable Filling for Sandwiches

3 tablespoons cream cheese

1 1/4 cups mayonnaise

2 teaspoons mild yellow mustard

2 small cucumbers

8 scallions

1 cup watercress leaves

2 medium-sized tomatoes

5 hard-cooked eggs

Salt and freshly ground black pepper

(Serves 8)

Soften the cream cheese by bringing it to room temperature. Blend in the mayonnaise and mustard. Peel the cucumbers, cut them in half, and remove the seeds with the tip of a spoon and discard them. Chop the pulp coarsely and reserve it. Trim the scallions, keeping 3 inches of the green tops. Rinse the watercress thoroughly and pat it dry, discarding any thick stems. Peel the tomatoes, cut them into quarters and shake out the seeds. Chop the scallions, watercress, tomato pulp and hard-cooked eggs. Combine these with the reserved chopped cucumber and the mayonnaise mixture. Season with salt and pepper to taste. Chill.

Shrimp Sandwich Filling

1 1/2 pounds cooked shrimp, shelled and deveined

6 scallions with 3 inches green top

1 1/2 cups mayonnaise

3 tablespoons capers

Salt and freshly ground black pepper

(Serves 8)

Chop the shrimp coarsely. Trim and finely chop the scallions and stir them into the mayonnaise. Mix the shrimp into the mayonnaise. Add the capers and salt and pepper to taste.

Tomato-Cream Cheese Sandwich Filling

1 1/2 pounds cream cheese	4 large tomatoes
6 tablespoons minced onion	Salt and freshly ground black pepper to taste
2 tablespoons sour cream	

(Serves 8)

Soften the cream cheese by bringing it to room temperature. Blend the onion and the sour cream into the cheese. Peel the tomatoes, cut them in half, and shake out the seeds. Chop the tomato pulp finely, and blend thoroughly with the cream cheese mixture. Season with salt and pepper.

Horseradish Ham and Cheese Spread

4 teaspoons fresh horse-radish, grated, or 2 tea-spoons bottled (well drained)	1/4 cup milk
	3 tablespoons minced cooked ham
1 teaspoon lemon juice	3 tablespoons minced parsley
8 ounces cream cheese, at room temperature	

(Serves 8)

Grate enough horseradish root to measure 4 teaspoons and drain thoroughly. Blend the cream cheese with the lemon juice and the milk to spreading consistency. Stir in the horseradish, ham and parsley. Use as filling for sandwiches, hors d'oeuvres or celery.

Refried Beans and Cheese Sandwiches

*The beans in this novel sandwich are Mexican, the
bread is Middle Eastern, the taste is divine.*

8 Pita (flat Israeli breads)
Mayonnaise
3 cups Refried Beans
(page 88)
16 tablespoons shredded
Jack or mild Cheddar
cheese

1 large sweet onion,
thinly sliced
1/2 head lettuce, shredded
16 thin slices avocado
16 thin slices tomato

(Serves 8)

Make a cut across the top center of each of the Pita. Spread
insides with mayonnaise and stuff the two halves of each bread
with equal amounts of the hot beans, cheese, onion, lettuce,
avocado and tomato. Serve immediately.

Preserves, Pickles, Butters and Relishes

Pickled Knockwurst

3 cups white vinegar
3 1/2 cups water
25 whole allspice
20 peppercorns
5 tablespoons sugar

6 cloves garlic, peeled
2 teaspoons salt
2 Bermuda onions
2 pounds knockwurst

(Serves 8)

Measure the vinegar and water into a saucepan, add the all-spice, peppercorns, sugar, garlic and salt. Place on medium-high heat and bring the mixture to a boil. Lower the heat, and cook for 10 minutes. Remove the marinade from the fire and set aside until lukewarm. Slice the onions and separate into rings. Cut the knockwurst into 1/3-inch slices. Alternate layers of onion and knockwurst in 2 1-quart mason jars, filling the jars to the top with the vinegar mixture. Cover, and place in the refrigerator for 3 days to age. (The knockwurst will keep in the refrigerator for 2 to 3 weeks.)

Tongue and Ham Pots with Chopped Pickles

1/2 pound cooked
  smoked tongue
1/2 pound cooked
  smoked ham
1 1/2 cups melted butter
1/8 teaspoon cloves
1/4 teaspoon nutmeg

1/4 teaspoon allspice
Salt and freshly
  ground pepper to
  taste
1/3 cup sweet pickles,
  finely chopped
Clarified butter

(Serves 8)

Cut the tongue and ham into 1/2-inch pieces and place in a blender along with the melted butter. Blend the meat and butter into a smooth purée. Stir in the cloves, nutmeg, allspice, salt, pepper and pickles. Spoon this tongue and ham purée into 2 small crocks and seal with clarified butter. Refrigerate and serve cold.

This potted tongue will keep about one month if kept in a cool place.

Pickled Carrots

15 to 18 young tender
  carrots
2 small cloves garlic,
  crushed
3 sprigs parsley
1 large bay leaf
1/2 cup vegetable oil
1/2 cup white wine
1 cup vinegar

1/2 cup water
1 1/2 tablespoons sugar
3/4 teaspoon salt
Pinch of thyme
2 sprigs fresh
  tarragon
2 tablespoons fresh
  parsley, minced

(Serves 8)

Peel the carrots and cut into quarters. Tie the parsley and bay leaf in a cheesecloth bag and place in a large saucepan with the garlic, oil, wine, vinegar, water, sugar, salt, thyme and tarragon. Bring this marinade to a boil and cook, for 5 minutes, stirring once or twice. Add the carrots and parsley; reduce the heat, cover, and simmer the marinade until the carrots are barely tender. Remove the saucepan from the fire and chill the carrots in this liquid. Discard the cheesecloth bag and place the carrots in jars. Strain the marinade over the carrots and cover the jars. Store the carrots in the refrigerator where they will keep for 2 to 3 weeks.

Pickled Mushrooms

20 small fresh mushrooms	inches green top,
3 tablespoons lemon	chopped
juice	1/2 teaspoon salt
3 tablespoons olive oil	1/8 teaspoon pepper
3 scallions, each with 3	

(Serves 8)

Rinse the mushrooms. Small fresh mushrooms need not be peeled. Mix the remaining ingredients. Add the mushrooms and stir well. Place in a jar, cover and refrigerate for at least 2 days, inverting the jar occasionally. Serve cold.

Pickled Mustard Cauliflower

These are so zesty you may want to make a double amount to keep for future picnics or cookouts.

1 small cauliflower	1/2 teaspoon curry powder
1 cup tiny whole white	2 tablespoons dry
onions	mustard
5 cups water	1/8 teaspoon pepper
1/4 cup salt	1 teaspoon turmeric
1/4 cup flour	1 tablespoon French-
1/2 cup sugar	style mustard
1/3 cup brown sugar	3 cups vinegar

(Serves 8)

Rinse the cauliflower and divide it into florets. Chop the stems and the core. Peel the onions, place them in a large saucepan along with the cauliflower and add the water and salt. Cover the saucepan and allow the vegetables to soak overnight. Place the saucepan over high heat and bring the liquid to a boil.

Remove from the heat, drain the vegetables thoroughly, and set aside. Combine the flour, both sugars, curry powder, dry mustard, pepper and turmeric in the saucepan. Blend in the French-style mustard and 1/2 cup of the vinegar, pressing out all lumps with the back of a spoon. Cook over low heat, adding the remaining vinegar a little at a time, until the mixture is thick and smooth. Stir in the cauliflower pieces and onions until they are heated and thoroughly coated with the mustard sauce, but do not let the mixture boil. Pour into a hot sterilized jar and seal tightly. Store in the refrigerator.

Grandma's Pickled Eggs

These old-fashioned red pickled eggs are ideal for a snack or for a picnic lunch.

5 medium-sized beets	2 cloves garlic, crushed
8 hard-cooked eggs	1 1/2 teaspoons pickling
1 1/2 cups cider vinegar	spices
5 tablespoons sugar	3/4 teaspoon salt

(Serves 8)

Cook the beets in an enamel pot until tender. Peel the beets and cut them in quarters. Shell the hard cooked eggs. Mix together the beets, vinegar, sugar, garlic, pickling spices and salt, and allow to stand for 45 minutes. Place the shelled eggs in a large jar. Add the beets with their marinade. Cover and refrigerate for a day or two—or three or even a week.

Marinated Pimiento, Olive and Anchovy Snacks

Marinate overnight.

1 7-ounce can pimientos	1/8 teaspoon salt
1/3 cup olive oil	16 flat fillets of anchovy
2 cloves garlic, crushed	16 pimiento-stuffed olives
1/4 teaspoon oregano	

(Serves 8)

Drain the pimientos on paper towels and lay flat. Slice into 1-inch squares and place in a jar that has a tight-fitting cap. Add the oil, garlic, oregano and salt. Cover the jar and shake it well. Refrigerate the pimiento squares overnight. To serve, drain off the seasoned oil, wrap an anchovy around each pimiento square and secure with a toothpick topped with an olive. Serve cold.

Spicy-Oriental Relish

1 head Chinese cabbage	2 teaspoons hot red chili pepper
3 tablespoons salt	
3 large cloves garlic	1 teaspoon fresh ginger root, grated
5 scallions	

(Serves 8)

Remove the outer leaves from the cabbage. Cut the remaining leaves into thin slices, taking care not to include any of the core. Place the sliced cabbage leaves in a bowl and mix well with 2 tablespoons of the salt. Set aside for 20 to 30 minutes.

Meanwhile peel and mince the garlic. Trim the scallions, leaving 3 inches of the green tops, and cut into 1-inch lengths. Mince the chili peppers. Place the garlic, scallions and peppers in a bowl and add the grated ginger root. Rinse the reserved cabbage leaves thoroughly under running water, and drain well. Combine the cabbage with the chili-scallion mixture and the remaining tablespoon of salt. Toss well to mix.

Place the cabbage relish in a large mason jar and fill to

the top with water. Cover the jar loosely and store in a cool place for several days, stirring from time to time.

Cover tightly and refrigerate until needed. Serve cool or at room temperature.

Red and Green Apple Relish

3 ripe tomatoes	2 tablespoons sugar
2 green tomatoes	1/4 teaspoon celery seed
1 red pepper	1/4 teaspoon dry mustard
1 green pepper	1 1/2 teaspoons salt
1 cucumber	1/2 cup cider vinegar
1 large onion	1/2 cup fresh orange
2 tart green apples	juice
1 large red apple	

(Makes 3 6-ounce jars)

Cut the tomatoes into quarters and shake out the seeds. Remove the seeds and the white pith from the peppers and peel the cucumber and onion. Coarsely chop the tomatoes, peppers, cucumber and onion. Core the apples and cut them into coarse dice. Measure the sugar, celery seed, dry mustard, salt, vinegar and orange juice into a saucepan. Place on medium-high heat and boil for about 6 minutes. Remove the orange-vinegar mixture from the stove, cool to lukewarm and pour over the chopped vegetables and apples. Mix lightly, making sure that the vegetables and apples are well coated. Pour into sterilized jars and seal tightly. Store in the refrigerator.

Cauliflower Relish

1 small head cauliflower	1/4 cup salt
1 cup small white onions	1 cup cider vinegar
1 sweet red pepper	1 cup sugar
1 green pepper	1/4 cup flour
2 carrots	1/2 teaspoon turmeric
1 cup small lima beans	1/2 teaspoon poppy seeds

248

(Makes 2 8-ounce jars)

Remove the leaves from the cauliflower, cut it into quarters, and cut away the hard core. Peel the onions. Remove the stem, the seeds and the white pith from the peppers. Scrape the carrots. Coarsely chop all of these vegetables and place in a large bowl along with the lima beans. Cover the vegetables with water, add salt and let soak overnight. Pour the vegetables and the liquid into a saucepan. Place on medium-high heat and bring to a boil. Drain off the liquid and reserve the vegetables. Place the vinegar, sugar, flour and turmeric in a large saucepan and cook, stirring constantly, until thickened. Add the reserved vegetables and the poppy seeds and cook until they are tender but not mushy, stirring from time to time to avoid sticking. Pour the relish into sterilized jars and seal tightly. Store in the refrigerator.

Pickled Blueberry Jam

*This unusual jam is spectacular with game,
duck or pork.*

4 cups fresh blueberries	1 teaspoon whole allspice
1 cup water	1 teaspoon whole stick
1/3 cup wine vinegar	cinnamon, crushed
2 cups sugar	1 teaspoon whole cloves

(Makes 3 jars)

Rinse the blueberries and place them in a kettle. Add the water, vinegar, sugar, and the spices (which have been tied together in a cheesecloth bag). Bring the mixture to a boil, then lower the heat and allow to simmer until it reaches the jelling point. Remove and discard the cheesecloth bag and spoon the hot pickled blueberry jam into 3 jars. Seal with paraffin.

Sweet Orange Rum Butter

*Try this tangy, sweet butter on biscuits or
French toast.*

Juice and zest of 2 oranges (grated outer rind)	1 1/4–1 1/2 cups confectioners' sugar 1 cup butter 1 tablespoon rum

(Makes 3 cups)

Squeeze the oranges and strain the juice. Add the sugar and the orange zest to the juice. Stir until smooth. Cream together the orange-sugar mixture, butter and rum until well blended. Pack the orange butter in a small crock, wrap tightly in aluminum foil, and freeze overnight or until needed.

Cantaloupe Butter

2 ripe medium-sized cantaloupes 1 1/2 cups light brown sugar 1/4 teaspoon ground ginger	1/4 teaspoon powdered cloves 2 tablespoons lime juice

(Makes 2 8-ounce jars)

Discard the seeds and skins from the cantaloupes and coarsely chop the pulp. Place in a kettle, cover, and simmer over very low heat for about 10 minutes, or until the fruit is soft. Purée the cooked melon by forcing it through a fine sieve. Mix in the sugar, ginger, cloves and lime juice and return the pulp to medium heat. Cook, stirring occasionally, until the mixture thickens to spreading consistency. Pour at once into hot sterilized jars and seal immediately.

Pear-Rum Butter

2 pounds pears
3/4 cup pineapple juice or other fruit juice
1/4 teaspoon orange zest (thin outer rind of the orange), grated

2 cups light brown sugar
3/4 teaspoon nutmeg
1/4 teaspoon powdered cloves
1/4 cup light rum

(Makes 2 8-ounce jars)

Peel the pears, slice in half, and cut away the cores and threads. Chop coarsely and place in a kettle with the fruit juice and the orange zest. Bring the fruit to a boil, reduce the heat and simmer, covered, until the pears are tender. Purée the mixture by pressing it through a fine sieve. Mix in the sugar, nutmeg and cloves and return to medium heat. Cook, stirring occasionally, until the mixture is thick. Pour 1 to 2 tablespoons of light rum into each hot sterilized jar, fill the jars with the pear mixture, and seal immediately.

Apple-Plum Butter

1 pound fresh plums
1 pound apples, cut into quarters
1 cup apple juice

2 cups light brown sugar
3/4 teaspoon cinnamon
1/2 teaspoon nutmeg
1/3 teaspoon ground cloves

(Makes 2 6-ounce glasses)

Place the unpitted plums and the apples in a large kettle; add the apple juice, and bring to a boil, then simmer until the plums are soft. Purée the mixture by forcing it through a fine sieve with the back of a spoon, discarding the pits. There should be about 1 quart of purée. Add the sugar and spices and cook over medium heat, stirring constantly, until the mixture reaches the consistency of butter. Pour at once into hot sterilized jars and seal immediately.

Drunken Peach Butter

3 pounds fresh ripe
  peaches
1 1/2 cups orange juice
2 cups light brown
  sugar
3 tablespoons lime juice
  (or lemon juice)

1 1/2 teaspoons cinnamon
1 teaspoon nutmeg
1/8 teaspoon ground
  cloves
1/3 cup bourbon whiskey

(Makes about 3 small jars)

Scald the peaches in hot water for a few seconds, then dip in cold water and slip off the skins. Chop the peaches and discard the pits. Place the chopped peaches in a kettle and add the citrus juices. Bring to a boil, cover, and simmer over low heat until the peaches are tender. Purée the mixture by forcing it through a fine sieve with the back of a spoon. Mix in the sugar, cinnamon, nutmeg and cloves, return to low heat, and simmer, stirring constantly, until the mixture reaches the consistency of apple butter.

Pour 2 tablespoons whiskey into 3 small sterilized jars. Fill the jars with hot peach butter and seal immediately.

Old-Fashioned Whole Strawberry Preserves

. . . Just like Grandmother used to make.

3 quart baskets firm, ripe
  strawberries

Sugar
3 tablespoons lemon juice

Pick over the berries, discarding any that are badly bruised, green or poorly formed. Wash the remaining berries and set to drain. Weigh the drained berries and place them in a large preserving kettle. Weigh an equal amount of sugar and add it, with the lemon juice, to the berries. Bring slowly to a boil; continue to boil for 8 minutes. Remove from the heat, cover, and cool to room temperature. Pour into sterilized jars and seal with paraffin.

Tomato—Peach Relish

Meat and fish become a special dish when accompanied by this fresh-tasting relish.

4 medium-sized tomatoes	3/4 cup cider vinegar
2 medium-sized peaches	3/4 cup sugar
1 small preserved red pepper	1 1/2 teaspoons salt
	1/8 teaspoon powdered ginger
1/2 large Spanish onion	1 1/2 tablespoons whole allspice

(Makes 2 6-ounce jars)

Dip the tomatoes and peaches in scalding water and slip off their skins. Cut the tomatoes into quarters and shake out the seeds. Cut the peaches in half and remove the pits. Hold the red pepper over a flame until the skin blisters. Remove the skin and the seeds from the pepper. Cut the tomatoes, peaches, the red pepper and the onion into coarse dice. Put the diced vegetables and peaches into a saucepan, along with the vinegar, sugar, salt and ginger. Secure the allspice in a small cheesecloth bag and drop this into the saucepan with the other ingredients. Place over medium heat and bring to a boil, stirring frequently. Lower the heat, cover, and simmer until the relish is thick. Remove and discard the spice bag. Pour the hot relish into sterilized jars and seal tightly. Store in the refrigerator.

Orange Slices in Rum Syrup

3 navel oranges	1/4 cup dark rum
1 1/2 cups sugar	1 cinnamon stick
1 1/4 cups water	
3 tablespoons lemon juice	

(Makes 1 jar)

Cut the oranges into 4 slices each, discarding the end pieces. Place the orange slices in a saucepan, cover with boiling water and simmer for 1 hour. Drain off the liquid and reserve the orange slices. Put the sugar, water, lemon, rum and cinnamon stick into a large saucepan and cook on low heat for 5 minutes. Add the orange slices and continue cooking gently for 1 hour, or until the orange slices are tender.

Carefully place the orange slices in a wide-mouthed mason jar and cover with the hot syrup. Seal the jar and keep in the refrigerator until ready to use.

Cooking
for a
Crowd

PIT BARBECUING is the conventional way to serve great feasts outdoors when feeding numbers of people. It is also a long-standing American tradition. Methods of cooking and the types of food served vary in origin, since each region of this vast and abundant country has contributed its specialty. Nowadays, cooking outdoors is a popular method of entertaining, easily adapted to any locale.

OPEN-PIT BARBECUING is broiling or spit-roasting over a deep bed of red-hot coals. Out on the Texas range, roasting the whole animal is often the procedure, but you may find a smaller side or roast more manageable. Dig a pit 3 feet deep, slightly longer and wider than your piece of meat, and start your fire of hardwood or briquettes several hours in advance, since it must burn down to a foot-thick bed of coals. Care should be taken to maintain a good bed of coals, so that the temperature will be even through the many required hours of cooking. The beef, lamb or pig may be marinated first, then trussed and secured on long rods. Suspend the ends of these rods on the ground at either end of the pit so that the lowest part of the meat is 1 foot above the coals. The meat may be turned from time to time. Baste frequently with barbecue sauce as the meat cooks to keep it from drying out too much.

CLOSED-PIT BARBECUING provides moist cooking similar to steaming for large-sized roasts, so the less tender (and also less expensive) cuts may be used. Dig a long narrow pit and line the bottom and sides with good-sized dry rocks or bricks. Build up a fire of hardwood or briquettes to a thick bed of hot glowing coals. Use roasts of approximately the same size, which may be marinated first. Wrap them well in a layer of cheese-cloth or muslin, brush them again with more marinade or a basting sauce, and cover securely with aluminum foil. When the coals are ready and the rocks are steaming hot, scatter hot sand over the ashes, or shovel the ashes out and line the bottom of your pit with green leaves or corn husks. Set your roasts on the bottom of the pit, cover with the hot ashes or another layer of green leaves, then place a large sheet of galvanized iron over the top to keep out the dirt. Finish by filling in with a foot of earth and tamp it down well. Work quickly so that too much heat does not escape. If steam appears to be escaping during the cooking process, shovel more dirt over the steam holes and pack it down firmly. Since the heat in a closed pit is moist, roasts may cook as long as 10 to 12 hours, but generally the timing depends on how hot the rocks are and the size of the meat portions.

CLAMBAKES traditionally take place at the seashore, but you may also improvise in your own backyard. The process employed is the same as in closed-pit cooking, except that layers of seaweed are required as insulation for your food. The essential foods prepared at a clambake are clams, white or sweet potatoes and corn; however, lobsters, frankfurters, chicken, fish or other shellfish are often included. Whatever is available at the seashore and the preferences of your guests really dictate the menu.

Dig a deep pit and line the sides and bottom with large, dry stones (wet stones are apt to explode when heated). Build a big fire of driftwood or hardwood, and let it burn down to a bed of incandescent coals. While the fire is heating, your guests may be set to gathering clams or seaweed, or fishing for the dinner menu. When the fire is ready, shovel out the embers and arrange a thick (6- to 8-inch) layer of seaweed over the bottom. Cover the seaweed with chicken wire or several yards of cheesecloth to prevent losing any small morsels, and set your food on top. The clams should be well scrubbed and soaked in water or seawater; a little cornmeal tossed into the water will help to make the clams void the grit inside their shells. Remove the silks from the corn but leave the husks intact. Pierce or cut the potato skins. Fish may be wrapped in foil, and lobsters must be cleaned. Chicken halves should have the skin crisply browned before being placed in the pit. If you're feeding a large crowd, put several inches of seaweed between the layers of food. Top all with a last layer of seaweed and cover the pit with a piece of wet canvas anchored securely with stones or sand to prevent the steam from escaping. Cook for 1 to 1 1/2 hours, depending on the amount of food and heat. Serve at once for guests to eat with their fingers, along with generous helpings of melted butter.

The LUAU is closed-pit cooking, Hawaiian-style. Cooking a whole suckling pig on a bed of banana leaves is traditional, but other cuts of pork, fish or chicken may be more suitable for your menu. Vegetables and fruits, especially sweet potatoes, pineapples, coconuts and bananas, may also be cooked in the pit. The fire is prepared as in closed-pit cooking, with stones or bricks over the bottom and sides. The pig may be rubbed with salt or a mixture of soy sauce and ginger. Hot stones are placed inside the body and the carcass is wrapped in foil and placed in the pit. If you decide on smaller pork roasts, wrap them in foil, too, and do the same to smaller portions of chicken, fish, seafood, fruits and vegetables. Spread your long white tablecloth on the ground and decorate it attractively down the center with fruits and flowers for an authentic feast. Traditional rum drinks, flavored with pineapple and coconut milk, and, of course, leis worn around the neck, help make the occasion festive.

The tailgate of a station wagon provides the modern version of the CHUCK WAGON of the old West: The food, traditionally steak and home-fried potatoes, is often accompanied by sourdough bread or biscuits. Apple pie and coffee complete the menu. The food is transported via the station wagon, cooked on a portable grill and served buffet-style from the tailgate.

BURGOO is the customary way to feed a hungry crowd down in Kentucky. It doubles as a soup and a stew, and is usually cooked in an oversized castiron soup kettle over a campfire. First into the kettle go the meats, which are simmered until tender. Vegetables, including the traditional okra which serve as a thickener, are then added and all are cooked until done; seasonings are blended in, and the Burgoo is ladled into cups. Each guest is liberally supplied with hot cornbread or corn dodgers, accompanied by lots of butter. Here is my favorite recipe for Burgoo.

Kentucky Burgoo

2 pounds each: beef, veal and pork shanks

2 pounds breast of lamb

2 whole chickens, cut in eighths

6 quarts water

8 medium-sized onions, diced

8 medium-sized potatoes, diced

8 medium-sized carrots, diced

2 green peppers, coarsely chopped

2 cups coarsely

chopped cabbage leaves

1 1/2 cups diced celery

3 cups diced okra

3 cups fresh whole corn kernels

2 cups fresh lima beans

8 cups tomato puree

Salt

Cayenne pepper

Worcestershire Sauce

A-1 Sauce

Tabasco Sauce

1/2 cup chopped parsley

(Serves 16)

Arrange the meat and chicken in a large, heavy soup kettle. Cover with the water. Bring to a boil, cover, and simmer slowly until the meat is tender enough to fall from the bones, about 3 hours. Remove from the fire and cool. Chop the meat and chicken, discarding the bones. Strain the stock and reheat, adding the meat and chicken. Add the vegetables and tomato purée to the stock. Stir in the spices and seasoning sauces, to taste. Use a light touch at first since cooking the burgoo strengthens the seasonings.

Stir occasionally while the burgoo slowly simmers for 6 to 7 hours. After it begins to thicken, stir constantly. The burgoo should be highly seasoned, so add more seasonings, if necessary, along with the chopped parsley, just before serving.

Beanhole Beans

Baking beans all day or all night under the ground in a fireless cooker has long been a favorite technique of outdoor cooks. The principle is the same as that used in cooking sides or roasts of meat in closed-pit barbecuing. Make a hole a bit larger and deeper than the size of the pot, and line it with dry rocks, which will retain the heat once the fire is underway. (A word of caution: always make sure the ground is sand or dirt before digging; fire will spread underground in peaty soil.) Build your fire of kindling and hardwood, and keep it going until the coals are about a foot thick and the rocks are thoroughly heated.

Your cooking pot may or may not be a cast-iron Dutch oven; but punch holes in the cover of any thin containers to allow the the steam to escape. Set your covered Dutch oven or pot over the layer of coals and ashes, raking some of the coals and ashes over the top and sides. A hot rock placed on the cover holds it down. If your pot has a handle, leave it in an upright position for easier removal when you're ready to eat. Top the pot with aluminum foil or a layer of green leaves to keep out the dirt, and shovel earth back into the hole to a depth of 4 or 5 inches, tamping it down well. It's not necessary to fill the hole completely. Now let the beans cook 6 to 8 hours. Here is my favorite method for preparing beans for a beanhole.

3 1/2 cups dried white pea beans

20 cups water

1/2 pound salt pork

4 tablespoons tomato paste

1 cup molasses

1/2 cup brown sugar

2 1/2 teaspoons dry mustard

1 teaspoon black pepper

1/2 teaspoon thyme

A pinch or two of cloves

2 onions, peeled

(Serves 10)

Measure the beans, pick them over, and place in a pot. Cover with 10 cups of cold water and soak overnight. Drain the beans and reserve the liquid. Cover the beans again with 10 cups fresh cold water and bring them to a boil. Immediately lower the heat and simmer the beans for 45 minutes. Drain the beans well once again, reserving the water. Cut a 1/4-pound slice of salt pork and place it on the bottom of the Dutch oven. Gently mix the tomato paste, molasses, brown sugar, dry mustard, pepper, thyme and cloves into the beans. Spoon the bean-mixture over the salt pork in the Dutch oven. Bury the whole onions in the center of the beans. Cut the remaining salt pork into 1/2 x 2-inch fingers and arrange these on top of the beans. Pour in the reserved bean liquid (plus additional boiling water if needed to bring the liquid high enough to cover the beans). Cover tightly and cook according to directions given.

Barbecue For 1000

If you happen to have 999 hungry friends, a full pocketbook and a day and a half of free time, why not plan a Barbecue For 1000? In addition to the barbecue beef itself you will need 250 pounds of cole slaw, 60 gallons of baked beans and 300 gallons of beer. Bon appétit!

20 20-pound boned sides
of beef

100 pounds medium-size
onions, peeled and
quartered

30 teaspoons salt

20 teaspoons black pepper

40 tablespoons chili
powder

40 tablespoons thyme

80 tablespoons wheat flour

80 tablespoons brown
sugar

60 cups sherry

40 6-ounce cans tomato
paste

Dig a pit 4 feet deep, 4 feet wide and 20 feet long. Reserve the dirt and mix it with sand. Line the sides of the pit with adobe brick and build a hard wood fire (using any wood but pine) the full length of the pit. When the fire has diminished to about 20 inches of hot coals, gently shovel 7 or 8 inches of the mixed sand and dirt over all. Place a well-soaked tarpaulin over the dirt.

Rub the meat with the salt, pepper, chili, thyme and flour. Place a 20-pound slab of meat and 5 pounds of onions in each of 20 double thick cotton flour or sugar sacks. Sprinkle 1 1/2 teaspoons salt and 4 tablespoons sugar over the meat in each bag. Mix the sherry and tomato paste and pour 4 1/2 cups of the mixture into each bag of meat and onions.

Place these 20 meat-filled bags in another 20 water-soaked canvas bags, fold the tops of the bags over and place these on top of the tarpaulin in the pit. Cover with another wet tarpaulin and an 8-inch layer of sand and dirt. Build another hardwood fire over the dirt. Allow the fire to burn heartily for about 24 hours.

When barbecue time rolls around, douse the fire with water, shovel the coals from the barbecue pit, lift a bag or two of meat from beneath the tarpaulin, place on a table, cut the bags open and serve immediately. Allow the remaining bags of meat to remain beneath the tarpaulins until needed and the meat will stay piping hot until the last bun has been filled.

HIKING
AND
BACKPACKING

Eating,
Drinking
and Cooking
on the Trail

THE EXTREME EXERTION that is part and parcel of hiking requires that the eating and drinking habits of the hiker be changed to meet the challenge of the trail. Breakfasts and lunches must be fairly light as opposed to the hearty ham, eggs and fried potato variety of the in-camp camper. Fats and proteins digest slowly, and a blood supply that is working overtime digesting food in the stomach cannot be at work simultaneously in the active muscles of the hiker and/or climber.

Although fat and protein are necessary, especially in the morning meal, carbohydrates are the best bet for quick energy and nourishment on the trail. It is far better to nibble snacks high in energy and vitamin content during the day and replenish your body more heartily at the evening meal.

Liquid must also be ingested wisely when backpacking. Cold drinks on a hot trail spell trouble. Water should be sipped, not gulped, and the evening meal should begin with a light soup to get the stomach ready for the heavier fare that is to follow. Remember that much body moisture is lost in perspiration during hiking, and care should be taken to replenish this supply, preferably during the long period of inactivity around the evening fire.

You will be unable to carry large quantities of heavy fruit in your pack, but all vitamin C requirements are easily met by carrying a small lightweight bottle of vitamin C tablets.

Although they are not recommended as a steady diet, dehydrated freeze-dried foods and drinks may be used with very great efficiency when hiking. Remove these lightweight foods from their boxes or jars, double wrap them first in waxed paper and then in plastic bags, and the makeup of many appetizing meals will fit conveniently in one pack. I am perhaps more interested in the taste of the meals on the trail than most hikers. Exertion and the resulting ravenous appetite does not seem to diminish my interest in the *taste* of the food. Trail-meals must be as delicious as possible. Always carry along some fresh potatoes, onions, carrots and apples. These do add weight to your pack but they make trail dinners taste "chunkier" and more like "real" food, and every day your pack gets lighter. Fruits are the one food in which drying does not seem to diminish flavor. True, dried fruits taste different from fresh ones, but the "new" taste is equally delicious. Nuts keep well, taste great and are good for you.

I am a great believer in the "pre-prepared" snack that is manufactured in your own kitchen.

The snacks in this section are tremendously high in vitamin and mineral content, with just enough fat and protein included to provide a well-balanced tidbit. Honey is a vital ingredient here because it need not be transformed by the body before it can be used. Honey also contains natural nutrients missing in sugar, and therefore it "pulls its own weight," nutritionally speaking. Energetic hikers who are anxious to hit the trail early in the morning and do not wish to spend time cooking may nibble several of the snacks in this section, drink a glass of juice prepared from citrus fruit crystals, and have a cup of herb tea (or if you really need it to get your motor started, a cup of coffee). Those hikers who do not mind a slower get-away may add fried eggs or pancakes to this menu. In either case you will have nourished your body with a meal that will not take long to digest, and your blood stream may get back to the important job of sending blood to your hiking muscles.

Trail lunches should be light for this same reason. Slowly sip a cup of any thin soup while you rest in the shade. Chew on dried chipped beef to replenish salt, eat a handful of nuts and dried fruits (chewing them slowly), eat a snack from this section, and drink a cup of tea. Rest a while longer, and then resume your hike.

The evening meal is the time to replenish your body from the day's output of energy, and to store up strength for tomorrow's hike. Simmer a pot of soup to sip as camp is being set up for the night. This prepares your stomach for the heavier food you will eat at dinner and also restores some of the water content your body has lost through perspiration. Prepare a hearty stew, a Beef Stroganoff or some other one-pot dinner where meat, starch, vegetables and sauce all cook together, one ingredient lending flavor to the other (and the cook has only one pot to wash). Follow the main course with a "skillet sweet" or a piece of fruitcake with steaming cups of tea or coffee. Anyone who is still hungry can dip individual nuts or dried fruit into a small dish of honey and have as much liquid as he or she desires (providing, of course, that water is plentiful).

I have never backpacked for more than 3 days at one time, so my advice and procedures may be less valid for longer trips, but I have found small butane stoves to be ideal for this kind of travel. The stoves themselves are tiny and lightweight and the cartridges neat and not overly bulky. I do not believe in building fires in the wild unless it is absolutely unavoidable. Campfires leave long-lasting scars on the landscape, endanger forests, and are generally an unnecessary indulgence. A Coleman lantern set in the midst of a group of campers may not be as romantic as a crackling camp fire, but a world that has been damaged and defaced and is devoid of unspoiled areas is not romantic either. It is well past time that we thought of something other than our own fleeting pleasures. Build fires in national camp grounds or along trails where fires have been previously lit. Build your fire on top of the old one, even if it means extra work. You or your children may come this way again, and if *everyone* who camps or hikes built his own fire in his own place, soon there would be no wilderness left *anywhere* for *anyone* to see. Cook with butane, propane or gasoline; it's better for the ecology and much, much easier, too.

Take
Along
Recipes

Sesame Squares

1/2 cup hulled sesame
    seeds
1 teaspoons orange zest
    (thin orange outer skin
    with none of the bitter
    white included),
    minced
20 pecan halves, chopped

2 eggs
1/2 cup natural organic
    sugar
6 tablespoons whole-
    wheat flour
1/4 teaspoon salt
16 pecan halves

(Makes 16 squares)

Place sesame seeds, orange zest and chopped pecans in a mixing bowl. Add the raw eggs, sugar, flour and salt, and mix thoroughly with your fingers. Place this batter in the bottom of oiled 8-inch pans. Arrange the pecan halves neatly in evenly-spaced rows in each pan. Bake for 30 minutes in an oven preheated to 350° F. Remove from the oven and cool for 5 minutes. Cut into 16 squares with a pecan half in the center of each. Loosen the edges, carefully lift the squares and arrange them on waxed paper until they are cool. Wrap each square in waxed paper and then in aluminum foil.

Sautéed Sunflower Seeds

A delicious snack for a hike.

3 cups hulled sunflower seeds	2 tablespoons butter or oil
	2 cloves garlic, halved

Shell the sunflower seeds and place them in the skillet with the butter or oil and the garlic. Stir over low heat until the seeds begin to pop. Eat hot or cold.

Persian Tidbits

1 cup walnut quarters	Confectioners' sugar
1 cup dates, pitted	2 tablespoons rum
1/2 cup dried figs	24 walnut halves
3/4 cup dried prunes, pitted	Coarse sugar

(Makes 20 confections)

Combine and finely chop the walnut quarters, dates, figs, and pitted prunes. Sprinkle confectioners' sugar on a flat pan or wooden board and work 2 tablespoons of rum into the chopped fruits and nuts until the paste is fairly smooth and well blended. Shape into a slender roll 1-inch thick. Wet a sharp knife and slice the roll into 24 pieces. Reshape the slices a bit if necessary. Dip each slice in coarse sugar, shake off any excess and place each slice on waxed paper. Lightly press a walnut half into each. Cover loosely and allow these fruit and nut confections to dry overnight. They may then be stored in a tin between pieces of waxed paper.

Walnut Snacks

Don't reach for a cookie, reach for one of these
nutrition-laden walnut treats. Tiger milk powder is
substituted for flour to produce a sweet with nearly
as much pick-me-up as a vitamin pill.

2 egg whites
9 dates
1/2 cup shelled walnut
 halves
5 heaping tablespoons
 tiger milk powder
1 tablespoon wheat germ
1/2 cup unsulfured golden
 raisins

1/2 cup unsulfured dark
 raisins
1 tablespoon honey
1/2 teaspoon powdered
 cinnamon
1/4 teaspoon ground
 nutmeg

(Makes 16)

Beat the egg whites until they hold a soft point when the beater
is raised. Chop the dates coarsely. Stir all ingredients together.
Use your fingers to form the mixture into 16 balls. Place on a
greased cookie sheet and bake for 12 minutes at 350° F. Remove from the oven. Allow the snacks to cool before wrapping
each in waxed paper. Double wrap with aluminum foil.

Stuffed Dates

Less is more if it's rich and sweet. Eat one of these
with a cup of herb tea and be satisfied.

10 unsulfured dates, pitted
10 walnut quarters

Natural organic sugar

(Makes 10)

Slit the dates, top each with a walnut quarter and a pinch of
sugar. Wrap the dates first in waxed paper and then in aluminum foil.

Honey-Coconut Balls

These energy-packed treats are ideal for backpacking.

4 tablespoons honey
4 teaspoons natural organic
   sugar
6 tablespoons water
4 tablespoons flaked
   coconut

4 tablespoons raisins
8 apricot halves, dried
4 tablespoons sunflower
   seeds

(Makes 20 1-inch balls)

Mix honey, sugar and water in a small enamel pan. Boil over medium heat until the syrup forms a soft ball when a small amount is dropped into a glass of cold water. Quickly stir in the coconut, raisins, coarsely chopped apricots and sunflower seeds. Grease a plate and your hands and form the candy into 1-inch balls. Cool. Wrap each in waxed paper. Twist the tops to secure. Wrap a second time in aluminum foil.

Fruit Snacks

13 prunes
1/3 cup pecan halves
   The zest or thin orange
   outer skin from 1 small
   orange

A generous pinch or
two each of powdered
anise and cloves
2 tablespoons natural
   organic sugar

(Makes 10)

Chop the prunes, pecans and orange zest together very finely. Add the spices and mix well. Shape into 10 "fingers," each approximately 2 1/2 inches by 1/2 inch. Roll each fruit finger in sugar, and cover each with a small piece of waxed paper. Double wrap in aluminum foil.

Bake-Ahead Pancakes

*Bake this sweet and crunchy confection and press
between waxed paper to form flat cakes. These
store well in your pack and may be eaten on
the trail with no reheating necessary.*

1/4 cup sugar
1/4 cup butter
1/3 cup honey

1 cup rolled oats
2 cups cornflakes
1/2 cup ground nuts

(Makes 16 cakes)

In a large bowl, mix the sugar and butter until well blended,
then stir in the honey. Add the rolled oats, cornflakes and nuts
and when the batter is thoroughly mixed, spread it over the
bottom of a well-greased 10-inch baking pan. Bake for 20
minutes in an oven preheated to 350° F. Allow the mixture to
cool before cutting into 16 bars. Form the bars into balls and
press between waxed paper to make flat cakes. Wrap the cakes
individually and unwrap as needed. These are light in weight
and may be eaten without further cooking. Serve with a steaming hot cup of coffee or tea for an energy-packed breakfast.

Fig and Nut Spread

*Take a small jar of this delicious fruit and nut paste
with you on your next hike or camping trip.*

8 small dried figs
1/2 cup raw cashew nuts,
   chopped
2 small tart apples, cored

1/4 teaspoon cinnamon
Generous pinch of
cloves

(Makes approximately 1 cup)

Finely chop and mix together all ingredients. Chill. Use within
24 hours.

Cooking

at

the

Site

Old-Fashioned German Mushroom Soup

1 medium-sized onion,
chopped
1 tablespoon butter
2 teaspoons flour
1/2 cup dried mushrooms
2 packages beef broth
mix

2 cups water
1/2 teaspoon Worcester-
shire sauce
Pinch of nutmeg
Salt and freshly ground
black pepper to taste
Garlic croutons

(Serves 2)

Heat the butter in a deep kettle and sauté the onions slowly
until transparent. Blend in the flour and cook the mixture for
30 seconds. Soak the mushrooms for 15 minutes and discard
the water. Cut into small dice and add with the beef broth mix,
water, Worcestershire sauce and spices to the onion mixture.
Simmer the soup, covered, for 5 minutes. Serve immediately
with the garlic croutons.

Scottish Bread Soup

*If Bread Soup sounds like fare more suited to
beggars than kings, you really should
sample this tasty old standby.*

1 cup bread cubes or
pieces (any dried bread
slices, cubed)

2 tablespoons butter or
oil

1 medium-sized onion

3 packages beef broth
mix

2 cups water

1/2 cup lima beans, canned

1/4 teaspoon sugar

Salt and freshly ground
black pepper to taste

2 tablespoons dry sherry
or any other alcoholic
beverage except beer

(Serves 2)

Sauté the bread cubes in butter in a skillet. Peel and chop the
onion and add it to the bread. Sauté 5 minutes more. Place
the sautéed bread cubes and onions in a bowl; set aside. Place
the beef broth mix and the water in the skillet, bring to a boil;
add the drained lima beans and heat to scalding boil. Add the
bread and onions, sugar, salt and pepper. Simmer for 5 minutes
without boiling. Stir in the sherry and serve immediately.

Dried Corn and Bacon Chowder

3/4 cup Pennsylvania
Dutch dried corn

4 cups water

1 1/2 teaspoons sugar

1/3 teaspoon salt

1/4 pound bacon, diced

1 onion, chopped

1/2 green pepper,
chopped; or 1 1/2

teaspoons dried green
pepper flakes

1 potato

1 cup milk

1 tablespoon flour

Salt and freshly
ground pepper to
taste

(Serves 4)

Measure the corn and 2 cups of the water into a large jar. Add
sugar and salt and soak the corn for 3 hours. You may seal the

275

jar and carry it in your pack while the corn is soaking. Add the remaining water and simmer the corn for 1 hour, or as directed on the package. Fry the bacon. Peel and chop the potato, Sauté the onion, pepper and potato for 15 to 20 minutes in the bacon fat until the potato is soft but not mushy. Stir the milk and flour together until smooth, add to the corn mixture and stir constantly until the soup comes to a boil. Lower the heat and simmer for 10 minutes. Season to taste and serve hot.

Sweet-Soy Nuts

2 tablespoons butter
2 cups pecan halves

2 tablespoons soy sauce
1 tablespoon sugar

(Serves 8)

Melt the butter in a skillet. Add the pecan halves and stir over medium heat for 1 minute. Sprinkle with soy sauce and sugar and continue to stir until the soy sauce disappears and the nuts are coated. Cool, dry on paper towels and store in a glass jar.

Wild
Edibles

WILD ONIONS, garlic and leek grow in every state within the continental U.S. None of these plants are poisonous and any of them may be used in stews, soups, etc. Although these wild plants are a bit tougher than the domestic varieties, this may be easily overcome by parboiling. When wild onions, garlic and leeks are used without parboiling as flavoring in meat and fish dishes that do not require much cooking, the onion may be discarded, if desired, for its rather strong flavor will have already added zest to the dish.

Wild onions are easily recognizable by their basal bulbs, their long flat or tubular leaves and their unmistakable onion odor. More to the point... they look and smell like onions or scallions, and both the bulbs and young leaves may be used in any recipe that calls for their cultivated cousins.

Wild Carrot (*Daucus carota*) has another, more common name... Queen Anne's Lace. I'm amazed that I picked the latter weed during my entire childhood for country bouquets and never realized that these lacy beauties were descendants of the domestic carrot. The roots may be scraped, simmered and used as a vegetable in soups and stews.

Wild Sunflower (*Helianthus Annuus*). The sunflower is the official state flower of Kansas, but sunflowers grow wild in every state within the continental U.S. Harvest the delicious seeds, dry or roast them and use in any recipe that calls for nuts. Sunflower seeds are 53 percent highly digestible protein and are prized for their nutritional properties by health food enthusiasts.

Wild Ginger (*Asarum Canadense*). This shy and beautiful little plant with soft, furry underleaves may be found blooming in the deep woods in the early spring. Two large heart-shaped double leaves grow from long slender surface roots which taste and smell like commercial ginger, although the two plants are not related.

Candied Wild Ginger and Ginger Syrup

2 cups sliced wild ginger root	3 cups water
	2 cups sugar

Scrape the roots and cut into 1/3-inch diagonal slices to measure 2 cups. Boil the ginger and water together for 1 hour, or until the roots are tender. Stir in the sugar and boil again for 20–25 minutes. Bottle the syrup, place the candied root on sheets of waxed paper, and dry overnight. The following afternoon sprinkle the roots with coarse natural sugar and dry 1 day longer. Use the syrup to flavor fresh picked wild fruit, curry or any Oriental dish and the candied ginger root in any recipe that calls for commercial candied ginger.

Wintergreen or Teaberry

*Hidden away in the still forests, these glossy green
leaves with the cheery, cherry red berries provide
a refreshing nibble on a brisk hike.*

TEABERRY TEA

30 teaberry leaves
6 cups boiling water

(Serves 4)

Crush or crumble the leaves and place them in a small glass or
enamel pot. Pour boiling water over the leaves and allow to
steep for 3 minutes. Strain into a teacup. Sweeten with honey
or natural sugar.

PEPPERMINT—M. piperita

*This fragrant wild plant has bright green opposite
leaves growing on a square stalk. Its flowers are a
dark lavender and the undersides of the leaves are
rough to the touch and strongly mentholated
to the taste.*

Spicy Mint Tea

6 cups boiling water
2 sticks cinnamon
4 whole cloves

4 whole allspice
2 cups fresh mint leaves

(Serves 4)

Bring the water, cinnamon, cloves and allspice to a boil. Boil
for 1 minute. Stir in the mint leaves. Remove from the heat and
steep for 5 minutes. Strain into cups. Sweeten with honey if
desired.

Sassafras Tea

*Northeastern Pennsylvania is a land of plenty. Most
of my childhood was spent there, and I cherish
memories of fruit-laden orchards and field after
golden field of heavy rippling grain. One of the
pleasant bounties nature provided was a sassafras
tree which grew just around the bend from my
house, near the edge of the forest. The rusty-
colored sassafras roots provided us with many
a pot of fragrant tea. Sassafras—warming in
the winter, cooling when iced in the summer,
and marvelous as a spring tonic.*

2 3-inch pieces sassafras　　　　　**4 cups boiling water**
root (or bark)

(Serves 4)

Scrub roots and cut into short pieces. Boil the roots and water
for 15 minutes or until the tea is red and strong. Serve hot,
sweetened with honey or natural sugar, or chill and serve with
ice.

Index

INDEX

HB6C